Julian the Apostate

DEBATES AND DOCUMENTS IN ANCIENT HISTORY

GENERAL EDITORS

Emma Stafford, *University of Leeds*, and
Shaun Tougher, *Cardiff University*

Focusing on important themes, events or periods throughout ancient history, each volume in this series is divided into roughly equal parts. The first introduces the reader to the main issues of interpretation. The second contains a selection of relevant evidence supporting different views.

PUBLISHED

Diocletian and the Tetrarchy
Roger Rees

Julian the Apostate
Shaun Tougher

IN PREPARATION

Roman Imperialism
Andrew Erskine

Roman and its Empire, 193–284
Olivier Hekster

Julian the Apostate

Shaun Tougher

Edinburgh University Press

For Barbara, Ian and Paula: Special Subject 1987–8

Edinburgh University Press Ltd
22 George Square, Edinburgh

Typeset in Minion
by Norman Tilley Graphics Ltd, Northampton,
and printed and bound in Great Britain
by Cromwell Press, Trowbridge, Wilts

A CIP record for this book is available from the British Library

ISBN 978 0 7486 1886 6 (hardback)
ISBN 978 0 7486 1887 3 (paperback)

Published with the support of the Edinburgh University
Scholarly Publishing Initiatives Fund.

Contents

Series Editors' Preface

Debates and Documents in Ancient History is a series of short books on central topics in Greek and Roman history. It will range over the whole period of classical history from the early first millennium BC to the sixth century AD. The works in the series are written by expert academics and provide up-to-date and accessible accounts of the historical issues and problems raised by each topic. They also contain the important evidence on which the arguments are based, including texts (in translation), archaeological data and visual material. This allows readers to judge how convincing the arguments are and to enter the debates themselves. The series is intended for all those interested in the history of the Greek and Roman world.

In this volume Shaun Tougher explores the much-discussed figure of Julian 'the Apostate', whose reign, though brief (AD 360–363), was significant for his attempt to revive paganism in the increasingly Christianised Roman empire. Opinions both ancient and modern have been widely divided: some have regarded Julian as a villainous opponent of Christianity, others as a hero making a gallant last stand in defence of classical culture, others again as an idiosyncratic fantasist pursuing an impossible dream. But where does the truth lie? And is there more to Julian than personal religious convictions? How far was he a product of turbulent times and tragic personal circumstances? We have an unusually rich supply of ancient source material on Julian, including the narrative history of Ammianus Marcellinus, partisan speeches and letters by other contemporaries, hostile accounts by later church historians, and the extensive writings of Julian himself, in addition to inscriptions, statues and coins. Drawing on all these sources, Shaun Tougher provides a lucid and even-handed introduction to Julian's life and times, enabling readers to come to an independent assessment of this fascinating character and his significance for the history of Christianity.

Emma Stafford
July 2006

Preface

Julian must be one of the most written about Romans. He symbolises the demise of the pagan Roman empire and the rise of its Christian counterpart, but he also stands against the backdrop of the larger transition from antiquity to the middle ages. He has been the subject of numerous studies, but has also inspired works of literature and art. There is no sign that the fascination with him is waning. The modern preoccupation with him, however, merely reflects the reaction of his contemporaries. As an emperor who attempted to restore the traditional predominance of paganism and undermine the status acquired by Christianity since the reign of his uncle Constantine the Great, he elicited sharply divided opinion. To this day Julian continues to divide opinion. This book is an attempt to provide an indication of the different views of Julian that exist and to supply a selection of the key evidence utilised in the construction of these divergent interpretations of him. It is hoped that individuals can thus make up their own minds about Julian, rather than being guided to a particular vision of him.

A fuller account of the reasons for the appeal of Julian as a subject and of the range of sources available for his study is provided in the initial chapter of Part I (Debates). The subsequent chapters focus on key aspects of Julian's life and reign, but also largely follow a traditional chronological path. These chapters contain cross-references to the sources in Part II (Documents). The cross-references are denoted by bold type in brackets, and may allude to the whole item (e.g. **II 2**) or to a specific section of it (e.g. **II 50 16.10.18–19**). The references to primary sources which are not in bold type indicate that they are not included in Part II. The key to the short references to secondary literature (by author and year of publication) is provided by the bibliography. Further supporting material is supplied in the form of a family tree, maps, a chronology, details of further reading, and a list of internet resources. Given the focused nature of the chapters in Part I and the limitations of space, full coverage of every detail of Julian's life and reign cannot be

ix

furnished, but this can be pursued through the listed sources, books, articles and resources.

The selection of material for inclusion in Part II has posed a particular challenge, simply because so much exists. It would not have been feasible to include everything of relevance, so I have had to be selective. I have striven to acknowledge the range of sources available, as well as providing key extracts. Readers are thus urged to consult also full translations of the appropriate texts. Most readily available is the Penguin translation of the history of Ammianus Marcellinus (Hamilton 1986), and consultation of the three-volume edition and translation of the works of Julian in the Loeb Classical Library series (Wright 1913 and 1923) is a must. Most of the sources furnished in Part II are extracted from extant translations, as is indicated in the Acknowledgements. Where I have provided translations of my own this will be made clear in Part II. Regarding the organisation of the sources in Part II, I have endeavoured to follow roughly a chronological plan, from earliest to latest (though material evidence is grouped at the end). This was an attempt to make clear the developing picture of Julian that emerges in the ancient sources and to stress in particular how much material predates Ammianus' privileged history. The sources provided in Part II should also be read in their entirety, not just when they are referenced in Part I. They provide much more information and detail than can be acknowledged there, and will supply inspiration for further thought.

Finally, I would like to take this opportunity to acknowledge debts of gratitude. Especial thanks are owed to John Davey and Carol Macdonald of Edinburgh University Press, for their unstinting support and patience. I could not have wished for better advocates. I am also grateful to Emma Stafford for helpful feedback. Over the years I have benefited greatly from the advice, encouragement and expertise of other historians, and would like to thank in particular (for services in the field of Julian) Nicholas Baker-Brian, John Drinkwater, Kate Gilliver, Mark Humphries and Michael Whitby.

S.F.T.
Cardiff, March 2006

Acknowledgements

Grateful acknowledgement is made to the following sources for permission to reproduce material previously published elsewhere. Every effort has been made to trace the copyright holders, but if any have been inadvertently overlooked, the publisher will be pleased to make the necessary arrangements at the first opportunity.

II 30   Pharr, Clyde; *The Theodosian Code and Novels and the Sermondian Constitutions.* © 1952 in the name of the author, 1980 renewed in the name of Roy Pharr, the executor. Reprinted by permission of Princeton University Press

II 31   H. W. Bird

II 32   Samuel N. C. Lieu

II 42   © Cambridge University Press

II 45   Samuel N. C. Lieu and Judith M. Lieu

II 46   H. W. Bird

II 47   Thomas M. Banchich

II 48   Samuel N. C. Lieu

II 49   Roger Pearse, The Tertullian Project

II 50   Reprinted by permission of the publishers and the Trustees of the Loeb Classical Library from *Ammianus Marcellinus: Volume I*, Loeb Classical Library ® Volume 300, translated by J. C. Rolfe, revised 1950, Cambridge, MA: Harvard University Press, Copyright © 1935, 1950 by the President and Fellows of Harvard College, and from *Ammianus Marcellinus: Volume II*, Loeb Classical Library ® Volume 315, translated by J. C. Rolfe, Cambridge, MA: Harvard University Press, Copyright © 1940 by the President and Fellows of Harvard College. The Loeb Classical Library ® is a registered trademark of the President and Fellows of Harvard College

II 51   Francis Cairns (Publications) Ltd

Abbreviations

AClass	*Acta Classica*
AE	*L'Année Epigraphique*
AJPh	*American Journal of Philology*
AncW	*The Ancient World*
BMGS	*Byzantine and Modern Greek Studies*
Byz	*Byzantion*
Byz Forsch	*Byzantinische Forschungen*
CIL	*Corpus Inscriptionum Latinarum*
ClPhil	*Classical Philology*
CQ	*Classical Quarterly*
EHR	*English Historical Review*
GRBS	*Greek, Roman and Byzantine Studies*
Hist	*Historia*
JEH	*The Journal of Ecclesiastical History*
JHS	*The Journal of Hellenic Studies*
JHSex	*Journal of the History of Sexuality*
JÖB	*Jahrbuch der Österreichischen Byzantinistik*
JRS	*The Journal of Roman Studies*
NChron	*Numismatic Chronicle*
PCPhS	*Proceedings of the Cambridge Philological Society*
VigChr	*Vigiliae Christianae*
YCls	*Yale Classical Studies*

Family Tree

(from G. W. Bowersock, *Julian the Apostate*, Duckworth, 1978)

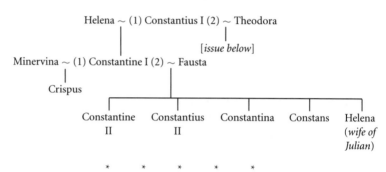

Helena ~ (1) Constantius I (2) ~ Theodora

[*issue below*]

Minervina ~ (1) Constantine I (2) ~ Fausta

Crispus

| Constantine II | Constantius II | Constantina | Constans | Helena (*wife of Julian*) |

*   *   *   *   *

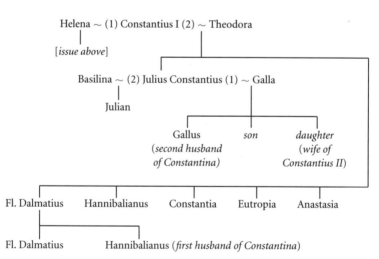

Helena ~ (1) Constantius I (2) ~ Theodora

[*issue above*]

Basilina ~ (2) Julius Constantius (1) ~ Galla

Julian

| Gallus (*second husband of Constantina*) | *son* | *daughter* (*wife of Constantius II*) |

| Fl. Dalmatius | Hannibalianus | Constantia | Eutropia | Anastasia |

Fl. Dalmatius   Hannibalianus (*first husband of Constantina*)

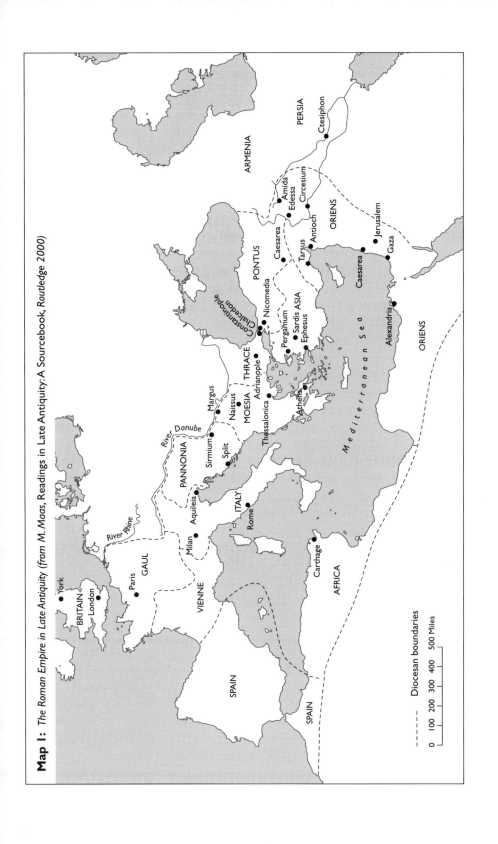

Map 1: The Roman Empire in Late Antiquity (from M. Maas, Readings in Late Antiquity: A Sourcebook, Routledge 2000)

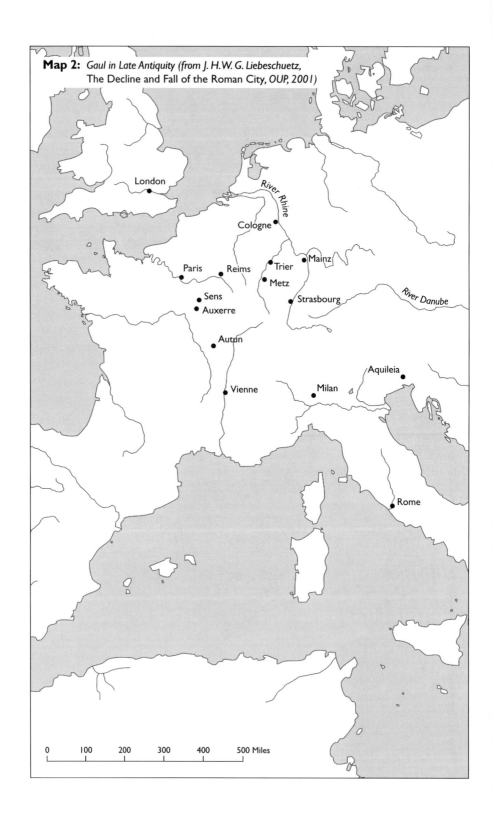

Map 2: *Gaul in Late Antiquity (from J. H. W. G. Liebeschuetz,*
The Decline and Fall of the Roman City, OUP, 2001)

London

River Rhine

Cologne

Paris Reims Trier Mainz

Metz

Sens Strasbourg

Auxerre

River Danube

Autun

Aquileia

Vienne Milan

Rome

0   100   200   300   400   500 Miles

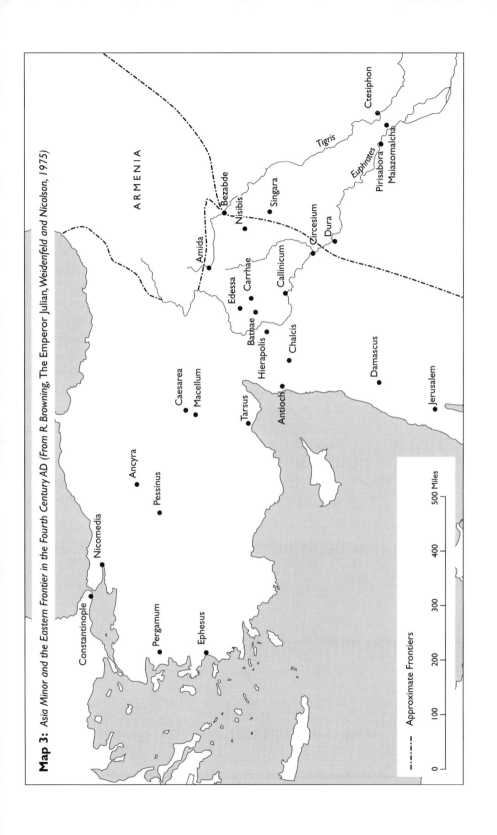

Map 3: *Asia Minor and the Eastern Frontier in the Fourth Century AD (From R. Browning, The Emperor Julian, Weidenfeld and Nicolson, 1975)*

ARMENIA

Ctesiphon
Maiazomalcha
Pirisabora
Euphrates
Tigris
Bezabde
Singara
Nisibis
Amida
Circesium
Dura
Carrhae
Edessa
Callinicum
Bathae
Hierapolis
Chalcis
Damascus
Caesarea
Macellum
Jerusalem
Tarsus
Antioch
Ancyra
Pessinus
Nicomedia
Constantinople
Pergamum
Ephesus

0   100   200   300   400   500 Miles

– · – · – Approximate Frontiers

Part I

Debates

The Fascination of Julian

The figure of Julian has proved fascinating for centuries. Ever since he provoked heated debate during his own lifetime he has continued to be discussed throughout human history, as numerous books on the emperor have emphasised (e.g. Bidez 1930: 332–47; Browning 1975: 220–35; Braun and Richer 1978–81; Murdoch 2003: 209–24). A famous example is Gibbon's treatment of Julian in the second volume of his celebrated *The History of the Decline and Fall of the Roman Empire* (1781: chs 19 and 22–4), but he has not been the preserve of historians alone. Julian is, for instance, the subject of a play by Ibsen (Meyer 1986), a painting by Edward Armitage (1874) (**II 67**), poems of C. P. Cavafy (Dalven 1976) and a novel by Gore Vidal (1964). More recently, Julian has inspired another novel, by Michael Curtis Ford (2002), the cinematic nature of which suggests that the hero may one day sally into the medium of film too.

The inevitable question is, why has there been such sustained interest in Julian? The obvious answer is religion. Julian was the last pagan emperor to rule the Roman empire. But it is the context of his times which further explains the fascination. In the early fourth century AD, a sea change in the imperial attitude towards Christianity occurred. Following a period of persecution of Christians which had been initiated under Diocletian (284–305), there was a declaration of religious toleration. Moreover, there emerged a desire to support Christianity actively. At the forefront of this development was the emperor commonly known as Constantine the Great (306–37), forever associated with the Christianisation of the Roman empire. Although he did not achieve this he certainly set the process in motion. It was this process that Julian wanted to stop, being a devotee of paganism. Ironically, not only had Julian been brought up a Christian, but he was also a relative of Constantine the Great: this emperor was his uncle. It was his abandoning of Christianity to return to traditional religion, when he was a young man, which earned Julian the title of 'The Apostate'. He symbolises the last stand against Christianity before it progressed to its seemingly inexorable triumph. This explains in large part the preoccupation with him, both for those antipathetic to his design and those sympathetic to it. Regarding the latter, Vidal observed 'Julian has always been something of an underground hero in Europe. His attempt to stop Christianity and revive Hellenism exerts still a romantic appeal' (1964: ix). Revealingly, Alice Gardner's study of Julian (1895) was published as part of the series *Heroes of the Nations*. There still exists today *The Julian Society*, 'a non-denominational religious order dedicated to the advancement of pagan religion' (www.juliansociety.org). Of course, the fact that Julian's life was cut short makes him more intriguing. He supplies one of the great 'What ifs' of history. Could he have achieved his religious ambitions? If he had, would we be living in a very different world today?

There are however other aspects of Julian which contribute to his appeal. He presents a rather tragic figure. Not only was he cheated of his hopes and consigned to an early death, but his childhood and youth were blighted too. He lost his mother while still an infant, and then his father was killed, along with several relatives, in the tense period that ensued after the death of Constantine the Great in 337. Subsequently Julian had little control over his own destiny, but was in the power of his cousin the emperor Constantius II. When Julian's half-brother Gallus was executed too in 354, having been elevated to the position of Caesar in 351, Julian faced an uncertain future. But he was made Caesar himself in 355, and thrust into the treacherous arena of public life. All this makes for a gripping and dramatic story, as Julian himself appreciated. It was not just one of tragedy, though, for he managed to stay alive and become emperor. There is a narrative of survival and success here too, which is no less compelling. Bound up in the tale are two distinct features of Julian which augment the interest in him: he was an intellectual and a soldier. His enthusiasm for learning marked him from a young age, and led to his studying in philosophical circles in Asia Minor. He became a prolific writer. His military career he came to later in life, but he embraced it with equal dedication. It was distinguished by great highs, such as his victory over the Alamanni at the battle of Strasbourg in 357, as well as great lows, such as the ending of his Persian expedition six years later in disaster and his own death.

It is not just religion and his personal circumstances, however, which account for the attraction of Julian as a subject. He lived in interesting times. Religion, especially Christianity, is a major theme of the Roman empire in the fourth century AD, but there were other key issues too. In the third century it is commonly agreed that the empire experienced severe difficulties, if not a period of crisis, following the termination of the Severan dynasty in AD 235. External threats intensified, there was internal division and fragmentation, reigns tended to be brief and end badly, and the economy was placed under strain. Of course, emperors attempted to respond to this situation, but it is Diocletian and Constantine that are credited with concerted efforts to tackle the problems. The world into which Julian was born, however, still had its difficulties. The northern and eastern frontiers were under pressure. How to maintain power was a concern, as was the effective functioning of the cities of the empire. Combined with these predicaments were distinctive features of the empire that were relatively new. The emperor had become a remote, sacred figure, surrounded by an expanded court and increased ceremony. Also, Rome was no longer the main residence of emperors. Provincial cities such as Trier, Milan, Sirmium, Thessalonica, Nicomedia and Antioch had become favoured as imperial residences, given their greater strategic value, and they had benefited from the ensuing patronage. Constantinople, the place of Julian's birth, is the famous example. Formerly the Greek city of Byzantium, it had been refounded as 'The City of Constantine' by Constantine the Great. This was the vibrant and challenging world in which Julian moved, the fortunes of which he sought to restore. It is this context which further explains the attraction of studying him.

Thus it is easy to understand why Julian has fascinated people for so long. However, modern historians can differ wildly in their interpretation of him. For some he is the flawed hero, very much in the mould of the image created by the Roman historian Ammianus Marcellinus, but a hero nonetheless (for example, the recent Renucci 2000). He is a man of integrity, motivated by the purest of reasons, attempting to do his best for the good of the Roman empire. Such readings can verge on the romantic (e.g. Athanassiadi 1992). For others, Julian is a much more complex and questionable figure (e.g. Bowersock 1978). He is a fantasist, out of touch with the realities of his age, attempting to restore a lost world. He is motivated by his own desires and attachments. Beyond these broad divergences of opinion a host of other issues are debated. Was Julian attempting to replace Christianity with his own demanding brand of pagan monotheism, in which Mithraism was key (Athanassiadi 1992), or was he in fact a much more traditional pagan, happy for the plethora of gods to have their devotees (Smith 1995)? Was he an isolated nervous misfit (Bowersock 1978) or a more grounded character with a wide circle of friends (Smith 1995)? Was he a genuinely modest and mild person, or in fact a ruthless autocrat? Was he deeply influenced by historical heroes such as Alexander the Great and Marcus Aurelius (Athanassiadi 1992) or not (Hunt 1995; Lane Fox 1997)? How gifted a soldier was he? Is he historically significant, or can he be dismissed as a mere blip in the advance of Christianity towards becoming the religion of the empire? The subject of Julian is marked by intense debate, and this compounds his inherent interest.

The fascination with Julian is further fuelled by the richness of the ancient source material available for studying him. Just as his project continues to elicit comment today, his contemporaries were moved to produce a mass of literature about him and his aspirations. This is polarised between the camps of pagan and Christian. Probably the most famous and influential writer on Julian is the historian Ammianus Marcellinus (**II 50**), undoubtedly the most written-about historian of the later Roman empire. Ammianus was a Greek, very likely a citizen of Antioch, who was of elite background. He had a military career, serving amongst the staff officers (*protectores domestici*). During this career he came into the orbit of Julian. Ammianus was in Gaul under his commander Ursicinus when Julian was posted there as Caesar in 355, though he departed with Ursicinus soon after in 357. More often remarked upon is the fact that he participated in the Persian expedition of 363. Such was the impact of Julian upon Ammianus, a fellow pagan, that the latter's history, written in Latin and published in Rome in the 390s, was in large part inspired by the emperor. Although Julian only reigned for a short time, Ammianus devotes a disproportionate amount of his history to him (just as Gibbon, an admirer of Ammianus, was to do). Further, the esteem in which Ammianus held Julian is clear; he speaks of his treatment of him as being akin to a speech of praise (**II 50 16.1.3**). This is not to say that the historian is blind to the flaws of his hero; Ammianus is notable for the criticisms he is prepared to level at Julian (e.g. the trials at Chalcedon; his anti-Christian teaching edict; his treatment of the *curiales*; his love of popularity). These critical comments have contributed to Ammianus' reputation for impartiality. Nevertheless, there is no mistaking the favouritism shown towards Julian, as well as the concomitant hostility shown towards Constantius II. There is no doubt, also, that Ammianus' vision has been tremendously influential on later historians. His preeminence as the major Roman historian of the fourth century has imbued him with authority. However, some historians have been alert to the danger of depending too heavily upon him. Bowersock (1978: 5–7) has stressed the lateness of Ammianus' account of Julian, and privileged instead the contemporary sources. Others are alive to the disingenuous nature of Ammianus' history (e.g. Barnes 1998). Certainly, at least, his verdicts do not always square with his narrative.

Prominent amongst the contemporary sources are two men on opposite sides of the religious divide: the pagan sophist of Antioch, Libanius (**II 33–41**), and the Christian bishop Gregory of Nazianzus (**II 43–4**). Both men had met Julian. When Libanius was teaching at Nicomedia Julian surreptitiously secured copies of notes taken at his lectures (**II 39 13–15**), and the two men communicated by letter and exchanged works before meeting in Antioch during Julian's sojourn there in 362–3 (**II 33**). Gregory was a student at the university in Athens at the same time as Julian's brief attendance there (**II 44 23**). Their contrasting takes on Julian are symbolised by the opposing literary genres they are famous for using when writing about the emperor: Libanius produced panegyrics, and Gregory invectives. Libanius' most famous speech on Julian is the funeral oration of AD 365 (**II 39**), but it is by no means the only one, and he was still taking the emperor as his theme at the end of the 370s, in a speech demanding that the murder of Julian should be investigated for the good of the empire (**II 40**). Gregory's attacks on Julian were written very soon after his premature death. Although these were Gregory's main contribution to the subject of the pagan emperor, Libanius produced many other relevant works, several dating from Julian's own lifetime. In addition to speeches to or about Julian, there survive letters written to or about him. Julian also features in Libanius' autobiography (**II 41**). The works of these two men clearly deserve the attention they have received, and the weight attached to them, as sources for Julian. However, they are emblematic of the difficulty of accessing an objective view of him.

Other contemporaries illustrate the same problematic polarisation. When the new consuls for 362 were inaugurated on New Year's Day in Constantinople, one of them, Claudius Mamertinus, delivered a speech of thanks to Julian (**II 32**). Like the speeches of Libanius this was panegyrical. It was demanded of the circumstances, but Mamertinus was a supporter of Julian anyway, having held official posts under him since 361. Significantly, he had been one of the judges at the recent trials conducted at Chalcedon. The speech provided him with the opportunity to celebrate Julian's accession to power, and to praise the agenda of the new regime, which he implicitly contrasts with that of Constantius II. As such it is a work of great interest, as much for what it leaves out as for what it includes (e.g. Blockley 1972b), and illustrates

that the art of spin is nothing new. An opposing voice is provided
by Ephrem the Syrian, a Christian who experienced the surrender of
Nisibis to the Sasanids thanks to the failure of Julian's Persian
expedition, and who saw the dead body of the emperor outside the city
as it made the journey to its resting place at Tarsus (**II 45 3.1–4**). Ephrem
articulated his hostility to Julian in four hymns, composed soon after
the death of the emperor (**II 45**). Their historical value has only begun
to be appreciated relatively recently (e.g. Bowersock 1978: 9–10; Griffith
1987; Lieu 1989: 100–1). A further hostile Christian commentator who
can be reckoned a contemporary is John Chrysostom, who became
patriarch of Constantinople at the end of the fourth century. John, an
Antiochene, was a youth at the time of Julian's prolonged visit to his
native city. Later in life (perhaps the late 370s) he wrote a homily on St
Babylas (**II 48**), in which he recalls events which occurred at that time,
when Julian had the relics of the saint removed from the precinct of the
temple of Apollo at Daphne, which subsequently burnt down. Part of
Chrysostom's agenda was to deride elements of Libanius' monody on
Julian (*Oration* 17). The ongoing war of words was not just directed
against the dead emperor.

Thus there is a wealth of literary sources devoted to Julian, dating
to his lifetime or shortly after his death, to set beside the history
of Ammianus. Further, Ammianus was not the only author to treat
Julian in a historical framework. Another contemporary of Julian who
participated in the Persian expedition was Eutropius, who included a
brief and largely positive account of his reign in his *Breviarium* (**II 46**),
which covered Roman history from Romulus to AD 364, and was
produced in the reign of Valens (364–78). Also on the expedition was
Magnus of Carrhae (possibly the Magnus distinguished at the siege of
Maiazomalcha: Fornara 1991), who composed a narrative too. This has
been lost, but informs the sixth-century chronicle of Malalas (**II 61
13.21 and 23**). Julian also features in such concise historical works as the
De Caesaribus of Aurelius Victor (**II 31**), the *Breviarium* of Festus (**II 47**)
and the *Chronicon* of Jerome (**II 49**), and appears in a history of the
empire written by the Christian priest Orosius in the fifth century
which was designed to show that the Romans had experienced disasters
when the empire was pagan (**II 55**). The other major history to provide
coverage of Julian was written by the sophist Eunapius of Sardis (**II 51**).
He was a pagan like his contemporary Ammianus, and as with
Ammianus, Julian was the hero of his history, a notoriously anti-
Christian work. Fascinatingly, for his information on Julian Eunapius
drew on a memoir of the emperor's doctor and friend Oribasius (**II 51**

15). Unfortunately, the history has been lost, though there survive fragments (such as the excerpts preserved in compilations produced under the tenth-century Byzantine emperor Constantine VII), and the *New History* of Zosimus (**II 60**), written in the late fifth or early sixth century, provides some indication of its contents as it drew upon it. The erratic and partisan nature of Zosimus' history does not inspire much confidence however. Something of Eunapius' treatment of Julian can also be gained by his references to him and the history in his other major work, the *Lives of the Sophists* (**II 52**). In particular this provides a memorable account of Julian's experiences with the Neoplatonic philosophers in Pergamum and his decision to seek out Maximus (**II 52 474–5**).

A distinctive set of historiographical sources for Julian are the church histories. This genre had been introduced by Eusebius of Caesarea in the early fourth century, and many authors were inspired to continue his narrative. Later in the fourth century Rufinus translated Eusebius' history into Latin and provided his own continuation, which included coverage of Julian (**II 54**). However it is the fifth-century church historians writing in Greek who are well known for their treatment of Julian. The most famous of these is Socrates of Constantinople (**II 57**), who was writing during the reign of Theodosius II (408–50). Socrates was perhaps a lawyer, and certainly displays a marked interest in education and intellectuals. It is usually observed that he was engaged in producing a more synthesised type of history, covering both ecclesiastical and secular events, and as such he marks a stage in the eventual emergence of the Byzantine chronicle. He is judged by some to treat Julian in a more considered manner than the other church historians (Krivouchine 1997; Urbainczyk 1997: 156–9), though his hostility to the emperor is in no doubt. The other church historians, however, are not without their interest. Although Sozomen, a lawyer, draws heavily upon Socrates, there are differences in tone, focus and content (**II 58**). Theodoret, bishop of Cyrrhus, is even more hostile to Julian, depicting the emperor as an outright persecutor (Penella 1993; **II 59**). Especially intriguing is the work of Philostorgius, for it provides a different perspective on church history, being sympathetic to the Arian position and thus to Constantius II. Unfortunately, however, the original text has been lost and we have to depend mainly on a summary made in the ninth century by the famous Byzantine intellectual and churchman Photius (**II 56**).

As has been indicated, Byzantine chroniclers such as Malalas continued to provide accounts of Julian and his reign. Another noteworthy example is the chronicle of John Zonaras, written in the twelfth century AD (**II 62**). The interest of this late source has been particularly emphasised by Michael DiMaio (1977, 1980, 1988), who attempts to identify the sources Zonaras used and suggests that he preserves some information from lost works.

The richness of the literary sources for the study of Julian is thus notable in itself, but further depth is added by the fact that the emperor was a prolific writer himself (**II 1–28**). Much of his work survives. This encompasses speeches, satires and letters, some written before he became sole emperor, but the majority of his work dates to his reign. Amongst his most famous creations are his speeches on the emperor Constantius II, and a companion piece on the empress Eusebia, all written during his Caesarship (**II 1–3**); his *Letter to the Athenians*, a justification of his decision to take up arms against his cousin, written in Naissus towards the end of 361 (**II 7**); *The Caesars*, his playful reflection on his imperial predecessors – and Alexander the Great – probably written at Antioch late in 362 (**II 25**); and, also written in Antioch, early in 363, his *Misopogon* (literally 'Beard-Hater'), an avowed satire on himself but really an attack on the Antiochenes who had provoked him and sent him up (**II 28**). Notable also is that Julian wrote an attack on the Christians, his *Against the Galilaens* (see for example Burr 2000). Unfortunately, but perhaps unsurprisingly, this does not survive intact, though something of it can be reconstructed from a Christian refutation of it written in the fifth century by Cyril of Alexandria. Julian's writings, of course, fuel the fascination with him, holding out the prospect of understanding his psychology better than that of any other Roman emperor, though this may be a misguided expectation.

In addition to this extensive stock of literary sources, a certain amount of documentary and material evidence relating to Julian survives. Inscriptions relate to his public career, both as Caesar and as sole emperor (**II 29**) (Conti 2004). Various laws have been preserved, mostly in the *Theodosian Code* (**II 30**), the compilation of imperial legislation produced under Theodosius II, which included material from the reign of Constantine the Great onwards. A limited number of artefacts such as statues, busts and intaglios are identified as being depictions of the emperor (Lévêque 1960, 1963). Probably the most famous portrait of Julian is a statue in the Louvre representing the emperor as philosopher and priest (**II 66**). The major source of images of Julian is his coinage (**II 63–5**), which has attracted particular attention (Webb 1910; Kent 1959; Gilliard 1964). Most familiar is his bull coinage (**II 65**), a large bronze issue dated to 332, though infamously its meaning is much debated (Vanderspoel 1998; Woods 2000; Tougher 2004). Monumental works produced in his name are virtually non-existent, though he is credited with building work in Constantinople, comprising a new harbour connected to a stoa, and a library within the stoa (**II 60 3.11.3**). The brevity of his rule may explain the lack of Julianic buildings, not just simple loss.

In general, then, there is no doubt that the amount of source material surviving for the study of Julian, especially the literary sources, would be described as abundant. Despite this fact the historian is still presented with many problems. The most obvious of these is the polarised nature of the sources between pagan supporters and Christian opponents, which perhaps explains the attraction of writers such as Ammianus Marcellinus and Socrates who can be thought to offer a more balanced, or at least less biased, vision. The conflicting images of Julian can make it difficult to assess him, and this allows for the co-existence of contrasting interpretations. In addition, despite the testimony of Julian himself, there are many gaps in our knowledge about Julian's life and reign. When was he born? What was the exact path of his education? What are the dates of his confinement at Macellum? Why did he embrace paganism? These are just some of the questions which still exercise those who study him. In part historians are victims of Julian's failure to provide a fuller account of his life, though the factors of chance lack of information and conflicting reports play an important part in creating uncertainty too. Surviving material evidence poses its own problems. What was the message of the bull coinage? How certain are identifications of images of Julian? Thus there is no shortage of matters for debate.

In the Debates section of this book I have devoted six chapters to aspects of the life and reign of Julian, focusing on key areas and the different views that exist about them. These six chapters also follow a chronological progression, from Julian's birth to his death, so there is an element of continuous narrative. I have attempted to treat the material and issues in an objective manner. However, if there is one thing that is clear from studying Julian, it is that he is a figure whom it is hard to remain objective about, even for modern historians. I do have my own views about him, and about his cousin Constantius II, and these will no doubt be apparent. Nevertheless, I have endeavoured to present alternative opinions, and urge readers at all times to make up their own minds. Indeed, that is the essential aim of this series.

CHAPTER 1

Family

1. Imperial blood

In the new imperial city of Constantinople a new member of the imperial family was born in the early 330s (either 331 or 332 – see Bouffartigue 1992: 30). This was Flavius Claudius Julianus, the future emperor Julian. It was through his father that Julian was of imperial blood, for Julius Constantius, like his half-brother the emperor Constantine the Great (306–37), was a son of the emperor Constantius I (293–306) (see the Family Tree). Julian's mother Basilina was of rather different stock to the Balkan military men of the Flavian dynasty; her family was of the traditional elite (Ammianus Marcellinus 25.3.23) and from Bithynia. Julian's family's status in the imperial house was less prominent than that of Constantine the Great's own children (his sons Crispus, Constantine II, Constantius II and Constans), but it seems that this situation altered in the 330s as Constantine began to promote his half-brothers and their children. Julius Constantius' brother Flavius Dalmatius was consul for 333, whilst Julius Constantius held the same honour in 335. In the same year Flavius Dalmatius' son Dalmatius was made Caesar and given authority over Moesia and Thrace, and another son Hannibalianus was acclaimed king of Armenia. The increasing significance of Julian's branch of the imperial family is also attested by marriage ties with the children of Constantine. In 336 Constantius II married the daughter of Julius Constantius whilst Constantine's daughter Constantina was married to Hannibalianus. Thus during Julian's early years the political profile of the descendants of Constantius I and Theodora was clearly being enhanced.

It has been suggested that this development occurred due to the death of Constantine the Great's mother Helena, since she may have been responsible for impeding their careers as she resented them as Theodora's descendants (Bowersock 1978: 21; and note Julian's hostile attitude to Helena preserved by Libanius: II 35). Certainly belonging to the imperial family was not without its dangers, as the mysterious case of Crispus and Fausta demonstrates. In 326 the Caesar Crispus was arrested and executed. Soon afterwards Constantine's wife Fausta was also killed, apparently steamed to death. These events are difficult to understand as key sources either fail to record them (e.g. Eusebius) or just mention them in passing (e.g. Ammianus Marcellinus 14.11.20). A full source is Zosimus, who relates that Crispus was executed since he was suspected of having an affair with his step-mother, and that Fausta was killed in order to appease the distraught Helena (**II 60 2.29.2**). This seems to be patent pagan propaganda however, since Zosimus uses the events to contextualise Constantine's conversion to Christianity, though this had occurred in the previous decade. Modern historians tend to turn to politics to account for these dramatic deaths (e.g. Odahl 2004: 206–7 with bibliography). Fausta may have been seeking to secure the inheritance of her sons Constantine, Constantius and Constans by bringing down her step-son Crispus, and when Constantine realised her treachery she was punished.

Julian was to discover the dangers of belonging to the imperial family in the aftermath of the death of Constantine the Great on 22 May 337. The details are hazy, but it is clear that several of the male relatives of Julian were put to death (including Julian's father Julius Constantius, his uncle Flavius Dalmatius and his cousins Dalmatius and Hannibalianus), and the empire was left securely in the hands of Constantine II, Constantius II and Constans, who shared it between them. Eusebius (*Life of Constantine* 4.68.2) hints at a military uprising in support of the sons of Constantine, which seems to have been the official line (as Julian himself indicates: **II 7 270C–271B**), but it is common to hold Constantius II primarily responsible (e.g. DiMaio and Arnold 1992). Julian does credit Constantius with the massacre in his *Letter to the Athenians* (**II 7 270C–271A**). However, it was advantageous to take this stance in this declaration of his right to oppose the emperor; there was certainly no point blaming Constantine II or Constans since they were dead (revealingly, after the death of Constantius Julian does widen the target in his *The Caesars*: **II 25 336B**). Constantius II has however found his defenders (e.g. Leedom, 1978: 132–6), and it is possible that circumstances were more complex than his opponents have allowed. In the absence of Constantine there may have been genuine anxiety about the future government of the empire, and Julian's side of the family could have had their own aspirations (**II 56 2.16**). Whilst the murders may shock us, they make political sense and fit into a larger pattern of competition for power in the later Roman empire, such as the events following the retirement of Diocletian from imperial office. The murders are also used by those hostile to Constantius II to make political capital. Julian emphasises the deaths in his *Letter to the Athenians*, whilst Ammianus asserts that Constantius 'destroyed root and branch all who were related to him by blood and race' (21.16.8). This latter claim is certainly an exaggeration, for there were survivors, most notably Julian himself and his half-brother Gallus. The latter was older than Julian, but supposedly spared due to his ill health, whilst Julian was allegedly thought too young to be worth killing (e.g. **II 39 10**). (There also exist, however, stories that Julian had to be actively saved: e.g. **II 43 91**.) It seems evident that the victims were selected as they presented a political threat; less threatening relatives were left alive. In addition to Gallus and Julian these included Constantius' wife, Julian's eponymous maternal uncle, Procopius the future usurper, Julian's maternal grandmother, and the bishop of Nicomedia Eusebius. As for Julian's mother, she had already died, not long after his birth.

2. Private lives

From the time of the family murders in 337 to his accession to sole power in 361, the figure who loomed largest in Julian's life was his cousin the emperor Constantius II (337–61). It was Constantius who ruled the eastern share of the empire, where Julian was to spend most of his life until 354, and by this year Constantius ruled the whole empire as his brother Constantine had been killed in 340 when he clashed with his brother Constans, and Constans had been murdered when the commander Magnentius usurped power in 350. Throughout this period it was Constantius who had direct control over Julian.

After the dramatic events of 337 it seems that Julian's maternal grandmother had a part to play in his upbringing. Julian waxes lyrical on a small estate in Bithynia which she had bequeathed to him, where he had spent time as a boy (**II 16**). At this period Julian was also taught by his mother's old teacher the eunuch Mardonius, to whom he says he was entrusted after his seventh year, and whom he credits as a formative influence, imbuing him with a love of Homer and Hesiod and their values (**II 28 351A–352C**). In his *Consolation to Himself on the Departure of the Excellent Salutius* he recalls his painful separation from his instructor (*Oration* 8 241C). Ammianus asserts that Julian was educated in Nicomedia by the bishop Eusebius (a distant relative) (**II 50 22.9.4**), but Julian himself makes no mention of this. Libanius' account of Julian's early education suggests that Julian and Mardonius spent time in Constantinople (**II 39 11**), and some have thought that they moved to the imperial city when Eusebius became patriarch. Julian's assertion that he was removed 'from the schools' (**II 7 271B**) certainly suggests that his education had become more formal and extensive by the time of his transfer to Macellum (now usually dated to AD 342). It should be noted however that Libanius' account is somewhat confusing as it omits the phase at Macellum (Bowersock 1978: 26).

Macellum was an imperial estate in Cappadocia, not far from the city of Caesarea (**II 58 5.2.9**). Constantius sent both Julian and Gallus to live on the estate, where they remained for six years (**II 7 271C**). Why Constantius took this step is not clear. Some link it with the death of Eusebius (Hunt 1998a: 44), which effectively forced the emperor to do something. Certainly Julian was heading towards puberty, which Gallus had already passed, so maybe Constantius felt the time was right to impose tighter control of their movements as they might become the focus for political opposition. The Macellum episode is a fascinating one to consider, as there are contrasting sources for it. Julian provides a memorable account in his *Letter to the Athenians*, where he conjures up an image of a miserable, isolated and sterile imprisonment (**II 7 271B–D**). An alternative, though equally slanted, view is supplied by Gregory of Nazianzus. He presents the period at Macellum as one of training of Gallus and Julian for imperial power, and also details their development as Christians, both being ordained lectors (**II 43 22–3**). Whilst Gregory's account may be suspect, it is recognised that Julian can give himself away. After the murder of the bishop of Alexandria, George of Cappadocia, in 361 Julian wrote a letter to Ecdicius the Prefect of Egypt requesting that he be sent George's books (**II 13**). In the course of this letter he reveals that his knowledge of George's library was due to the fact that George had lent some books to him to copy when he was in Cappadocia. This has led some to suggest that George had replaced Eusebius as the new Christian tutor (Athanassiadi 1992: 23; Hunt 1998a: 45), but perhaps this pushes the evidence too far. What is more significant is that Julian was not entirely deprived of intellectual stimulation as he claimed. It is also known that there was at least one visitor to Macellum, Constantius himself. This is recorded in the *Letter to the Athenians*, though not in the passage on Macellum (**II 7 274A**). Startlingly Julian asserts that this was the first time that he and Constantius had ever met, which may say more about family relationships generally than it does about the emperor specifically. (Julian's own relationship with Gallus does not seem to have been a close one either, despite their shared experiences.) It is likely that there was more traffic at Macellum than Julian admits, given its proximity to the travel network between the cities of Constantinople and Antioch (Hunt 1998a: 45).

The termination of the residence at Macellum in 348 is more puzzling than its initiation. If Constantius was concerned about the potential danger of Gallus and Julian, why did he let them go? The case of Julian is more perplexing, as it seems that Gallus simply swapped Macellum for the imperial court itself, though he was not to become Caesar until 351. Ammianus records that after the fall of Gallus in 354 Julian was accused of having left Macellum without permission (**II 50 15.2.7**), which suggests an odd lack of clarity, though perhaps the imperial court was grasping at straws: Julian was able to refute the charge. Unlike Gallus however, Julian was free to remain at large. He devoted his time to furthering his education. Julian's pursuit of learning gave him a great deal of mobility. He moved from Constantinople to Nicomedia and then on to Pergamum and Ephesus, and perhaps was able to meet up with Gallus as he journeyed east to take up residence in Antioch as Caesar (Libanius *Oration* 18.17, but see below). At Constantinople he studied rhetoric with the pagan Nicocles and the Christian Hecebolius (**II 37; 39 12; 57 3.1.10**), and perhaps attended the philosophy lectures of Themistius (Smith 1995: 26–7). Libanius asserts that Julian was moved on to Nicomedia since Constantius feared that he would attract too much attention in the imperial city, though this may just be spin (**II 39 13**). Libanius also records that Julian was not allowed to attend his lectures in Nicomedia (Libanius taught there c. 343–9), though he secured notes from someone who had attended. At Pergamum Julian extended his study of philosophy under the pupils of the Neoplatonist Aedesius (himself a pupil of Iamblichus), and from there the trail led to Maximus in Ephesus (**II 52 474–5**). Once again however, in 354, Constantius II intruded into the life of Julian.

3. Return to the imperial arena

Constantius' reintervention in the life of Julian was prompted by the emperor's recent political circumstances. In 350 Constantius found himself the sole surviving son of Constantine the Great, and thus master of the whole of the Roman empire. Such a position was unusual, as power-sharing had been the norm ever since Diocletian took Maximian as his colleague in 285. It seems that one of the purposes of the subsequent establishment of the tetrarchy had been to ensure control of the empire, and though Constantine had striven for sole power, he utilised his relatives, especially his sons, to help him rule. In 350 Constantius II still had no sons of his own, but was faced with the problem of the usurper Magnentius. In this difficult situation Constantius decided to have recourse to Gallus. On 15 March 351 Gallus was made Caesar at Sirmium, and to cement his relationship with the emperor he was married to Constantius' sister Constantina, who had previously been married to Hannibalianus. Gallus was then despatched to the east, to the city of Antioch where Constantius himself had already spent so much of his career. The emperor stayed in the west and took on Magnentius. In September 351 the latter's army was defeated in the Balkans at the battle of Mursa, though Magnentius himself escaped. He was subsequently forced back into Gaul, and defeated again in the summer of 353 at Mons Seleucus, and not long afterwards he committed suicide. Thus Constantius had secured the empire, but also a reputation for being victorious in civil war (e.g. **II 50 21.16.15**).

As for Gallus, his grip on imperial power proved to be brief. In 354 he was recalled to the imperial court at Milan, and as he approached Italy in October he was arrested, deprived of his rank, and taken to a place near Pola where he was questioned and then executed (Ammianus Marcellinus 14.11.19–23). It seems that Gallus' administration had been erratic, and he even opposed Constantius' personnel to the point of treason. Few lamented Gallus' end (Zosimus is an exception). His wife was already dead; Julian's protest in the *Letter to the Athenians* has to resort to special pleading, recognising Gallus' inherent brutal character (271D–272D); Ammianus, no lover of Constantius, condemns Gallus, and presents him as Domitian to Julian's Titus (14.11.28), though the historian was probably biased in favour of the Antiochene elite. The fall of Gallus however had ramifications for Julian. Given their association he too fell under suspicion and was also summoned to Milan.

Yet again, Julian is a key source for the events of his own life. His experiences in the years 354–5 are described in the *Letter to the Athenians* (**II 7** 272D–273A), but also in his earlier *Panegyric on the Empress Eusebia* (**II 2**). Julian recalls that for seven months his movements were controlled and he was kept under guard (and in the *Letter to the Athenians* he also says he lived in the same city as Constantius – Milan – for six months: **II 7** 274A; Ammianus Marcellinus 15.2.8 reports a brief stay at Como), and that he was only finally released due to the influence of the empress Eusebia, Constantius' new wife from Thessalonica. He emphasises that he only saw the emperor once during this time, an audience secured by Eusebia. Julian is vague about the charges that were brought against him, but Ammianus specifies them as leaving Macellum without permission and meeting with Gallus in Constantinople (II 50 15.2.7). This latter information makes sense of Julian's vociferous assertion in the *Letter to the Athenians* that he had not seen Gallus. The familiar joyful conclusion to this episode of detainment is that Julian was sent to attend the university of Athens, once again at the inspiration of Eusebia. But, as Julian makes clear, this did not immediately follow his release. At first he was freed to return to his maternal home in Bithynia, but his journey was cut short and he was redirected to Greece. One might imagine that Julian was delighted to be allowed to pursue his studies again, this time in the famous and distinguished city of Athens. Julian's panegyric on Eusebia certainly conveys this impression as does his letter to the Athenians (when he laments his departure from the city: 274A–B) (and see also his *Letter to Themistius*: II 9 260B). However, perhaps one should be cautious in accepting these declarations at face value (e.g. Drinkwater 1983: 368–9). It is also important to appreciate the brevity of Julian's residence in Athens (Bouffartigue 1992: 47). He may have attended the lectures of the Christian Prohaeresius, befriended Priscus (a pupil of Aedesius) and Himerius (son-in-law of the Platonist Nicagoras), and been initiated in the mysteries at Eleusis, but he was soon recalled to the imperial court in Italy.

Once again difficult circumstances had persuaded the still childless Constantius to seek a partner in power. Since the usurpation of Magnentius the frontiers of Gaul had been weakened, and in 355 another usurper had arisen, the Frank Silvanus, Master of Infantry in Gaul (Ammianus Marcellinus 15.5). Like Gallus before him, Julian was to become Constantius' Caesar, and was elevated to this position on 6 November 355. In this development the sources indicate that a significant role was played by the empress Eusebia, just as was the case when Julian fell under suspicion following the execution of Gallus. Zosimus asserts that the idea to make Julian Caesar was the intelligent Eusebia's alone (II 60 3.1.2), but Ammianus (II 50 15.8.3) and Julian himself (II 2 121B–C) reveal her as a supporter of the proposal rather than its initiator. It is possible that Constantius had already formed this plan earlier in the year, and this may be why Julian was redirected to Athens, to be closer at hand if the court required him. It is also possible that throughout the dealings between Julian and the court in the period 354–5, the empress Eusebia had been deliberately assigned the role of Julian's protector and spokeswoman so as to ease the tensions between the cousins who had such a difficult history (Tougher 1998b). Julian thus found himself transformed. He was shorn of his philosopher's beard, dressed in imperial garb and acclaimed Caesar. He was also given a wife who was a member of the dynasty (in this case Constantius' sister Helena), just as several of his now dead relatives had been before him. He was then despatched to Gaul.

A key question is, what was Julian's reaction to this rapid alteration in his circumstances? Ammianus conjures up a vivid sense of Julian's fear at the greatness that had been thrust upon him, the new Caesar whispering to himself the following Homeric line, 'By purple death I'm seized and fate supreme' (**II 50 15.8.17**). Given the history of his family, fear would have been a natural response, and he himself certainly attests his reluctance to accept the position (**II 2 121B–D; 7 274B–D** and **277A**), though one should remember that these assertions are not the simple outpourings of his heart; to declare desire for power would not have been politic. But perhaps there was also a thrill of anticipation at the opportunity being afforded him.

4. Julian on the Flavian dynasty

As well as having a part to play in the history of his family, the Flavian dynasty, Julian also provided much reflection on it in his writings. This could be both ostensibly positive (e.g. his imperial panegyrics) and overtly negative (e.g. his treatment of Constantine I in his *The Caesars* and of Constantius II in the *Letter to the Athenians*). Julian's verdicts are especially intriguing due to his membership of the dynasty; he was in a good position to comment, though he was of course not disinterested.

The majority of his coverage is of Constantius II, the member of the dynasty who most affected him, but Constantine the Great also receives attention due to his attitude to Christianity and the effect this had on the empire. In the *Letter to the Athenians* Constantius emerges as a suspicious, treacherous and cruel man, an image familiar from other authors, not least Ammianus Marcellinus. This impression can even be conveyed in the imperial orations; in his panegyric on Eusebia Julian asserts that the emperor had been harsh towards him, thus accounting for why Eusebia had to spring to his defence (**II 2 118A–B**), and in the first panegyric on Constantius he acknowledges the emperor's lack of control over the crimes of others (*Oration* 1 16D–17A). As for Constantine, he is ridiculed in *The Caesars* (**II 25 317D–318A, 329C–D,** and **336A–B**). He is selected by the gods to be in their competition to decide who had been the best emperor only because he represented a devotee of pleasure, and as such was not even admitted into their presence but had to stand at the door. When Constantine made his case he is depicted as realising the meagreness of his achievements in comparison with those of Alexander the Great, Julius Caesar, Octavian, Trajan and Marcus Aurelius, and his ignorance is exposed when he does not understand the meaning of 'gardens of Adonis'. Constantine is also characterised as money-loving, self-indulgent and vain in his attention to his appearance. His attraction to Christianity is portrayed as resulting from its easy forgiveness of sinners, an allegation found in Zosimus too (**II 60 2.29.3–4**). A striking account of Constantine and the dynasty is also provided in Julian's *Against the Cynic Heraclius* (**II 14**). Demonstrating to Heraclius how a myth should properly be composed (Smith 1995: 49–50), Julian creates one about his own life. In this he relates how he was called upon by the gods to rectify the crimes of his family. The greed of Constantine is specified again, and the complex family relationships are identified, due to successive marriages and intermarriage, dismissed as 'marriages that were not marriages'. The conflicts and murders that occurred within the family after the death of Constantine are mentioned, and the poor behaviour of his sons is attributed to Constantine's failure to train them in virtue. The religious activity of the sons of Constantine also features, the destroying of temples and the building of churches. The character of Constantius II and his regime are focused on. He is depicted as neglectful, distracted, deceived and a prey to flatterers, served mostly by rapacious shepherds.

Thus Julian could be a critical observer of the Flavians, unsurprisingly given his history and enthusiasms. However, his stance is not so simple, for Julian's claim to power rested on the fact that he was a member of the dynasty. This is demonstrated by his attitude to Constantius II once he was dead; Julian gave him a full imperial funeral and participated in this ceremony (e.g. **II 44 17**). His pride in belonging to the imperial family is strongly asserted in his hymn to Helios, a boon he presents as coming from the god himself (**II 26 131B**). Julian's more positive and traditional take on the dynasty is reflected in the panegyrics on Constantius, which naturally deal with the ancestry of the family. In these Julian follows the party line in tracing the imperial origins of the dynasty to the emperor Claudius II Gothicus (268–70) (**II 1 6D–7A; 3**). He also stresses the intense imperialness of the dynasty, noting for instance that Constantius II had two imperial grandfathers, Constantius I and Maximian (father of Fausta) (*Oration* 1 7A). Notably in the second panegyric Julian is also more confident in declaring his own membership of the dynasty. It is obvious that the figures of

Claudius Gothicus and Constantius I were of huge significance to Julian, for they represented for him the unsullied pagan ancestors of the dynasty, and are depicted as worthy emperors. This is especially clear in his *The Caesars*, since Julian declares that the punishment meted out to the Flavian dynasty by the gods on account of its impiety and in-house murders was alleviated 'on account of Claudius and Constantius' (**II 25 336B**). This perception is also evident in the family myth found in *Against the Cynic Heraclius*. Julian notes that amongst the votive offerings stolen from the temples by the sons of Constantine were those that their own ancestors had made (**II 14 228C**). Julian presents the dynasty as having abandoned Helios, and himself as a child of the god, given his divine mission 'to purify [his] ancestral house' out of the gods' 'respect for [his] ancestors' (**II 14 234C**). It is well known that the sun god had been the favoured deity of the dynasty (e.g. Barnes 1981: 36–7).

Finally, Julian also comments on the ethnic origin of the dynasty. In his *Misopogon* he thrice refers to the Thracian origin of his family (**II 28 348C–D** and **367C**; see also 349C–D). He uses this to set himself apart from them, for he is contrastingly Hellenised and a Hellenophile. It is perhaps this aspect of his identity that was crucial in his conversion from his family's recently-adopted Christianity to their traditional Roman religion. This conversion is the subject of the next chapter.

CHAPTER 2

Conversion

1. Evidence and arguments

One of the puzzles about the conversion of Julian from Christianity to paganism is that he tells us so little about it. The main statement he makes is that he was a Christian until his twentieth year, thus placing his conversion around AD 351 (**II 24**). He also remarks on his attraction to the sun and stars from his childhood, but such an enthusiasm was presumably not unique to him and only acquired significance in the light of his subsequent religious transformation (**II 26**). Given the lack of evidence from the horse's mouth historians have been forced to hypothesise about Julian's motivations. Interpretations can vary drastically, usefully illustrated for example by the contrasting views of Athanassiadi (1992) and Smith (1995).

To understand Julian's actions some historians have veered into the territory of psychoanalysis, an understandable temptation given the amount of evidence that survives and that much of it derives from the pen of Julian. However, such an approach can be dangerous due to the contrived nature of the sources. There has been a tendency, for example, to assert that Julian's traumatic trials as a child at the hands of a Christian emperor, and his unhappy experiences at the hands of Christian teachers such as Hecebolius and George of Cappadocia, may have led to Christianity becoming repellent to him (e.g. Bowersock 1978; Athanassiadi 1992). However the image of the trauma suffered at the hands of Constantius owes much to Julian himself, not without an eye to the political advantage. This approach also privileges Julian's experiences, ignoring the traumas experienced by others, such as Gallus and even Constantius himself. As for Hecebolius and George, there are questions to be asked about the evidence concerning the character of the former and the exact nature of the relationship of the latter with Julian.

Historians have also pursued other explanations for Julian's religious transformation. It is clear that Julian had a deep love of Hellenic culture, as he testifies in works such as the *Misopogon* and as is evident from his actions, for example his own literary activity. It is possible, then, that his paganism was simply an expression of this enthusiasm. Crucial in Julian's hellenophilism was his education. He himself describes the impact that his tutor the eunuch Mardonius had on him, instilling a love of Homer and Hesiod and an appreciation of their values. Another key figure was the philosopher Maximus, whom Julian sought out at Ephesus. Indeed Maximus is often thought to be the key figure in Julian's conversion. Libanius declares the vital role of the philosopher in a speech delivered to the emperor (**II 36**), whilst Julian's indication of the timing of his abandonment of Christianity coincides with the period of his studies with the philosophers in Asia Minor. This evidence can be taken to indicate that Julian's religious transformation occurred at a specific moment, but some historians have argued rather that his conversion was an extended process (e.g. Athanassiadi 1992).

The different interpretations do not stop there. It has been suggested that Julian was never a committed Christian, so 'conversion' would not be the right term for Julian's experience. Further, there is also the issue of the nature of Julian's paganism. One view is that his Neoplatonic initiation was quickly followed by initiation in the cult of the sun god Mithras which became central to Julian's identity as a pagan and to his plans for the revival of paganism in the empire (Athanassiadi 1992). However the centrality of Mithraism in Julian's devotion and religious ambitions can be questioned (e.g. Smith 1995; Renucci 2000), and some have even doubted that he was a Mithraist at all (Turcan cited by Smith 1995: 127). It is clear then that much about Julian's 'conversion' is debated. In this chapter the evidence and hypotheses shall be explored in the context of his youthful experiences and education.

2. Early education

Julian was born into a Christian family and raised as a Christian. This did not preclude a traditional classical education, though there is evidence that Christians could be wary of the dangers of pagan literature as well as alert to its advantages (e.g. Nimmo Smith 2001: xvi–xxiii). Regarding his early education, Julian himself emphasises his instruction at the hands of Mardonius (**II 28 351A–352C**). Mardonius is described as a eunuch and a Scythian, so he was presumably a slave, though he may have been freed. The tag 'Scythian' is understood as a deliberate archaism and it is assumed he was of Gothic origin. He became Julian's tutor (*paidagogos*) after his seventh year, having previously taught Homer and Hesiod to his mother Basilina. Julian credits the eunuch with a deep impact upon his character, moral values and literary tastes, of which the primacy of Homer is acknowledged. The impression that Mardonius made is also attested by others, such as Libanius (**II 39 11**), though it is likely that this was just echoing Julian. Modern historians have been happy to follow this line too, and there seems no reason to doubt it. If support is sought, maybe it is found in Julian's teaching edict of 362 (**II 22**), which perhaps assumes that teachers had a high degree of influence on their students. The question of Mardonius' own religious convictions remains open. It might be assumed that a Christian family would not employ a pagan tutor (Bowersock 1978: 24), but such a stance can be challenged. Maybe the positive manner in which Julian treats the eunuch in his recollections suggests that he thought he was a pagan.

It is important to appreciate that Julian's account of his early education is highly selective; there is much that he does not tell us. He does not mention the role of the bishop Eusebius, which Ammianus records (**II 50 22.9.4**). He does indicate that he also went to school when Mardonius was his tutor, but reveals no more (**II 7 271B**). Regarding his years at Macellum, he recalls the pain of his separation from Mardonius and in the *Letter to the Athenians* conjures up the impression of an intellectual desert. However, as we have seen, he did have access to the library of the Christian George of Cappadocia (**II 13**). He knew that it contained Christian texts, but also works on philosophy and rhetoric, and he admits that he copied some of them when he was at Macellum. Some have argued that George's relationship with Julian was a formal one, that he was his tutor or minder (e.g. Athanassiadi 1992: 23; Hunt 1998a: 45). The impression Julian gives in the letter to Ecdicius is of more informal contacts, though it is possible that he has not revealed the true picture. The view that George's vile character alienated Julian from Christianity is hard to substantiate. It is evident that Julian loathed George, judging by his reaction to his death in Alexandria in 361 (**II 12**), but this may have been an attitude common to pagans. The contact with George does however reveal a Christian dimension to life at Macellum. (Perhaps Julian even copied some Christian texts from George's library!) This aspect of the Cappadocian sojourn is explicitly revealed by other authors. Gregory of Nazianzus relates how Julian and Gallus were engaged in erecting a monument to Christian martyrs, though he utilises this to make a point about Julian's paganism, as his building work collapsed (**II 43 24**; Sozomen names a specific martyr, St Mamas:

II **58** 12). Whilst the lesson of the anecdote may be informed by hindsight, it is possible that such Christian activity did occur. Gregory also records that the half-brothers were ordained lectors (II **43** 23), a role which Julian apparently later took up in Nicomedia (II **57** 3.1.20). Thus at Macellum Julian continued his studies but also maintained the identity of a Christian.

With the termination of his residence in Cappadocia Julian returned to more formal studies in Constantinople. He says little about this directly, and our earliest witness is Libanius (II **37** and **39** 12), though the allusiveness of the information he provides means that we are grateful for provision of specifics by later sources (e.g. II **57** 3.1.10). Julian was taught rhetoric by a pagan and a Christian, Nicocles and Hecebolius respectively. Libanius' presentation of these two men has been very influential, with Nicocles as the admirable developer of Julian's appreciation of Homer and Hecebolius as the incompetent knave who alienated Julian further from Christianity. It is recognised that Libanius is hardly a reliable commentator, having no love for Hecebolius due to professional conflict and having a fluctuating attitude towards Nicocles (e.g. Bouffartigue 1992: 41–2; Smith 1995: 26–7). Whilst other sources castigate Hecebolius too, it seems noteworthy that Julian wrote a letter to him (ed. Wright 1913–23, vol. 3: Letter 63) but never mentions Nicocles. What remains is that Julian's education continued, and in a world where Christians could study under both pagan and Christian teachers. Indeed it seems that at this time Julian was also taught by the famous pagan Themistius (agent of so many Christian emperors), or at least attended his lectures on Plato (Smith 1995: 27). (On Julian's relationship with Themistius see for example Brauch 1993b; Vanderspoel 1995: 115–34.)

From Constantinople Julian moved on to Nicomedia. Our knowledge of this phase of his education derives from the account of Libanius (II **39** 13–15). Libanius attributes the change of location to Constantius' nervousness at Julian's presence in Constantinople. This sounds like a gratuitous dig at the emperor, but it tends to be accepted as accurate, apparently supported by Julian's later mention of the dangers he faced at that time (II **9** 259B–C). It has the merit at least of providing an explanation for the move, but perhaps there is no need to resort to imperial politics; an educational reason could be equally valid (Hunt 1998a: 45). However, at Nicomedia there was an element of control, for Libanius reports that Julian was not allowed to attend his lectures. He asserts that the ban was imposed by Hecebolius, but that despite the prohibition Julian obtained copies of the lectures. Libanius proudly records that such was the influence of his style on Julian that it was thought that he had in fact been Libanius' pupil. Given the self-glorification of Libanius' narrative, and the fact that there is no independent testimony, some have doubted these details (e.g. Bouffartigue 1992: 42). However Julian did demonstrate respect for Libanius, for instance sending him his own work from Gaul (**II 33**; for a later example see **II 41**). If the story of Julian's exclusion from Libanius' lectures has any validity, it is notable that it suggests that his interest in the pagan Libanius was due to concern about rhetoric rather than to concern about religion. The account of Libanius is also frustrating as it does not reveal what studies Julian did pursue in Nicomedia. Did he simply remain under the instruction of Hecebolius? Following another oration of Libanius (*Oration* 13.11) Athanassiadi (1992: 31) suggests some contact with pagan philosophers in the city, which was to lead Julian to the Neoplatonic philosophers at Pergamum, the next stage of his intellectual journey.

Before turning to consider this it is useful to establish some preliminary conclusions. It is clear that education was a key aspect of Julian's youth. Whilst it has been observed that this was hardly unusual for young members of the Roman elite, Julian's enthusiasm does seem notable and probably authentic despite being reported with hindsight. Also, Julian was not a typical member of that elite; he was related to the imperial family (though denied an imperial role himself) and was of concern to Constantius, whatever is made of reports of the emperor's character and motivations. As such, Julian probably felt the uncertainty of his position, and maybe viewed intellectual activity as a safe outlet. This is not to deny his personal passion, but perhaps it fed it. On the question of religious preference, it is hard to judge from the limited evidence. However the hypotheses about his gradual alienation from Christianity can be questioned, and there remains his assertion that his conversion came at a specific time. It is this key moment that will be considered next.

3. Continuing education

The main source for Julian's experiences with the philosophers of western Asia Minor is Eunapius' *Lives of the Sophists*, where Julian is treated within the account of the career of Maximus of Ephesus (**II 52 473–5**). This narrative of Julian's time with the philosophers is generally accepted, though there are oddities about the information supplied by Eunapius. For instance, his description of Julian's education prior to coming to Pergamum is severely condensed and vague. He seems to confuse Mardonius with palace eunuchs who were charged with Julian's instruction. Details of Julian's activity after encountering Maximus seem to conflict with other evidence too. He asserts that Julian went directly from Ephesus to Athens and under his own steam, which can cause confusion (e.g. Bowersock 1978: 30–1). Perhaps Eunapius was simply not that concerned with the exact details of all of Julian's experiences; his focus here was the philosophers. On the other hand, one might expect him to have been better informed, given the writing of his *History* and its focus on Julian.

According to Eunapius Julian had imperial permission to travel in pursuit of his education, and relates that he came to Pergamum as he had heard about the wisdom of the philosopher Aedesius. This appears to support the notion that Julian had already had contact with philosophers, who would have provided such information. Further, it suggests that Julian wanted to take his education to a higher level. Aedesius subscribed to Neoplatonism, that is the system of Platonic philosophy initiated in the third century AD by Plotinus (Wallis 1995; Smith 2004). The pupils of Plotinus, including Porphyry, had promoted the movement, and Aedesius' own master Iamblichus had been a pupil of Porphyry. By the time Julian met Aedesius the philosopher was very old, and he entrusted Julian to two of his pupils, Eusebius of Myndus and Chrysanthius of Sardis. Eunapius depicts these two men as representing different aspects of Neoplatonism. Whilst Chrysanthius was an adept of theurgy, that is ritual magic (Dodds 1947; Shaw 1985), Eusebius insisted on the primacy of dialectic. Eunapius asserts that Julian revered Eusebius, but became intrigued about the other dimension of Neoplatonism which the philosopher rejected. This led Eusebius to relate a story about an exponent of theurgy, Maximus of Ephesus, another pupil of Aedesius. He described how Maximus had seemed to animate a statue of the goddess Hecate, making her smile and laugh and the torches she held to burst into flame. The aim of the story was to ridicule Maximus, but, so says Eunapius, Julian was instead enthused and departed for Ephesus to study with him, where they were soon joined by Chrysanthius.

As has been seen, it is thought that Julian's tutelage under Maximus marked his transition from Christian to pagan. Libanius directly credits the philosopher, and Julian's indication of the timing of his conversion seems to fit. In addition, Julian was evidently devoted to Maximus: he wrote to him (e.g. **II 8** and **10**), expressed his attachment to him when he became emperor (e.g. **II 50 22.7.3**), and he had him join his retinue (e.g. **II 50 25.3.23; 52 477–8**). Julian's idolisation of the Neoplatonic theurgist Iamblichus (e.g. there are several acknowledgements in his hymn to Helios) also seems to be an expression of the debt Julian owed Maximus (this is supported by **II 14 235A–C**). What exactly happened with Maximus in Ephesus is not clear however. Gregory of Nazianzus (**II 43 55–6**) indicates that Julian was initiated into the Neoplatonic mysteries in a cave (e.g. Athanassiadi 1992: 37; Smith 1995: 130; Renucci 2000: 80–1), but his report is slight and hostile. As to why Julian took this step, one can only resort to hypotheses. Perhaps it was a logical progression from his devotion to Hellenic culture; perhaps it was a reaction against his experiences at the hands of Christians; perhaps he was looking to find meaning in his life; or perhaps it was simply the Maximus effect. There is also the view that Julian's action can be read as typical student rebellion, but it may be felt that this at least is an inadequate explanation as it belittles the experience. Regarding the question of whether the conversion was a process or an event, the case for the latter is supported by Julian's own comment on the chronology and by the role ascribed to Maximus. However, perhaps it is possible that both positions can co-exist: a developing attraction culminating in a specific moment.

Associated with Julian's new identity as a pagan is the question of his attachment to the sun god Mithras. Athanassiadi (1992: 38) has argued that Julian's initiation in this well-organised and hierarchical cult quickly followed his transformation. This is, however, a controversial issue. Some have doubted that Julian was ever an initiate, but his own assertion in *The Caesars* should not be underestimated (**II 25 336C**). What is a matter for debate is the timing of the initiation. Smith (1995: 136–7) has suggested a more appropriate context might be Julian's residence in Gaul, when he acquired not only an imperial role but a military one too: as is well known the cult of Mithras was particularly popular among Roman soldiers. The question of Julian's Mithraism also relates to the nature of his religious ambitions for the Roman empire, but this will be discussed in a more appropriate place below (Chapter 5).

4. After Ephesus

Following his watershed experience in Ephesus most historians agree that Julian returned to Nicomedia. Bouffartigue (1992: 45) has argued that in fact Julian was still in Ephesus when summoned to Milan in 354 as he visited Ilium on his journey, but this seems to ignore good evidence for Julian's life in Nicomedia. It is possible that Bouffartigue's point could still be valid, if the suggestion that Julian attended Gallus' elevation as Caesar (Barnes 1987: 209) is followed. Maybe he did travel from Ephesus via Ilium, but in 351 not 354. However, since Julian asserts that he had only seen Constantius twice before the meeting in Milan in 355 (II 7 274A: at Macellum and in Milan in 354), this must remain doubtful.

Despite his dramatic religious transformation Julian had to conceal it from the wider world (II 39 19). He was, essentially, in the closet. He could be open with a select few but otherwise he had to maintain a pretence of Christianity. On his return to Nicomedia he served as lector (II 57 3.1.20), but on the estate he had inherited from his grandmother he hosted intellectual discussions (II 16; see also II 39 20). Julian also alludes to his role as patron and protector in Ionia and beyond (II 9 259C–D). In spite of the need for concealment it seems that Julian's behaviour did attract attention. Philostorgius records that Gallus was concerned by his half-brother's activities and despatched his Christian adviser Aetius to Julian to bring him into line (II 56 3.27; a letter from Gallus to Julian also refers to this episode, but it is considered to be invented: ed. Wright 1913–23, vol. 3: Letter 82). Perhaps Julian was able to convince him that his interests were purely intellectual. The actions of the bishop Pegasius also suggest suspicion of Julian's concern for the gods, or in fact knowledge from a pagan insider. When Julian was journeying to the west he visited Ilium on the way and was given a guided tour by Pegasius, during which the bishop indicated his own attachment to the gods (II 27). Whether Julian's religious conversion led to any political ambitions is a moot point. Libanius declares that pagans who were in the know wanted Julian to become emperor, and that Julian did countenance such a suggestion, but only for the good of paganism and the empire, not for the sake of personal power or wealth (II 39 21–3). This question will be explored further in the following chapter.

In the light of his religious secret, Julian's anxiety when summoned to Milan after the fall of Gallus must have been intensified. As far as can be gathered, though, he was viewed by the government simply as an intellectual; witness the decision to send him to the university in Athens. Some have seen the empress Eusebia's interest in Julian as that of a fellow intellectual (Aujoulat 1983: 80). She was certainly alert to Julian's enthusiasm, evidenced also by the later gift of books to take to Gaul (II 2 123D–124A). However, there is little to support the notion that she was educated beyond normal limits, still less that she was a secret pagan too (Aujoulat 1983: 81).

Julian's attendance at the university of Athens was to mark the termination of his formal education, but it also witnessed the formation of further influential relationships and the embracing of further religious experience. It is often confidently asserted that Julian was taught by the Christian Prohaeresius and the pagan Himerius, but there is no direct evidence to this effect (Bouffartigue 1992: 46). It is known that Julian was in Athens at the same time as Basil of Caesarea and Gregory of Nazianzus (**II 44 23**; also Gregory of Nazianzus *Oration* 43.21), and that they were taught by Prohaeresius and Himerius (Socrates 4.26.6 and Sozomen 6.17.1), and so it is assumed that Julian was taught by them too. We do know something of Julian's subsequent relationship with these two men. He wrote to Prohaeresius later (ed. Wright 1913–23, vol. 3: Letter 14), and apparently exempted him from the teaching edict (**II 49 2f**), whilst Himerius visited the court (**II 52 494**), perhaps summoned by the emperor (Barnes 1987: 220–2). That they were his teachers in Athens can only be conjecture. What is certain is that at Athens Julian befriended Priscus the Thesprotian or Molossian, another of Aedesius' pupils. The fact that the relationship was not a formal one has been seen by some as indicating that Julian was deliberately keeping his distance from the pagan so as not to attract suspicion (Bouffartigue 1992: 46), but they were clearly in each other's company anyway. They seem to have become close. Julian corresponded with Priscus from Gaul and invited him to visit (e.g. **II 5**; see also ed. Wright 1913–23, vol. 3: Letters 1 and 5), and Priscus was with him on the Persian campaign (e.g. **II 50 25.3.23** and **52 478**). Julian also seems to have made friends with his fellow student, the Christian Basil of Caesarea, for he later invited him to court (ed. Wright 1913–23, vol. 3: Letter 26). Beyond these relationships, we know that Julian sought out the hierophant of the cult of Demeter, who was later to visit him in Gaul (**II 52 475–6**). Julian is presumed to have been initiated in the Eleusinian mysteries, but the role of Himerius (son-in-law of the Platonist Nicagoras, one-time torch-bearer at Eleusis) in this development is again hypothetical. This initiation tends to be neglected compared to the attention devoted to his induction into the cult of Mithras, though a case for its importance has been made (Renucci 2000: 99–105; but see also Geffcken 1978: 139). (This will be considered further in Chapter 5 where Julian's religious identity will be explored.) How Julian's experiences in Athens would have developed is a matter for conjecture given his quick recall to Milan, his elevation to the position of Caesar and his despatch to Gaul. It is the crucial Gallic phase of his career that is the subject of the following chapter.

CHAPTER 3

Gaul

1. A partial account

The Gallic phase was the most critical period of Julian's career. It marked his first experience of administrative and military duties, as well as his emergence as a major political figure, culminating in his arrogation of the position of Augustus in 360. For this vital segment of his life historians are, however, largely dependent on pro-Julian sources (Bowersock 1978: 34; Hunt 1998a: 49). Most obviously there is his own *Letter to the Athenians*, written to justify his conflict with Constantius. In addition the account of Ammianus begins to come into its own as a history of Julian, signalled clearly by the start of Book 16 which also indicates the extent of his admiration for his subject (**II 50 16.1.1–4**). Mamertinus, Libanius, Eunapius and Zosimus all have their contributions to make too. It is important to recognise the bias of these sources. However, whilst Julian set the tone, they do not necessarily speak with the same voice. Differences can be revealing of the degree to which Julian's version of events has been doctored to suit his purposes. Further, his account can be both questioned on its own evidence and augmented by other of his writings.

2. Julian's initial role and authority

In his *Letter to the Athenians* Julian presents a striking image of his limited role and authority in Gaul (**II 7 277D–278B**). He asserts that Constantius intended him to be a mere figurehead and ordered that he was to be closely observed for signs of revolt, and he comments on his lack of opportunity to take charge of the army. He relates that he was sent to Gaul with only 360 soldiers and that the generals held military authority, despite the fact that he was involved in campaigning from 356. He goes on to say that this situation altered in 357, when Constantius gave him control of the troops, after which amongst his achievements was the recovery of Cologne.

The jaundiced nature of this account of his early experiences in Gaul is evident even without consulting other sources. Since Julian had no experience of political and military leadership it seems quite natural that Constantius would have been concerned to have him monitored, and for others to make major decisions. Neither should one forget the difficulties Constantius had faced in the 350s with usurpers and the Caesar Gallus, so this would have added to his wariness (Hunt 1998a: 50). The fact that Julian was despatched with a limited number of troops can be understood in a less sinister light; they were probably just an escort as the majority of the troops were already in Gaul (Bowersock 1978: 36).

Resorting to other evidence proves illuminating. The placing of the recapture of Cologne in 357 can be challenged (Bowersock 1978: 36). Ammianus (15.8.19) indicates that Cologne fell in 355, and since Julian himself says he retook it ten months later this must have been in 356. Perhaps, then, the Caesar's military authority was not checked for as long as he asserts. Ammianus also reveals that Constantius was willing to support Julian in the face of internal opposition in the episode of Marcellus the Master of the Cavalry (II 50 16.7.1–2; see also 16.4). When Julian was besieged in Sens in the winter of 356–7 Marcellus did not come to his assistance. When this was reported to Constantius the emperor sacked Marcellus (an event the *Letter to the Athenians* alludes to), and did not countenance his allegations that Julian was nurturing higher ambitions. (Odd behaviour for a suspicious emperor keen to keep his Caesar in his place!) In addition, Ammianus testifies that the military activity undertaken in Gaul against the Alamanni was planned to coincide with attacks on them from the south (II 50 16.11.3), a scheme followed as early as 356 (Bowersock 1978: 38; Hunt 1998a: 50–1). The participation of Julian in such a defined strategy makes the claim that he was simply a figurehead look disingenuous.

There is reason to believe, then, that Julian's position in his first years in Gaul was less bleak than he alleged. Bowersock's assertion that 'Julian had full authority as Caesar, was glad of it, and used it' (1978: 36) is borne out by a consideration of his early military and administrative endeavours.

3. War and money, 356–8

Julian's achievements in these spheres are not just hailed by himself and his ancient supporters, but also by modern historians, such as Athanassiadi who speaks of Gaul's 'renaissance' under the Caesar (1992:

60). Julian is depicted as a super soldier and an economic whiz kid. The *Letter to the Athenians* sketches his military triumphs (**II 7** esp. **280C–D**). He first makes clear the poor condition of Gaul at the time of his arrival, recounting how the Germans had sacked towns and taken up residence near some of these, and emphasising the extent of their penetration and of the devastation they had wrought. In addition to celebrating his recovery of Cologne he mentions in particular the battle of Strasbourg in 357, describing it as a famous victory. Julian claims that Gaul was transformed, with all the barbarians being driven out, the towns recovered, and Roman ships able to navigate the Rhine. This is not the end of his feats, however, for he records how he went on the offensive against the Salii and Chamavi in 358. He concludes with a summary of his achievements. In the account, his economic successes are bound up with his military ones, as the latter aided the former. He mentions especially his abandoning of the policy of paying the barbarians to secure passage on the Rhine, a policy that had been devised by Florentius, the Praetorian Prefect. Julian also refers generally to his opposition to Florentius' greed.

This vision is largely supported by the other sources, though they can go into more detail and add further information. The account of Ammianus, who was in Gaul from 355–7 under the general Ursicinus, is recognised as the major testimony. Julian's energetic military activities prior to the capture of Cologne are described (16.2), including his recovery of Brumath, as are those prior to the battle of Strasbourg (16.11), such as the assault on those Alamanni who had sought refuge on islands in the Rhine. The account of the battle of Strasbourg forms an extended set piece (16.12), celebrating the Caesar as a military hero (Blockley 1977: 219–20). It seems that Ammianus is following Julian's lead here, since he wrote his own account of the battle (**II 34 25; 51 Fragment 17**). (Julian's observation that the Athenians may have heard of the famous victory is perhaps an allusion to his work.) Whether Julian included the detail that he had been hailed Augustus by the army after the successful conclusion of the battle (**II 50 16.12.64**) is of course unknowable. Julian's further achievements of 357 and 358 are also described by Ammianus: the campaigning against the Alamanni but also the Franks, including the Salii and Chamavi (17.1–2; 17.8; 17.10). He emphasises that some of this occurred on the far side of the Rhine, a feature Julian showed himself proud of in the *Letter to the Athenians*.

When it comes to the Caesar's financial measures, Ammianus fleshes out Julian's thin account (Matthews 1989: 89–90). The figure of Florentius looms large again. Julian opposed his proposed additional

levies on top of the standard taxation and got his way, despite
Constantius' caution in defence of the Praetorian Prefect (**II 50
17.3.2–5**). Ammianus adds that the Caesar was granted the administration of Belgica II, and kept the taxation at manageable levels (**II 50
17.3.6**). He also reports that for the whole of Gaul Julian was able to
reduce taxation for each individual from twenty-five to seven gold
pieces (**II 50 16.5.14**).

Thus one is presented with an extremely positive assessment
of Julian's conduct of war and administration. This needs to be
interrogated. Julian's *Letter to the Athenians* is designed as an attack
on Constantius, and an element of this is to contrast the Caesar's
embracing of an active military role with the Augustus' preference for
buying peace and taking the credit for the successes of others. Julian
dwells on the fact that it was Constantius who celebrated the triumph
for the victory at Strasbourg, and gained the glory of exhibiting
the captured king Chnodomarius (**II 7 279B–C**). Constantius is also
depicted as being soft on barbarians, willing to negotiate with them and
pay for passage on the Rhine, rather than fight them (**II 7 279D–280B**).
Julian was intent on denigrating Constantius, and this hostility to the
emperor also imbues the other accounts of Julian's Gallic career. The
question is then begged, was Julian prepared to exaggerate his own
achievements also?

In terms of his military success, some modern historians have indeed
wondered if Julian overstated the extent of the German problem in Gaul
so as to enhance his reputation (Hunt 1998a: 49–50; and see more
generally Drinkwater 1996). The fact that Julian wrote an account of the
battle of Strasbourg shows that he was willing to blow his own trumpet,
the sound of which reverberates in the work of others. Despite this, the
narrative of events seems to speak for itself. In addition, Ammianus
provides explanations for Julian's effectiveness as a soldier. He notes his
speed of action (**II 50 16.2.5**; see also 17.8.1–2), as well as his learning of
caution (16.2.11); his appreciation of when to make peace (16.3.2;
17.1.12; 17.10.3–4), and of when to be ruthless (17.8.4; 17.10.5–9); and
his intelligence (17.2.3). In particular Ammianus comments on Julian's
relationship with his troops. He records that Julian adopted the lifestyle
of an ordinary soldier (**II 50 16.5.3**; see also 16.5.5) (and see also the
testimony of Gregory of Nazianzus: **II 43 71**), and provided personal
leadership (**II 50 16.12.29**). The Caesar also knew the importance of
allowing his troops to rest (16.4.4), but had the ability to encourage
them to further action when necessary (16.12.41; 17.1.2). (Another
method of firing up the troops is related by Libanius (*Oration* 18.45):

Julian put a bounty on the heads of the enemy.)

Ammianus adds then to the picture of Julian as a super soldier. Interestingly, however, he can also provide some corrective to it. As has been observed the Caesar was not just acting alone. It is clear that his activities were part of an organised campaign to resecure the Rhine, in which trapping the Alamanni in a pincer movement was a key tactic. Co-operation was the name of the game. Ammianus also stresses the quality of the Master of Cavalry Severus (**II 50 16.11.1**), who had been despatched by Constantius to replace the disgraced Marcellus. It is possible that he was instrumental in the successes of 357 and 358, though it is stated that his enthusiasm and courage wilted when they crossed the Rhine (17.10.1–2). (He was replaced by Lupicinus in 359: 18.2.7.) In addition to these factors, Ammianus can even indicate less successful aspects of Julian's military career. He reports that in 357 the Caesar wanted to delay engaging the Alamanni, but was overruled by the determination of his soldiers and the chief officials, especially Florentius (**II 50 16.12.13–14**). If Julian's preference had been followed perhaps the famous victory of Strasbourg would not have occurred (Matthews 1989: 91–2). (Some even view Strasbourg as an easy victory anyway: Murdoch 2003: 57.) It is also related that Julian earned the wrath of his troops in 358 due to a lack of food supplies (**II 50 17.9.3–6**). Ammianus details the insults they hurled at Julian, but then turns the spotlight on Constantius for keeping the Caesar short of funds. Nevertheless, it is clear that in this instance Julian had made an error of judgement (17.9.2). Elsewhere, Ammianus can give the impression that Julian is successful in spite of himself (**II 50 16.2.5**).

The narrative that Ammianus constructs can also be read differently by modern historians, to the detriment of Julian. Whilst Ammianus praises Julian's successes and criticises the actions of Marcellus and Barbatio, an alternative interpretation is possible. Julian can be seen to engage in reckless independent actions which jeopardise the larger objectives (Bowersock 1978: 39, 41; Matthews 1989: 299–300; Hunt 1998a: 51). In such a scenario it is understandable that other officers would come to resent him. This has application for his dealings with Florentius too (Hunt 1998a: 54).

Whilst Julian's economic measures did lead to a clash with the Praetorian Prefect, his sensitivity to the ability of tax payers to meet the demands of the government seems creditable. Such generosity was not unknown in Roman rulers, witness Constantine the Great's own actions in Gaul (*Panegyrici Latini* 5.10.5–13.1). Perhaps there is a sense that Julian was seeking to make his mark with a popular action. Perhaps the improving situation in Gaul and the booty raised from successful campaigns lent themselves to such cutbacks.

To an extent then, Julian's account of his achievements can be questioned and tempered. Nevertheless, that he did have a measure of success and made a deep impact cannot be doubted. The fact that this was accomplished by a bookish youth with no experience of public life makes it all the more remarkable, and makes one wonder how he accomplished it. Ammianus indicates that Julian did receive some military training (**II 50 16.5.10**). Modern historians can fall back on the factor of his bookishness itself: Julian had learnt the lessons of history (Bowersock 1978: 36; Athanassiadi 1992: 55). (Julian supports this view himself, for in his panegyric on Eusebia he acknowledges the practical use of books for military inspiration (*Oration* 3 124B–D).) The major impression one is left with, however, is that Julian threw himself into the role of Caesar as he had nothing to lose. His actions bespeak a reckless resolve, a desire to prove himself and make a difference. Ammianus contributes significantly to this reading of Julian's motivations; in addition to the material already cited there are noteworthy passages on Julian's determination (16.2.2), his fury (16.11.8) and his lack of fear (16.12.3). Despite the picture which he helps to create, Ammianus rebukes the contemporary notion that Julian only embraced an energetic military role as he thought he might die anyway (**II 50 17.1.14**), but the fact that this was a current belief speaks volumes. The extent of Julian's boldness is reflected by the fact that he was even prepared to challenge the wishes of the emperor. Of course, without the addition of some ability, such behaviour would probably not have got him very far.

4. Usurpation

The central event of Julian's Gallic career was his acclamation as Augustus in Paris early in 360. Whether it was a spontaneous reaction to events or engineered is a matter for debate, as is the degree of Julian's complicity, if indeed it was deliberately brought about. The immediate context was the command Constantius despatched to Gaul that troops should be transferred from there to the east to assist in opposing the Persians, a move that is also open to interpretation: was it intended to weaken the Caesar, or was it an entirely genuine demand? Before these issues can be explored it is necessary to establish the details of the request and the sources' varied presentation of what occurred.

Ammianus reports that the conveyor of Constantius' demand was the tribune and notary Decentius, and that the terms of the demand were that Julian should relinquish his auxiliaries (the Heruli, Batavi, Celts and Petulantes) as well as 300 men from each of the remaining units of his army (**II 50 20.4.2**). This was to be overseen by Lupicinus, the Master of Cavalry, whilst the *tribunus stabuli* Sintula was to commandeer choice members of the Scutarii and Gentiles of the palace guard also (20.4.3). The latter task was accomplished, but complications with the former arose as Lupicinus was away in Britain. (The task was also fraught as Julian had assured his German troops that they would not have to serve south of the Alps: 20.4.4.) Finding himself in charge, Decentius decided to gather the departing troops at Paris, which Julian had made his residence after the campaigns of 357. There the soldiers expressed their discontent by acclaiming Julian Augustus.

In his *Letter to the Athenians* Julian is keen to declare his loyalty to Constantius and his innocence in this development, and emphasises that it was the work of the gods (**II 7** esp. **284A–C**). He acknowledges that circumstances were difficult, as not only was Lupicinus absent but so was Florentius. He also admits that there was discontent: an anonymous letter was written to the Petulantes and Celts in Paris attacking Constantius for his treatment of the Gauls and of Julian (**II 7 282D–283B**). Thus there was urgency for Decentius, as well as Nebridius (the Quaestor) and Pentadius (the Master of Offices), to hurry the departure of the troops. Julian recalls that he met the legions when they gathered (as was customary, he adds pointedly), but encouraged them to be on their way. He is at pains to assert that he knew nothing of their plans to make him Augustus until his palace was surrounded at sundown, swearing this on diverse pagan gods. He also avers that he only consented, and reluctantly at that, to the call to be Augustus when Zeus gave him a sign to accept.

Julian's account can, however, be augmented by other sources. Ammianus concurs that Julian met with the troops and urged them to depart to Constantius (20.4.12). However, he adds that the Caesar invited the officers to dine with him, sought their requests, and thus heightened their anguish (**II 50 20.4.13**). This led to their outcry at nightfall, and Julian's reluctant acceptance of the offered honour. Zosimus adds the extra detail that further anonymous letters were distributed by superior officers ('taxiarchs') in the evening, praising Julian and warning of the danger he was in, which further inflamed the troops (**II 60 3.9.1–2**).

Thus the accounts of what happened point to the anxiety created by Constantius' orders, but also to the fact that this anxiety was deliberately increased. The events and their interpretation have been much discussed by modern historians (e.g. Bowersock 1978: 46–52; Drinkwater 1983: 370–83; Matthews 1989: 93–9; Athanassiadi 1992: 70–5; Buck 1993; Hunt 1998a: 56–8). Views vary sharply. Some see Constantius' request as a hostile action (Athanassiadi), just as Ammianus presents it, some see it as entirely legitimate given the critical situation in the east (Amida had fallen to the Persians in 359) and the improved conditions in Gaul (Bowersock), and some see it is a more subtle combination of the two (Drinkwater). It is agreed, however, that the number of troops to be removed was substantial, variously estimated as one-third, one-half or two-thirds of Julian's forces (Bowersock 1978: 46; Hunt 1998a: 56). As for the acclamation, some see Julian as complicit (Bowersock), some point rather to the crucial role of others such as officers and members of the Caesar's entourage (Drinkwater; Hunt; Matthews), and some accept his innocence (Athanassiadi; Buck). In these debates the evidence cited is discussed further, and other evidence brought into play. For instance, the absence of Lupicinus and Florentius is noted, which some consider as rather convenient as it facilitated the usurpation (Drinkwater 1983: 378–9; Hunt 1998a: 57), whilst others argue that their absence is explicable and in fact made things more difficult for Julian (Matthews 1989: 95–7). Testimony which seems to support the idea of a deliberate conspiracy on the part of Julian is drawn from Eunapius' *Lives of the Sophists* (**II 52 476**), which relates that there was a pagan plot to overthrow Constantius, and emphasises in particular the crucial role of the doctor Oribasius, a member of Julian's entourage, a friend and a fellow-pagan (Bowersock 1978: 50–1; Drinkwater 1983: 370). This apparently damning evidence has however been challenged by Buck. He argues that the statement that Oribasius made Julian emperor refers rather to the effect he had on his character, and that the consultation with the Hierophant and the decision to bring down Constantius' tyranny occurred after Julian had already been acclaimed Augustus.

Given such division of opinion one can feel a little bewildered. It is instructive to step back and consider further the attitudes of Julian and Constantius towards one another during the former's Caesarship, up to the issuing of the demand for troops. Concerning Julian's attitude, it is usual to establish a trajectory from desire to appease to personal ambition, with the victory at Strasbourg and the first acclamation as Augustus being pivotal. This is established by Julian's words and actions. The desire to appease is thought to be demonstrated by Julian's *Panegyric on the Emperor Constantius*. This is usually dated to 356, and is typically interpreted as a diplomatic gesture towards the emperor, assuring him of his loyalty (Bowersock 1978: 37; Cameron 1993: 89). Some have seen a marked contrast with the subsequent panegyric on Constantius, dated to 358 and thus located in the context of the after-glow of the military victory of 357. Athanassiadi (1992: 63–6) argues that this oration is willing to recognise conflict with Constantius, and seems to be more concerned with Julian's own ideas about rulership than those of the emperor (see also Curta 1995). Whilst others have read the second panegyric as an attempt at diplomacy too (Bowersock 1978: 43–4; Cameron 1993: 89), there is no doubt that by 358 Julian had revealed an independent attitude and a capacity for self-appreciation; witness his military and administrative actions and his writing of an account of the battle of Strasbourg. The train of Julian's thoughts is revealed by a letter he wrote to Oribasius in 358/359 (**II 6**). He reports he had a dream, and describes it to the doctor. It seems clear that it alludes to the supplanting of Constantius by Julian, but the Caesar declares he does not understand its meaning. Drinkwater (1983: 374) sees this letter as confirming the role ascribed to Oribasius by Eunapius, and notes that it was the doctor who had initiated the exchange by reporting a dream of his own. Some have seen Julian's embracing of a more defensive military strategy in 359, devoting himself largely to the rebuilding of recovered forts, as an indication that he was preparing for the coming clash with Constantius (Müller-Seidel 1955), though this interpretation has been questioned (Matthews 1989: 95). Nevertheless, it is clear that Julian had aspirations of his own. It can be argued, however, that these did not crystallise just through the agency of the events of 357. As has been seen, Julian was quick off the mark in 356, despite his attempt to conceal this in the *Letter to the Athenians*. In addition, the first panegyric on Constantius need not be read as a passive document. Athanassiadi (1992: 61–2) asserts that Julian sticks so closely to Menander Rhetor's advice on how to write a *basilikos logos* that he is in effect distancing himself from the content of his speech. This assessment is not strictly accurate for Julian does divert from the guidelines of Menander's handbook, but it can be argued that there is indeed an element of subversion to the text (Tougher 1998a: 107–8; see for example **II 1 8D–9A, 16D–17A** and **47A**). This impression is increased when one considers also the panegyric on Eusebia, thought to have been written as a companion piece to the first panegyric on Constantius (though the oration on the empress dates to after her visit to Rome in 357). This is often read as a straightforward, heartfelt expression of gratitude to Eusebia for helping him in 354–5, but in fact it is more preoccupied with constructing an image of Julian, and can criticise Constantius, both directly and implicitly (Tougher 1998a; e.g. II 2 118A–B). Thus Julian's independence of mind is apparent even in the early stages of his Caesarship. Perhaps Marcellus had been on to something.

As for Constantius, it has been seen that he was anxious about Julian but also willing to defend and indulge him. Most notably he ignored Marcellus' allegations that Julian was preparing himself for higher flight (II 50 16.7.2), but he also gave him leeway to reject Florentius' proposals concerning additional taxation and paying the barbarians to access the Rhine. The more controlling aspect is revealed by the initial detailed instructions he wrote for Julian (II 50 16.5.3) and the restrictions he placed on his access to funds (II 50 17.9.6, and 22.3.7), although these can be understood as perfectly sound actions. If a deterioration in relations from Constantius' perspective can be detected it seems to follow upon the victory at Strasbourg. Constantius appropriated the glory for this, which was entirely normal, but it clearly rankled with Julian, as well as with Ammianus (II 50 16.12.70). Perhaps this is what encouraged Julian to write an account of the battle. Such a step on the Caesar's part was hardly a sensitive one, or a sensible one: it may have alerted Constantius to Julian's ambitious nature for the first time. If the emperor knew that Julian had been hailed Augustus after the victory this would have disturbed him too. The fact that Salutius, also a pagan, was recalled by Constantius in 359 is often seen as an attempt by the emperor to rob the Caesar of a potent friend and adviser (Athanassiadi 1992: 68–70). Julian certainly understood it in these terms: in his *Consolation to Himself on the Departure of the Excellent Salutius* he observes that Salutius was thought of as Laelius to his Scipio (II 4). The *Letter to the Athenians* also recalls this event, placing it in the context of the increased observation and hostility he faced from Constantius' agents (naming Pentadius, the infamous notaries Paul and Gaudentius, as well as the Praetorian Prefect Florentius) (II 7 282B–D). Julian suggests that Constantius was jealous of his Caesar's successes, and perhaps their contrasting fortunes were a source of aggravation to the emperor (Hunt 1998a: 55–6). Drinkwater may well be right then, that when Constantius gave the order for the troops to be sent from Gaul (an action reputedly suggested by Florentius: II 50 20.4.2) he was motivated both by legitimate military reasons and by desire to contain Julian.

In the light of the relations, attitudes and events which preceded the usurpation of 360 one cannot help but agree with those who judge that it was inevitable (Drinkwater 1983: 372; Matthews 1989: 99). The question of the complicity of Julian remains. One must make up one's own mind. For some it is inconceivable that he would have worked for his own advancement given his beliefs and values (Drinkwater 1983: 372; Athanassiadi 1992: 72). It might be felt, however, that this is hard to accept, for Julian was certainly an ambitious and determined individual, and arguably an artful one too. His appeal to Zeus, described in the *Letter to the Athenians*, may not be a sign of reluctance, but rather of the momentousness of what was about to happen and of the uncertainty of the resolution: he had lit the blue touch paper, but did not know what the result would be. His appeal was, of course, also indicative of a desire for divine validation. Some do accept that Julian was involved in the managing of the usurpation, but that it was a spontaneous reaction to the events of the day (Bowersock 1978: 51). This too can be questioned, given the direction of Julian's thoughts ever since he became Caesar. It may be that the context of the requisitioning of the troops provided the specific impetus, but it can be argued that Julian was hardly unprepared. In addition to his political aspirations one must not forget his religious enthusiasms. Is it likely that Julian did *not* dream of undoing the Constantinian revolution? Libanius certainly thought he did (**II 39 22**).

5. Collision course

The narrative of what happened after Julian's acclamation as Augustus is well known. Particularly familiar are the continued campaigning of Constantius and Julian against foreign foes; the splitting of Julian's forces into three parts and their rapid progress eastwards in 361; Julian's waging of a propaganda war from Naissus; and the timely death of Constantius from a fever on 3 November whilst returning from the eastern frontier for the final showdown. However, to conclude this chapter it is worth exploring two questions: could civil war have been avoided, and could Julian have defeated Constantius in a civil war?

The fact that Julian had been acclaimed Augustus, and accepted the honour, did not necessarily mean that there would have to be conflict between the imperial cousins. After all, multiple Augusti were not unknown; Constantius himself had reigned with his brothers. It seems that Julian held out some hope of sharing the empire (**II 7 285D–286A**), apparently expressed in a letter he entrusted to Pentadius and Eutherius to take to Constantius (**II 50 20.8.18–19**). The emperor, however, could not countenance such trespassing on his authority: Julian was commanded to remain as Caesar (Ammianus Marcellinus 20.9.4). Ammianus reports that Julian also sent an additional letter which was less diplomatic (**II 50 20.8.18**), surely not a wise decision if he did want to come to a power-sharing arrangement with Constantius. However, the accuracy of this information has been doubted by some (Bowersock 1978: 52). What is clear is that Julian was not prepared to back down; whilst he asserts that he continued to identify himself as Caesar in letters to Constantius (**II 7 285D**), coinage produced in the west acknowledged him as Augustus (Kent 1959: 110–12; e.g. **II 64**). Further, he now made his own appointments, and celebrated his *quinquennalia* at Vienne in appropriate style (**II 50 21.1.4**). The loss of the imperial women Eusebia and Helena has been seen by some as a significant factor in the intractable position of the two men (Browning 1975: 97 and 111; Athanassiadi 1992: 75–6). These wives died in quick succession during this critical period (**II 50 21.1.5** and **21.6.4**). However, it seems unlikely that their existence would have made a difference. Constantius did not show much concern for his sisters previously, and even if Eusebia was a defender of Julian she could hardly argue with the fact that he had over-reached himself. Essentially, neither Constantius nor Julian was prepared to concede to the other's wishes.

To wonder how the situation would have resolved itself if Constantius had not died when he did is of course to indulge in speculation, but it is an exercise not without interest. On the face of it, Constantius appears to have had the upper hand. He was a legitimate emperor with a record of winning civil wars. He also had control of the majority of the Roman army. Even Julian recognised the numerical weakness of his position (**II 7 287A–B**). On the other hand, Julian had proved himself in conflict with barbarians, and had won the support of his troops. An extra element in Julian's arsenal was propaganda, as the *Letter to the Athenians* illustrates. This was not the only document that he produced in defence of himself. Letters were also despatched to Corinth, Sparta and the senate of Rome (**II 35; 50 21.10.7; 60 3.10.3–4**). In addition, he got much mileage out of letters that Constantius had apparently written to the Alamanni encouraging them to attack Gaul and so distract Julian (**II 7 286A; 39 113; 50 21.3.4**). Libanius asserts that the effect of these tactics was positive, and Bowersock argues that Julian did win support on his journey eastwards (1978: 60–1), but it is possible that such reactions were pragmatic. Further, there are signs that not everyone was impressed with Julian. Ammianus records that the senate rebuked Julian for his ingratitude to the emperor (**II 50 21.10.7**). He also describes the more active resistance demonstrated by two legions of Constantius which Julian had despatched from Sirmium to Gaul: they led Aquileia into opposition (**II 50 21.11.2**).

If one had to place bets on the outcome of a civil war between Julian and Constantius, it is likely that one would favour the latter as the winner (Ammianus Marcellinus 21.7.3; Hunt 1998a: 60). Yet it was Julian who emerged as sole Augustus after the sudden death of his opponent. He had luck on his side, if not indeed the gods. They would soon receive their reward.

CHAPTER 4

Emperor: Style and Reform

1. Introduction

Despite the shortness of his reign, an immense amount is known about the desires and deeds of Julian during this time. Obviously his religious and military concerns attract significant attention from historians, and these aspects of his programme will receive separate treatment in Chapters 5 and 6. However, there are other noteworthy elements of his regime, such as the nature of his emperorship, his interest in the cities of the empire, and his continued preoccupation with financial affairs. These issues will be discussed in this chapter under the umbrella of 'style and reform'. Key in the debates that persist about Julian is the question of how his actions should be understood. Was he a man out of his time, seeking to restore a lost world (e.g. Bidez 1930), or was he in fact a recognisable contemporary product, attempting to address the issues of his day? Was Julian a high-minded idealist (e.g. Renucci 2000), or a more down to earth realist (e.g. Smith 1995)? The consideration of the specific topics examined in this chapter will keep these larger debates in mind.

2. The realities of power

For an appreciation of the character of Julian it is instructive to examine two phenomena from the early days of his sole reign: his attitude to the deceased Constantius and the trials of agents of Constantius' regime, which were conducted at Chalcedon. When news of the death of Constantius reached his cousin at Naissus, Julian had only recently been assaulting the character of the emperor. However, soon after his arrival in Constantinople on 11 December 361, Julian was to preside over the state funeral of Constantius, conducted according to Christian rite (II 32 27.5; 39 120; 44 17). Demonstrating respect to his dead cousin, Julian laid his body to rest in the church of Holy Apostles. Such behaviour calls for explanation. The sources favourable to Julian emphasise his magnanimity, but other interpretations are possible. Gregory of Nazianzus asserts that in part Julian had no choice in the matter; the support that still existed for the deceased legitimate emperor exerted a certain pressure. But perhaps Gregory overstates his case, for it was in Julian's interest to be seen as observant of the memory of Constantius, as his claim to power rested on his membership of the Flavian family, if not on the fact that Constantius had indeed declared Julian his heir (Ammianus Marcellinus 21.15.2). If Julian really did hate Constantius he was prepared to put such feelings aside, probably with a view to securing his position.

Certain agents of Constantius were not to be so fortunate. Julian initiated a series of trials at Chalcedon, described by Ammianus (**II 50** **22.3.1–9**). The emperor did not preside over proceedings himself, but appointed Salutius Secundus (Praetorian Prefect of the east) to this role. Making up the judges were Nevitta (Master of Cavalry), Jovinus (Master of Cavalry in Illyricum), Agilo (Master of Infantry), Arbitio (Master of Cavalry) and Claudius Mamertinus (Praetorian Prefect of Illyricum). Amongst those on trial were infamous officials of the previous regime: the eunuch Eusebius (Constantius' grand chamberlain) and the notary Paul 'the Chain'. Both these men were executed. Of the other officials on trial, there has already been reason to mention several: Florentius (who had been Praetorian Prefect in Gaul), Palladius (the ex-Master of Offices) and Pentadius (one time notary and former Master of Offices). Florentius was sentenced to death in his absence, Palladius was exiled to Britain, but Pentadius was acquitted. The reaction of Ammianus to these events is intriguing; despite being an admirer of Julian he expresses disquiet at some aspects of the proceedings, and outrage at one verdict in particular. Whilst he approved of the treatment meted out to Apodemius (one of Constantius' *agentes in rebus*), Eusebius and Paul, he has reservations about the other verdicts. He comments on the lack of impartiality of the judges, highlighting especially the death sentence pronounced on Ursulus the Count of the Sacred Largesses. Ammianus indicates that Ursulus was condemned since he had criticised the army after the fall of Amida to the Persians in 359 (see also Ammianus Marcellinus 20.11.5). But the historian's wrath is focused not so much on the army as on Julian, since he had allowed this fate to befall Ursulus, instead of intervening to save him in return for the services the Count of the Sacred Largesses had rendered him in Gaul. Ammianus famously declares about the death of Ursulus that 'Justice herself seems to me to have wept, and to have accused the emperor of ingratitude.' (Interestingly, Libanius indicates that Julian was sensitive about the death of Ursulus: *Oration* 18.152.) Whilst it is possible that Julian was deliberately keeping his distance from the trials in order not to be accused of influencing the judgements, Ammianus detects self-interest on the part of the emperor in the appointment of Arbitio as a judge. Since Arbitio had been one of Constantius' men himself it looks as if Julian was attempting to win his favour and thus secure his own position.

Whilst some modern historians have sought to defend Julian's reputation against the criticisms of Ammianus (e.g. Bidez 1930: 210–12), others have deduced even more pragmatic motivations in the organisation of the trials of Chalcedon (e.g. Bowersock 1978: 66–70). Bowersock points out that Julian was not just interested in winning over Arbitio (and Agilo, another of Constantius' generals) but the army of Constantius as a whole. Most of the judges were military men, and the trials were conducted in the presence of the generals and tribunes of the Joviani and the Herculiani. Further, all those on trial were civilian officials, and the sacrifice of Ursulus demonstrates that the military were being given their head. Thus the trials at Chalcedon reveal Julian's practical streak: in order to establish his rule he had to make compromises to secure the support of the army. In addition, several of the verdicts also served the emperor's personal vendettas. Most of those who had been involved in the fall of Gallus and who had crossed Julian received their comeuppance, notably the eunuch Eusebius, whom Julian seems to have held responsible for his difficult relations with Constantius (**II 7 274A–B**). (It should be noted that other executions also marked the early stages of the reign, and that one of the victims was the son of the Marcellus who had opposed Julian in Gaul: Ammianus Marcellinus 22.11.1–2.)

It can be argued then that the beginning of Julian's reign exhibited the new emperor's grasp of the realities of power. He was interested in avenging the past, but not to the extent of endangering his future.

3. Imperial style

By late antiquity Roman emperors are usually deemed to have forged a new character and manner of self-presentation compared to their predecessors. They are considered authoritarian, impassive and remote. They are said to dress extravagantly, copying the Persian model of royalty, in order to reflect their enhanced status. This transformation in imperial style is often associated with the emperor Diocletian (284–

305), who can be seen as a reformer and restorer of the Roman empire, though perhaps the alteration in the nature of the emperor was as much an evolutionary process (Cameron 1993: 42). A famous example of this new imperial style is Ammianus Marcellinus' description of Constantius II during his ceremonial entry to Rome in 357 (**II 50** 16.10.9–10). Such was the perceived distinctiveness of later Roman emperors that their period of rule has been termed the 'Dominate'.

Julian bucks this trend. He seems to have preferred a simpler imperial style: less domineering, less luxurious and more accessible. This aspect of his identity is already clear from his time as Caesar in Gaul, when he embraced the life of a soldier. Several illustrations can be drawn from his reign as Augustus. At the inauguration of the new consuls for 362 (Claudius Mamertinus and Nevitta), both Mamertinus and Ammianus comment on Julian's unusual behaviour during this event: the emperor attended on foot (**II 32 28.1–30.4; 50 22.7.1**), modest behaviour that Constantius would never have contemplated. The fact that Julian attended meetings of the senate in Constantinople is also thought worthy of mention (**II 39 154; 50 22.7.3; 57 3.1.54**). Socrates is wide of the mark when he says Julian was the first emperor since Julius Caesar to make speeches in the senate, but the observation still speaks volumes. His rejection of luxury is symbolised by his reaction to an encounter with a well-rewarded palace barber: he was led to conduct a purge of palace personnel (**II 50 22.4.9–10**). Whilst Ammianus does not spell it out, it seems that the eunuchs of the imperial court were particular victims of the change of regime. Libanius asserts that the palace eunuchs were 'more in number than flies around the flocks in spring', and these were expelled with the other domestic staff (**II 39 130**). The use of eunuchs has been associated with Diocletian and his enhancement of the status of the emperor (Hopkins 1963, and 1978: 172–96), though again this might have been a gradual development (Stevenson 1995). Mamertinus testifies in more general terms to Julian's reaction against the extravagance of the court (**II 32 11.1–4**).

It is natural to ask why Julian sought to challenge the new imperial style. For some it is an aspect of his desire to return to the traditions of the past: he was attempting to recreate the ideal of the citizen emperor (Bidez 1930: 214–16). This is certainly the interpretation of Libanius (**II 39 190–1**). Here the influence of a particular imperial model may be at work: the philosopher emperor Marcus Aurelius (161–80). Eutropius asserts that Julian endeavoured to imitate Marcus Aurelius (**II 46 10.16**), a view echoed by Ammianus (**II 50 16.1.4**) and expressed by Julian himself (**II 9 253A–B**). In *The Caesars* Julian also made the emperor one of those competing to be judged the best by the gods, a contest that Marcus won (e.g. **II 25 317B–D and 335C–D**). However the importance of Marcus Aurelius to Julian has been questioned by Hunt (1995). Perhaps, then, the simpler style and rejection of luxury has more to do with Julian's character and personal tastes than with archaic ideals. He was certainly renowned for his ascetic values, which formed part of his religious identity. An additional possibility is that Julian was making deliberate comment on the style and court of Constantius II. Certainly his cousin is depicted by Ammianus as a despot overly influenced by his eunuchs (Tougher 1999). Interestingly though, Julian was not the only fourth-century emperor to attempt to reduce the role that eunuchs had attained at the later Roman court: Magnus Maximus (383–7) also exerted himself to this end (**II 60 4.37.1–2**). The biography of Severus Alexander (222–35), included in the intriguing late antique text the *Historia Augusta*, is notable for its approval of his anti-eunuchs measures (Cameron 1965). Perhaps Julian's actions were taken against the backdrop of a discourse about the nature of imperial rule. Kelly observes that contrasting imperial values co-existed in the fourth century (1998: 150).

If Julian was hoping that his style would find him favour he faced some disappointment. Ammianus records critical reaction to elements of Julian's behaviour. He reports that the emperor's attendance of the inauguration of the consuls on foot was seen by some as affected and cheap (**II 50 22.7.1**), and that the emperor's spontaneous dash out of the senate house to greet Maximus and his subsequent introduction of the philosopher to the house could be considered unseemly and to demonstrate his love of empty glory (**II 50 22.7.3**; but see Libanius' positive take on the same episode: **II 39 155–6**). (Note also Libanius' defence of Julian's unseemly behaviour in his *Autobiography*: **II 41**.) As for his streamlining of imperial personnel, Socrates reports that some thought he was undermining the dignity of the imperial office (**II 57 3.1.53**). Most famously, Julian experienced ridicule in Antioch during his stay there from July 362 to March 363. Whilst the reasons for this reaction to the emperor were multiple and varied, there is no doubt that part of the response was elicited due to Julian's different imperial style and tastes. This is made clear in the emperor's *Misopogon*, his retort to the satires the Antiochenes had composed about him (**II 28**). They targeted his lack of attendance at shows and chariot racing, his beard, his neglected physical appearance, his asceticism, his lack of a sub-stantial entourage, and his desire to be seen as their friend rather than their master. In essence, they preferred his predecessor (**II 28 357A**). It seems that Constantius' style was what some people expected and wanted of their emperor; even Ammianus admired his dignified manner.

Aspects of Julian's behaviour suggest that he himself had not fully reconciled his desire to be a more modest emperor with the reality of his autocratic position. During the circus games following the inauguration of the new consuls Julian trespassed on the authority of another magistrate, and as punishment fined himself ten pounds of gold (II 50 22.7.2). This seems to signify a tension between how he wished to present himself and the nature of his office. His reaction to events in Antioch is instructive also. Despite his aspiration to be a more approachable emperor, relations with the people of the city deteriorated to such an extent that his answering satire descends into bitterness. On his departure, Antioch was left in no doubt about his wrath: he threatened not to return, and appointed as governor of Syria a man of ill repute, Alexander of Heliopolis (II 50 23.2.3). In spite of his avowed friendliness, Julian still presented the figure of a later Roman emperor who was not to be crossed.

4. Julian and the cities

During his short reign Julian demonstrated a particular concern for the cities of the empire and their successful functioning, a concern that is clear not just from his preserved legislation but also from the literary sources. To an extent, such an interest on the part of the emperor is not surprising, given the fundamental importance of the cities to the Roman empire. In effect the empire consisted of a patchwork of cities and their territories (Jones 1964: 712), and their well-being was crucial for the success of the larger entity. However, in the case of Julian it is often asserted that his preoccupation was in tune with his Hellenism (Athanassiadi 1992: 98). The cities, especially those of the eastern half of the empire, were for him not just political entities but representative of his beloved Greek cultural heritage.

Julian was particularly intent on revitalising the city councils (II 39 146). The councillors ('decurions') of cities were drawn from the freeborn local elites and served in the interests of their communities. They were vital for the continued existence of the traditional urban facilities and lifestyle. The emperor pursued a number of measures to increase the effectiveness of the councils, which had been failing in this period. One solution was to increase the membership of some councils in order to lighten the burden, a method he attempted at Antioch (II 28 367D).

In addition he sought to cut back on those who were granted exemption from serving on councils (such as Christian clergy: **II 30 12.1.50**), and expanded the pool from which selection could be made (such as eligible citizens of other cities: **II 30 12.1.52; 50 22.9.12**) (see also Ammianus Marcellinus 25.4.21). He also ruled that those who evaded their duty were to be recalled (**II 39 148**). As well as addressing issues of membership, Julian took direct measures to ease the financial pressure on the decurions. The city properties and taxes which had been previously confiscated by Constantine and Constantius II were restored (**II 30 10.3.1**). This placed resources at the disposal of the councillors which would help fund their civic activities. He also ruled that they did not have to make up the shortfall in the gold and silver tax (the *chrysargyron*) that was levied on merchants (**II 30 12.1.50.1**), and emphasised that the gift of crown gold was voluntary (**II 30 12.13.1**).

The significance of Julian's actions to benefit cities and their councils is open to different interpretations. As mentioned above, it has been suggested that Hellenism was a motive factor for the emperor. Athanassiadi admits, however, that Julian's laws hardly convey this impression (1992: 10). Associated with the Hellenism argument is the view that Julian was attempting to turn back time, to restore a transformed world to an earlier condition (Bidez 1930: 236; Bowersock 1978: 73). This interpretation casts the emperor as a man out of touch with the reality of the mid fourth-century empire, but it is important to realise that other emperors were equally concerned about the state of the cities and their councils, as some have demonstrated (e.g. Jones 1964: 748). Attempts to secure the service of councillors had already been made. Following his initial exemption of clergy, Constantine had had to take steps to prioritise the needs of the city councils (**II 30 16.2.3**), whilst in 361 Constantius forbade decurions from entering the senate and those that had managed to gain membership were ejected (**II 30 12.1.48**). Thus the councillors were being forced to maintain their traditional roles. Julian's step of restoring city properties may have been an unusual one, and his Hellenism may have added a different flavour to his work, but in general he was in tune with the intense imperial interest in city councils that distinguished his age.

One should also enquire what success Julian's measures met with. It seems that those who were qualified to serve on councils did not necessarily share the enthusiasm of the emperor. It is clear that the attempt to strengthen the council of Antioch ran into difficulties. The emperor alleges that the councillors obstructed his work, and cites the instance of a rich candidate being allowed to seek a more lucrative role in public life and being substituted by a poor citizen (**II 28 368A–B**). In September 362 he ruled that the nominations lately made to the council were void, and ordered an investigation into the matter (**II 30 12.1.53**). The complaints that Ammianus levels against Julian for his methods of stocking councils are suggestive of wider discontent (**II 50 22.9.12**; see also 25.4.21). The fundamental problem was that the elite of the cities wanted to escape their burdensome traditional role and take advantage of the new opportunities that were available, such as working in the expanded imperial administration, entering the new senate of Constantinople or embracing careers in the Church. Ironically, since the empire was providing these attractive alternatives, it had created the problem itself. This is evident even in the case of Julian, for he did allow some exemptions to stand (**II 30 6.26.1** and **6.27.2**). Essentially, he was attempting to address a problem that faced all late antique emperors, and which forms part of the larger debate about the transformation and fate of the cities of the empire (e.g. Liebeschuetz 2001; Ward-Perkins 1998).

5. Finance and reform

During his time in Gaul Julian demonstrated a concern to address economic issues, apparently keen to ameliorate the situation of the empire's subjects. As sole emperor he continued to show interest in such matters, as can be seen in his attempts to ease the burden on the councils, and his purging the court of what he considered excessive and expensive personnel. Other measures illustrate this also.

He exhibited solicitude regarding the imperial courier system (*cursus publicus*) (see for instance Kolb 1998). He limited the number of journeys that were to be allowed, as well as the number of officials who could grant permits (**II 30 8.5.12**) (see also **II 39 145; 43 75**). Julian also reduced the number of *agentes in rebus* (**II 39 135**). These changes would have had positive financial repercussions. However, perhaps there was an element of Julian commenting on the regime of Constantius. This emperor's uses of the public post to facilitate the travel of bishops and of *agentes in rebus* (such as Apodemius) were considered infamous aspects of his reign (**II 50 21.16.18**; see also Ammianus Marcellinus 22.3.11). (The *agentes in rebus* tend to be viewed as spies or secret service agents.) It should not be overlooked, however, that Constantius himself had already shown concern about the numbers of *agentes in rebus* and the *cursus publicus* (**II 30 1.9.1** and **8.5.5**).

As in Gaul, taxation preoccupied the emperor. He declared his intention to monitor the imposition and collection of taxes (**II 30 11.16.10**), and ruled that tax collectors were to be open to prosecution every sixth year (**II 30 8.1.6**). Specific cases reveal the emperor in action. When the Thracians implored him to waive their arrears he agreed to remit a portion of their debt, emphasising his concern for his subjects (**II 17**). The Antiochenes also received a remission in taxes (**II 28 365B** and **367D**).

Clearly Julian wanted to be seen as a fair and caring emperor, and Ammianus' verdict on his financial measures is very positive (**II 50 25.4.15**). However, it is instructive to consider the emperor's attempts to address inflation in the city of Antioch during his residence there. The price of consumables rose in the city following a drought and crop failures, a situation apparently aggravated by the hoarding of goods by the rich (**II 28 368D; 39 195**) and the demands of the imperial army (**II 57 3.17.2**). At first Julian instructed the city council to resolve the problem, but since they did not he intervened in October, establishing fixed prices and importing grain which was then sold at a reduced price (**II 28 368C–369B**). However, the rich exploited the latter measure for their own benefit: they purchased the cheap grain and sold it at a marked up price in the countryside (**II 28 369C**). The emperor's decision to sell 3,000 lots of city land so that it could be cultivated was also taken advantage of by the rich, for they acquired it for themselves (**II 28 370D**). Julian was frustrated by the perversion of his plans, but Ammianus records the critical reaction of the councillors to his decision to set fixed prices (**II 50 22.14.1–2**) (and see also **II 39 195**). Modern historians can be critical of the emperor's efforts as well, pointing out that he should have tightly controlled the selling of the cheap grain and the civic land, and branding Julian 'naïve' (e.g. Bowersock 1978: 99–101). The Antiochene episode certainly tempers the view of Julian as a financial whiz kid, though he was certainly not the first emperor to run aground on the rocks of economy, witness Diocletian's ill-fated edict on maximum prices. Whilst his economies may have eased the burden on his subjects, the shortness of his reign makes a significant assessment of his measures difficult.

It is apparent that Julian has the image of an emperor concerned about the economic well-being of his subjects. However, it is likely that most emperors wanted to have such a reputation (Cameron 1993: 93). As was seen in the case of Gaul, Julian is not the only emperor to display such acts of generosity (acts perhaps even taken when there was little alternative). A motive factor in Julian's enactments may have been the desire to provide a sharp contrast with Constantius, though presumably his cousin had thought the funding of court personnel and the transport of bishops a necessity. It is worth remarking that Julian was happy to subsidise the travel of friends and philosophers to visit him (e.g. **II 8** and 11; see also ed. Wright 1913–23: vol. 3, Letters 43 and 54).

6. Conclusion

Julian was an emperor concerned with image. He wanted to be seen as a citizen emperor, a reliever of the burdens of his subjects and a supporter of the cities and their councils. This does not necessarily make him a man out of his time, a traditionalist seeking to restore a lost age. His concerns were shared by other emperors of the fourth century, both those who succeeded him and those who preceded him. His more modest imperial style distinguishes him, but it can be argued that this was due to his religious and intellectual identity rather than to archaism. It should also be appreciated that other emperors could demonstrate similar concerns about style. Further, it is clear that he could have difficulties restraining his autocratic nature. What really set Julian apart from Roman emperors from Constantine onwards was his enthusiasm for paganism and his hostility towards Christianity. These aspects of his regime form the subject of the following chapter.

CHAPTER 5

Religion

1. Introduction

Religion is inextricably associated with Julian, due to his attempt to restore paganism to its traditional dominance in the wake of the favour shown to Christianity since the reign of his uncle Constantine. Thus Julian is more often referred to as 'the apostate' or 'the last pagan' than as, simply, 'the emperor'. Despite our knowledge of his imperial measures regarding religion, there is still debate about his aims and attitudes. Was he an inimical opponent towards Christianity from the start of his reign or did his hostility increase over time? Was there a deeper objective behind his infamous teaching edict, which banned Christians from teaching the classics? Regarding paganism, was he attempting to enforce adherence to a strictly controlled monotheistic moralistic religion that suited his own taste, or was he in fact a less unusual pagan than has been assumed, largely content for paganism in all its forms to have its devotees? The major questions are of course whether his religious ambitions could have succeeded, and whether he was doomed to fail anyway. This chapter will consider his religious measures and their interpretation before exploring these latter issues.

2. Coming out

Before discussing the main topics, there remains the question of when Julian came out of the closet and revealed himself to be a pagan. Julian dates his conversion to his twentieth year, but he did not declare this to the world at large at the time, presumably because of his precarious political position, since it was still possible to exist as a pagan (though a law issued under Constantius and Julian in 356 laid down the penalty of capital punishment for those who engaged in sacrifice or worshipped images: **II 30 16.10.6**). Certain individuals knew of his transformation, and others may have guessed, but on the whole Julian sought to keep his religious identity secret. His celebration of the Christian feast of Epiphany in 361 is well known (**II 50 21.2.5**). But when did he drop the mask? Ammianus implies that Julian only publicly acknowledged his paganism when he was installed in Constantinople and in occupation of the palace (**II 50 22.5.2**). This would seem sensible, as Constantius was safely dead and power had been successfully transferred to his cousin. However, it is often remarked that Julian contradicts Ammianus. In a letter to Maximus, written when Julian was still at Naissus, he tells the philosopher that he now worships the gods openly (**II 8**). It is often assumed that this letter postdated the death of Constantius (Bowersock 1978: 61), but this is by no means certain. In any case, in his *Letter to the Athenians*, also written at Naissus, Julian had already outed himself as a pagan, acknowledging the role of the gods in his successes in Gaul and swearing his devotion to Constantius on them (**II 7 280D**; see also **II 7 282D** and **284B–C**). Further, Libanius asserts that Julian reopened temples in Greece (*Oration* 18.114). It seems then that Julian had pinned his flag to the mast even before the death of Constantius. Given the importance he attached to the gods in his endeavours, and that a final showdown with his cousin was approaching, perhaps this is not unsurprising.

3. Christianity: toleration for all?

Once he had become sole emperor Julian was faced with the practicalities of restoring the worship of the traditional gods and undoing the privileged position Christianity had acquired. His initial response to the latter task seems to have been undertaken in a spirit of toleration, though the altered circumstances were nonetheless clear. He reverted to the stance of tolerating all religions, and recalled those Christians who had been exiled under Constantius (e.g. **II 11** and **23 435D–436B**; also **54 10.28** and **58 5.5.6**). At the same time, however, his personal attachment to paganism was not in doubt, which probably influenced the religious attachments of some of his subjects, as had been the case under Constantine and his sons (Gregory of Nazianzus acknowledges that there were Christians who apostatised: *Oration* 4.11). In his *Letter to Atarbius* (**II 21**) he asserted that the Christians were not to be persecuted but that the 'god-fearing' (i.e. pagans) were to receive preferential treatment. (Unsurprisingly, Julian deprived Christians and the Christian church of the benefits they had acquired since the time of Constantine (e.g. **II 30 12.1.50**).) However, it is often observed that later in his reign Julian was not above turning a blind eye to attacks on

Christians by pagans, such as those at Gaza and Emesa (e.g. **II 28 357C; 43 86** and **93; 58 5.9.12–13**), and that he introduced active discrimination against Christians, such as the teaching edict (see below). This has led to the view that Julian's attitude towards the Christians developed over time, that from a position of toleration he moved to one of hostility, which could be described as undeclared persecution (Bidez 1930: 261–5, 310–14).

This vision has been challenged (Bowersock 1978). The profession of tolerance may have been pragmatic. Julian knew from the example of the Great Persecution conducted under the Tetrarchs (Rees 2004: 59–71), and of previous assaults on Christians, that such measures tended to fail, producing only discontent and martyrs. This does not mean that Julian's opposition to Christianity lacked intensity of feeling. Ammianus declares that the recall of the exiles was a devious move, designed to bring about the self-destruction of the Christians (**II 50 22.5.3–4;** this is echoed by others, e.g. Sozomen: **II 58 5.5.7**). This may be overstated, but it did cause uncertainty amongst the Christian communities. A letter of Julian's to the Alexandrians reveals how the recalled Athanasius had seized the bishop's throne in Alexandria (**II 15**), but also the emperor's impatience with such behaviour, which could lead him to threaten harsh action. In fact, it is an earlier episode in Alexandrian history which makes a nonsense of the view that he became gradually more hostile to Christians. When George of Cappadocia, bishop of Alexandria, was killed by a mob at the end of December 361, Julian's response was simply to give the Alexandrians a telling off (**II 12**). No punitive measures were enacted. It is clear from the letter that Julian had no love of George, and that he deemed the bishop had deserved an even more gruesome end. Such sentiment leaves one in no doubt about the emperor's personal preferences, and is in keeping with his later responses to events such as those at Gaza and Emesa. His loathing of Christianity is clear from his writings, such as the depiction of the myth of his own life in *Against the Cynic Heraclius* (**II 14**), which emphasises his mission to restore the gods; his hymn to the Mother of the Gods (**II 19**), which calls for the stain of atheism (i.e. Christianity) to be removed; the portrait of Constantine and the identification of the appeal of Christianity in *The Caesars* (**II 25**, esp. **336A–C**); and above all his *Against the Galilaeans*. Indeed, the emperor's use of the term Galilaeans for Christians was a sign of opposition in itself.

Yet Julian did not embrace outright persecution, he followed a more subversive path. It is in this light that other of his measures touching on the Christians have been interpreted (for example, his legislation on funerals: **II 30 9.17.5.1**; on this see for example Bidez 1930: 292). Most familiar is his ban on Christians teaching the classics. This has been associated with the law issued on 17 June 362 (**II 30 13.3.5**). This is in fact inexplicit, but there is no doubt about the meaning of his so-called *Rescript on Christian Teachers* (**II 22**; on these documents see Banchich 1993). Julian asserts that it was inappropriate for Christians to give instruction on the works of pagan authors of the past, and suggests that they teach the gospels in churches instead. (Of course, if they converted, they would be able to keep teaching the pagan classics.) On the face of it, it looks as though Julian was simply outraged that Christians could make a living teaching the works of authors whose religion they rejected. Some historians have suspected deeper objectives. Bowersock (1978: 84) argues that Julian was intent on making Hellenism the preserve of the Hellenes (i.e. pagans), which would result in Christians becoming excluded from the educated elite and thus a redundant force. However, Julian did not ban Christian pupils from attending the classes of pagan teachers, so a good classical education would still have been available. Nevertheless, Smith (1995: 214) suggests Julian's subversive objectives would still have been obtained: either Christian families would keep their sons away from pagan schools and so deprive them of vital education, or the Christian students would be so influenced by their masters that they would become pagans themselves, an expectation informed by the emperor's own experiences. If these were indeed Julian's hopes, and are not just Smith's hypotheses, they seem to ignore the facts that Christians could be entrusted to pagan teachers, and that these pupils did not inevitably experience any crisis of religious identity, witness the example of Libanius and his students. It is possible that Julian's measure against Christian teachers was indeed motivated purely by a sense of outrage.

Another infamous design of the emperor relevant here is his desire to rebuild the Temple of Solomon in Jerusalem (e.g. **II 45 4.18–20; 50 23.1.2–3; 54 10.38**). This may have been a gesture of respect to the Jewish religion, which perhaps impressed Julian as an ancient monotheistic religion which included the rite of sacrifice, an enthusiasm of his own. However, there was probably anti-Christian sentiment to the plan too. Any support for the Jews was a slight to the Christians (witness the reaction of Gregory of Nazianzus: **II 44 3**). Julian may also have had in mind the prophecy of Christ that the temple would not be rebuilt (e.g. Matt. 24.2). To disprove this would have been a coup for the pagan emperor (Bowersock 1978: 89), though as it turned out the project was abandoned (see, for example, Gregory of Nazianzus *Oration* 5.4).

Thus, despite his avowal of toleration, Julian's despising of Christianity was evident from the early days of his reign. This could lead him to act without an even hand. He sought to undermine the religion without resorting to outright persecution.

4. Paganism: a new model?

Julian was concerned not just to weaken the position of Christianity, but to promote that of paganism. It was nearly forty years since Constantine had come to sole power, and Julian had much ground to recover. On becoming emperor he reopened the pagan temples, and restored the rite of sacrifice (**II 50 22.5.2**). Some temples had to be reconstructed, which necessitated reclamation of building materials (**II 30 15.1.3; 39 126**). Inscriptions testify to the actions of Julian, hailing him, for instance, as restorer of the temples (e.g. **II 29**; and see Lee 2000: 104–5; Smith 1995: 210–11; Geffcken 1978: 157–8).

More controversial are the issues of to what extent Julian recast the organisation of paganism, and whether he was attempting to enforce a particular brand of paganism. Concerning the first issue, it is a common view that Julian sought to introduce a 'pagan church', in which morally-upstanding imperially-appointed provincial archpriests played a crucial guiding role. Some of Julian's letters are written to such priests (**II 18** and **20**), and other sources identify further examples (e.g. **II 52 501**). The *Letter to Arsacius* suggests that the emperor was inspired by the model of Christianity. Julian asserts that this religion has flourished because the Christians care for strangers, tend the tombs of the dead and lead apparently dignified lives. He ordered that pagan priests should imitate such virtues, hostels should be established, and charity dispensed (see also **II 43 111**). Athanassiadi has described the emperor's priests as the 'shock troops of Julian's religious reform' (1992: 181). However, whether Julian was an innovator can be questioned, for the Tetrarch Maximin (308–13) was also associated with the introduction of a 'pagan church' in which archpriests played a key role (Eusebius *Church History* 9.4.2–3; Lactantius *On the Deaths of the Persecutors* 36.4–5). Whilst Nicholson (1994) argues that both emperors were building on extant pagan organisation anyway, he also notes that the character of the priests of Maximin and Julian differed. Maximin's priests were leading public figures with a political role, whilst Julian's were meant to be holy and removed from the taint of secular public life. In this respect, Nicholson suggests that Julian was influenced by the example of Christianity.

The issue of the type of paganism Julian was attempting to enforce has been reopened by Smith (1995). It had become common to accept the view that the emperor was championing his own monotheistic Neoplatonic beliefs and practices rather than the diverse traditions of paganism. Athanassiadi emphasised in addition the centrality of Mithraism in Julian's religious goals, declaring 'What his uncle had done with Christianity, Julian dreamed of repeating with Mithraism' (1992: 153). Bowersock saw in Julian's attacks on the Cynics the emperor's 'hostility to other forms of paganism than his own' which 'showed the character of a bigot and a puritanical one at that' (1978: 82). The influence of Christianity upon the emperor has been suspected here too (e.g. Fowden 1998: 547). However, Smith has challenged the interpretation of Julian as a narrow-minded missionary. As has been seen, the degree of Julian's attachment to Mithras is open to question, and his devotion to Helios is much more apparent. At the same time Julian was enthusiastic for the range of pagan deities, who sat quite comfortably within his Neoplatonic world view. As for his hostility to the Cynics, Smith argues that this was inspired by very specific circumstances, and was a traditional stance anyway. Certainly Julian had his personal convictions, but this does not mean he was intolerant of all other forms of paganism or expected everyone to follow his path. His primary desire was devotion to the old gods. Smith is able to conclude that Julian's 'plans for a pagan restoration were less outlandish than might be supposed' (1995: 177).

5. Success or failure?

Central to considerations of Julian's religious ambitions is the question of whether he could have achieved them. Was it possible that he could undo the preeminence that Christianity had achieved and restore paganism to its traditional favoured position in the empire? Answers to these queries run into difficulties due to the shortness of his reign. How can one judge? If he had reigned for longer, and been succeeded by a committed pagan emperor (like Salutius, the favoured candidate: Ammianus Marcellinus 25.5.3), perhaps his goals were attainable. Yet Christianity had proved itself a persistent and vital force, and what was to prevent a pro-Christian individual from gaining imperial power in the future? Despite the feeling that a response can only be provided by having recourse to the realms of hypothesis, one can examine more concrete evidence from the reign (and its aftermath) in the hope of securing some firmer ground.

Since Julian was not an outright persecutor of Christianity, there were limits to what he aimed to achieve vis-à-vis the religion. Certainly he sought to undermine it, by fair means and foul, but if persecution in the past had not destroyed it, his less overt methods were unlikely to succeed either. Essentially, Julian was seeking to sever the ties that had developed between Christianity and the Roman empire, especially since the time of Constantine. Hence his removal of imperial favour, and his equating of Hellenism with paganism. This was enough to alarm Christians. The most famous Christian response was supplied by the invectives of Gregory of Nazianzus (**II 43** and **44**). These express outrage at the emperor's underhand tactics. The reaction to the teaching edict is particularly well known, objecting to Julian claiming Greek for paganism alone (**II 43 4–5**). Notably Ammianus also criticised the ban on Christians teaching rhetoric and grammar (**II 50 22.10.7**; see also Ammianus Marcellinus 25.4.20), indicating that pagans themselves could consider the emperor's treatment of Christians overly harsh. Julian himself testifies to the intense Christian reaction against him, in his *Misopogon* (**II 28**). This was a response to the difficulties that he faced in Antioch during his residence there from July 362, including Christian hostility. He records that the Antiochenes declared that they preferred the Kappa (Constantius) and the Chi (Christ) to him and the gods (**II 28 356D–357D**). Some Christians are credited with direct action against paganism and the emperor. For instance, Gregory of Nazianzus reports the anti-pagan actions of two Christian youths (*Oration* 5.40). The cause of the destruction of the temple of Apollo at Daphne may have been Christian arsonists. A plot hatched by soldiers against Julian in Antioch (**II 39 199**) is given Christian motivation by some sources: **II 43 83–4** and **59 3.11**. It was even rumoured that Julian's death was the work of a Christian (**II 39 274–5**).

The flipside of Julian's attempt to weaken Christianity is of course his effort to restore paganism. It is easier to discuss his potential success in this arena since there is evidence to suggest that he was already encountering difficulties before his death. In his letter to the archpriest Arsacius, Julian exclaims that Hellenism (i.e. paganism) is not yet flourishing as well as he would wish, and he blames its devotees (**II 20 429C**). At the end of the same letter he pressurises the citizens of Pessinus to devote themselves to their resident goddess, the Great Mother (Magna Mater), for he says only on this condition will he support the city (**II 20 431D–432A**). The sense of his disappointment with the pagans is also reflected by the report that he reproached those of Caesarea for not saving the temple of Fortune from destruction by the Christians (**II 58 5.4.1–3**). In addition, there is the famous episode, early in the period of his residence in Antioch, when Julian turned up at the temple of Apollo at Daphne to celebrate the annual feast of the god but found in attendance only the priest with his personal offering of a goose (**II 28 361D–362B**). From such indications it has been argued that Julian's restoration of paganism was in trouble (Bidez 1930: 314; Bowersock 1978: 93). The typical explanation for this is that the emperor was to blame, having alienated the pagans himself with his unusual brand of religion (e.g. Cameron 1993: 95). Certainly there was some bemusement at Julian's zeal for blood sacrifice. Several times Ammianus criticises the emperor on these grounds, reporting that Julian earned the nickname 'axeman' (victimarius) rather than the title of priest, and joking that there would have been a shortage of cattle if Julian had survived the Persian campaign (**II 50 22.12.6** and **22.14.3**; see also Ammianus Marcellinus 25.4.17). For Julian, this practice was a vital part of his Neoplatonic beliefs, for, as the tract *Concerning the Gods and the Universe* explains, prayers without sacrifice were just words (**II 42**). (Perhaps Julian's attachment to the rite was viewed as excessive due to its increasing rarity.) There is the sense, then, that Julian's esoteric religion was a hindrance to his projected restoration.

However, Smith has provided grounds to challenge this interpretation, arguing for Julian's more catholic vision of paganism. It is also important to distinguish between reaction to the emperor as an individual and reaction to paganism in general. Further, the signs of difficulty in the attempted restoration can be tempered. The key evidence of the *Letter to Arsacius* in fact declares that the revival is going well, only not as well as Julian would wish. This says more about the expectations of the emperor than the state of paganism in the empire. Given that the letter was written less than a year into his reign, Julian can be convicted of impatience, if not a lack of realism. His complaints about the pagans of Caesarea not defending the temple of Fortune can also be read in such a light, since it appears that they were significantly outnumbered by the Christians. (Perhaps this also supports the view that he was thinking in Christian terms; did he expect pagans to be willing to be martyrs?) In the specific case of Antioch, one should also note that when Julian first arrived in the city the annual festival of Adonis was being celebrated (Ammianus Marcellinus 22.9.15), and that in the *Misopogon* Julian alludes to the Antiochenes attending temples

(344B), suggesting that the miserable episode of Daphne was not the whole story.

However, even if one accepts that the restoration was not necessarily in trouble, there is the argument that Julian was already too late, that the pendulum had swung irrevocably towards the Christians (e.g. Fowden 1998: 548). It is true that Christianity had established a strong hold in certain communities, most famously from Julian's perspective the city of Antioch, but also Nisibis for instance (**II 58 5.3.5**). However, there also existed strong pagan communities, such as at Gaza (**II 58 5.3.6**). There is evidence indicating that there was enthusiasm for the restoration, and there was no shortage of pagan supporters who lamented Julian's passing. No doubt if Julian had reigned longer he would not have been able to eradicate Christianity, but this was not necessary anyway. The crucial achievement would be to undo its association with the Roman empire. It is common to think of Julian as marking a mere blip in the Christianisation of the Roman empire, but Jones argued that the emperor had a clear effect despite the shortness of his reign (1964: 149–50). Paganism won a reprieve, and the emperor Valentinian I (364–75) notably sought to observe religious toleration. It was the momentum that built up again under Ambrose the bishop of Milan (374–97) and the emperor Theodosius I (379–95) that signalled a new onslaught on paganism. It remains valid to consider what Julian might have been able to achieve if he had had a longer reign (Jones 1964: 137).

With hindsight it is known that the Persian expedition witnessed the termination of Julian's life and his religious ambitions. However, from his point of view, the military undertaking was no less significant. Here was the opportunity to prove himself the divinely favoured saviour of the Roman empire, which would have added impetus to his programme of restoration. It is the expedition that will be considered in the following chapter.

CHAPTER 6

Persia

1. Introduction

Julian's Persian expedition of 363 holds a particular fascination for historians. This is not just because of the magnitude of the undertaking, or the fact that the emperor met his death during the campaign, but also since so many questions hang over the enterprise. What motivated Julian to launch the expedition? What were his objectives? Why did it end in disaster? These uncertainties have led to the Persian expedition being one of the most studied subjects of later Roman history (Kaegi 1981: 209). The topic was equally important to those Romans who wrote about Julian, signifying for good or ill the collapse of the emperor's dreams for the empire. The major narrative source, the history of Ammianus Marcellinus, creates a sense of impending doom when relating the progress of the expedition (e.g. **II 50 23.5.4** and **24.6.17**; Matthews 1989: 132; Smith 1999). Combined with the apparent loss of text at the crucial moment of the campaign, when the army is before the Persian city of Ctesiphon (e.g. Austin 1972: 301), this adds to the difficulties of understanding the expedition. The nature of other sources also causes obfuscation, be it the triumphalism of Christian authors or the optimism of pagans such as Eutropius and Zosimus, who hail the success of Julian (**II 46 10.16; 60 3.29.1**). This chapter will first discuss Sasanid Persia and its relations with the later Roman empire, and then explore the motivations, objectives and assessments of the expedition.

2. Sasanid Persia and the later Roman empire

Amongst the problems facing the Roman empire in the third century AD was renewed conflict with the Persian empire, associated with the establishment of a new ruling dynasty early in the century (AD 224), the Sasanids (Dodgeon and Lieu 1991). This is famously symbolised by the capture in 260 of the Roman emperor Valerian (253–60) by the Persian

shah Shapur I (242–c. 272), following the latter's invasion of Roman
Mesopotamia. The humiliation of the Romans was famously com-
memorated in rock and by the skin of Valerian himself, preserved and
exhibited after his death. Although relations between Rome and Persia
were less tense after 260, they flared up again under Diocletian when
Narses (293–302) became shah. This thorn in Rome's side was temporarily plucked when the Tetrarchy brought the Sasanids to peace
through the efforts of the Caesar Galerius (Blockley 1992: 5–7). The
treaty of 299 firmly instituted Rome as the winner. She regained
territory, and even established authority beyond the Tigris. Armenia, so
crucial in the struggle for power between Rome and Persia, was aligned
to the former and protected from invasion by the latter. However, by the
end of his reign Constantine the Great was preparing to launch a major
campaign against Persia following a renewal of conflict under Shapur II
(309–79), who sought to make amends for the disadvantageous treaty
of 299. Constantius II inherited the war. His reign witnessed such
infamous events as the battle of Singara in 348 (or maybe 344), which
took its toll on both Roman and Persian forces, and the destruction of
Amida by the Persians in 359, as well as Shapur's repeated attempts to
capture Nisibis. It was the difficult situation with Persia that justified
Constantius' demand that troops be transferred to the east from Gaul,
during Julian's Caesarship. When Constantius died in 361, the Persian
problem was still unresolved.

3. Motivations

An obvious answer to why Julian undertook the Persian expedition,
then, is that he was simply responding to a current concern that needed
attention (Murdoch 2003: 156). However, the evidence suggests that
there was more to it than this, that the emperor had deep personal
reasons for attacking Persia. Ammianus reports that Julian dismissed
calls for him to engage with the Goths, seeking instead a better enemy
(**II 50** 22.7.8). One may suspect that the story of Julian's rejection of a
campaign against the Goths gained currency in the aftermath of the
battle of Adrianople in 378, but there is no reason to doubt his
determination to engage with the Persians. Ammianus asserts that
the emperor was intent on winning the name of Parthicus (**II 50**
22.12.1–2). Julian's rejection of Shapur's overtures to negotiate a peace
confirm this picture (**II 39 164**), as does the rapid move to Antioch to
prepare the expedition. Thus it can be argued that there seems to be an
element of obsession to the emperor's decision.

To explain this, one solution has been to point to the influence of certain of Julian's idols upon him, namely the Macedonian king Alexander the Great and the Roman emperor Trajan (e.g. Browning 1975: 190). Both these rulers were renowned for the military victories they scored over the Persians. In the fourth century BC Alexander had won the Persian empire for himself, and in the second century AD Trajan had annexed Mesopotamia and momentarily won authority in Parthia after a successful attack on Ctesiphon. The concept of the importance of Alexander to Julian is especially well known. The church historian Socrates alleges that the emperor believed that he possessed the soul of Alexander, that he was in effect the reincarnation of the king (**II 57 3.21.6–7**). This may be a Christian attempt to mock Julian, akin to one of the versions of the emperor's death reported by Gregory of Nazianzus (**II 44 14**). Gregory relates that Julian wished to throw himself into the Tigris so that his body would not be found and that it would be thought that he was divine, a story that had been told of Alexander the Great. Nevertheless, the fact that these writers make any connection between Julian and the Macedonian king seems telling. There are other sources which do so, most notably Julian's *The Caesars*, written at Antioch in 362 (but see also **II 9 253A–B**; Libanius *Oration* 17.17 and 18.260 and 261). In it the emperor has the gods include Alexander in their competition to identify the best ruler from amongst the Romans, and the Macedonian was one of the six candidates selected by the deities from whom they would make their final choice (e.g. **II 25 316C–D**). As for Trajan, he too had the distinction of featuring in *The Caesars* as one of the final contestants. However, perhaps the interest in this emperor is just another expression of Julian's concern with Alexander. At the end of *The Caesars* Trajan flocks to the Macedonian, his own inspiration (**II 25 335D**).

Amongst modern historians of Julian, Athanassiadi particularly argues for the importance of the impact of Alexander upon the emperor (1992: 192–3 and 224–5), though Baynes (1912) was a strong advocate too. Others are not so convinced (e.g. Smith 1995: 12–13). Lane Fox (1997) observes that Julian was able to view Alexander dispassionately, recognising his negative qualities as well as his positive ones, and argues that this hardly amounted to an obsession. He shows that an interest in Alexander was not unusual for a Roman emperor concerned with Persia, witness the *Itinerary of Alexander* written for Constantius II. As with the question of the influence of Marcus Aurelius upon Julian (Hunt 1995), there can be a tempering of accepted wisdom.

Certainly, there are other reasons why Julian would have wanted to take on Persia. Julian would not be the first or last leader to recognise the political advantages of war. As a newly established emperor, military success against the old enemy would have been a useful asset, potentially bringing him glory and popularity. It would also serve to provide a specific contrast with his immediate predecessor, Constantius II, who had not resolved the Persian problem by the time of his death. Of course, Julian had an even more urgent desire to prove himself, given his ambitions for the empire, especially in the sphere of religion. A victory over the Persians would indicate that he was divinely favoured (Matthews 1989: 140). This urgent desire can only have been intensified following his unsettling experiences in Antioch. A further factor in Julian's determination may have been his own record of success. He had survived to become Caesar, achieved unexpected glory in Gaul, and become sole emperor upon the timely death of his cousin. Taking on Persia, and anticipating winning, can only have seemed natural.

Thus one does not have to resort to the explanation of the impact of heroes upon Julian to understand his decision to undertake the Persian expedition. At the same time, however, it is perhaps unwise to dismiss this dimension completely. It is possible that a range of factors motivated Julian, and that these could evolve, as Athanassiadi states. The Alexander factor may not be that surprising, but just because it is a stereotypical association does not make it unimportant. Since Julian was a hellenophile, the figure of Alexander may have had more significance for him than for other Roman emperors. It is the degree of significance which is the matter for debate.

4. Objectives

More intractable than the question of Julian's motivations is that of the immediate objective of the expedition. The details of the progress of the expedition are known, but the emperor's aims are uncertain. Ammianus gives an extended account of events, up to the arrival of Julian's forces at Ctesiphon (23.2–24.6): the gathering of the expedition at Hierapolis, the crossing of the Euphrates into northern Mesopotamia, the sending of Procopius and Sebastianus with a force eastwards, the feint of Julian and his army towards the Tigris and their return to the Euphrates, the joining of the fleet with the expedition, the capture of Pirisabora and the sacking of subsequent fortresses, the sailing of the fleet via a reopened canal to the Tigris above Ctesiphon, and the engagement of forces before Ctesiphon. There follows the abandonment of the siege of Ctesiphon, the burning of the fleet, the move inland and the advance north, the pursuit by the Persians, and Julian's death following a wound received in a skirmish (24.7–25.3). This narrative leaves Julian's objectives obscure, a feature shared with other accounts of the expedition.

Part of the explanation for the difficulty in understanding what the emperor hoped to achieve may be the secrecy with which Julian shrouded his plans. Libanius asserts that this was deliberately done to prevent information falling into the wrong hands (**II 39 213**). Nevertheless, it is Libanius himself who indicates one of the possible objectives of the expedition: regime change. In a letter written whilst the campaign was underway, the Antiochene anticipates Julian returning with Shapur as a captive, having entrusted Persia to Hormisdas (**II 38**). This Hormisdas was Shapur's brother, who had sought refuge in the Roman empire during the reign of Constantine the Great (Dodgeon and Lieu 1991: 147–9). Hormisdas was indeed a member of the expedition (e.g. **II 39 258**; see also Ammianus Marcellinus 24.1.2), but perhaps the part envisaged for him by Libanius was the result of guesswork. Ridley (1973: 325) observes that a lack of understanding of the plans of Julian, as well as of his actions during the expedition, had the consequence that 'rumour and legend have been substituted for fact'.

What is clear is that the arrival at Ctesiphon marked the high point of the campaign. Presumably reaching this city was a major goal of the expedition. It is certainly in keeping with the actions of the Roman emperors who had launched invasions of Mesopotamia prior to Julian (e.g. Hunt 1998a: 75), the most recent example being that of Carus in 283 (or possibly Galerius in the subsequent decade: Barnes 1976: 183–5). Beyond the possible desire to effect regime change, there are other potential explanations for the targeting of Ctesiphon. Perhaps its capture was to be the prelude to further assaults on Persia, as in the case of Trajan. Regime change might have had a part to play in this scenario, unless Julian was thinking of a more radical undermining of Persia, as also suggested by Libanius (Blockley 1992: 25; see also Seager 1997: esp. 262–6) (and perhaps Constantine the Great had had such ambitions: Blockley 1992: 12). The capture of Ctesiphon may, however, have been an end in itself, a demonstration of force facilitating a position of strength from which to negotiate with Shapur (Matthews 1989: 139).

Thus there are diverse readings of Julian's objectives, but one further possibility exists. Maybe the emperor was keeping an open mind, responding as events unfolded. If this was the case, his goals could be fluid rather than fixed. It could also account for the uncertainty of what he was planning.

5. Assessments

Although the motivations and objectives of Julian's Persian expedition are debated, its outcome is not in question: it failed. The death of Julian was followed by the conclusion of a treaty that swung the favour back in Persia's direction (Ammianus Marcellinus 25.7.5–14). The terms of the compact of 299 were abandoned, and Persia regained territory west of the Tigris, as well as the fortresses of Nisibis (see also **II 45 3.1–2**) and Singara. Armenia was left exposed to Persian attack. Ammianus blames the new emperor Jovian (363–4) rather than the dead pagan emperor for this 'shameful treaty', which seems unjust given the difficult situation Jovian found himself in. Whether Julian was to blame for the failure of the expedition itself is a key debate in the discussions of the subject.

Ignoring the motif of impending doom attached to the expedition by Ammianus, and his assertion that the gods deserted Julian, there are a number of decisions made by the emperor which have attracted criticism. Ammianus records that Julian's resolution to ship troops across the Tigris at night to the Persian-held shore by Ctesiphon was opposed by his generals (**II 50 24.6.4–5**). The difficulties these troops faced on landing were only eased by Julian's decision to ship further men across. The bank was secured and a victory won, but then came the abandonment of the siege of the city, which seems puzzling given the effort to reach it. Ammianus reports that it was said that Ctesiphon was impregnable and that Shapur was imminent, so the undertaking had to be given up (**II 50 24.7.1**). One would think that such obstacles should have been anticipated. (Libanius, perhaps optimistically, asserts that it was only lack of alacrity that prevented Ctesiphon being captured: **II 39 255**.) Associated with the move inland from Ctesiphon is Julian's most infamous act, the burning of the fleet (e.g. **II 60 3.26.2–3**). Gregory of Nazianzus presents this in a critical light, alleging that the emperor was incited by a treacherous Persian deserter (**II 44 11–12**). Strikingly, Ammianus echoes this assessment, giving it weight in the eyes of certain historians (e.g. Bowersock 1978: 114–15). Ammianus relates the distress caused to the troops and the attempt to save the ships (**II 50 24.7.3–6**), and modern historians can agree that the burning of the fleet would have had a negative impact on Julian's men (e.g. Hunt 1998a: 76). (See also the view of Theodoret: **II 59 3.20**.) Austin (1972: 304) talks of a 'crisis of morale'. Some commentators suggest that bringing a fleet in the first place was a mistake, since it would have slowed down the expedition and endangered the element of surprise (Hunt 1998a: 75).

Beyond controversial individual decisions, larger problems have been identified. There is a sense that Julian was overconfident, an attitude explicable given his previous success. After his arrival at Ctesiphon he rejected Persian peace overtures (**II 39 257–9**), and perhaps also even after the difficulties that ensued following the move inland from the city (Libanius *Autobiography* 133). In addition to his self-belief, Matthews suggests that Julian had underestimated the lengths the Persians were prepared to go to in order to thwart the invasion, specifically the destruction of their own territory (1989: 159–60). This can be associated with other gaps in the emperor's planning. Since the discovery of the 'Trajanic' canal (Matthews 1989: 157) which linked the Euphrates to the Tigris was entirely accidental (**II 50 24.6.1–2**), this gives the impression that Julian did not have an adequate knowledge of the terrain (Hunt 1998a: 75). Hunt even proposes that the emperor had not considered what to do beyond attacking Ctesiphon. Certainly the campaign can appear shambolic once the city had been reached. This view feeds back into the question of the objectives of the expedition.

A further, larger, problem is the relationship between the emperor and his army. There are signs of tension on the expedition. Julian was moved to inflict severe punishment on scouts that had fled a Persian attack, putting ten men to death (**II 50 24.3.1–2**). There was also a near mutiny at Pirisabora since the emperor offered the troops too small a financial reward (**II 50 24.3.3–8**). It is often observed that Julian was in a very different position with the army compared to the situation he experienced in Gaul. He was now an openly pagan emperor, no longer just dependent on men with whom he had established a good rapport. The shadow of the Christian Constantius loomed large. The exposure of a plot hatched by soldiers against Julian at Antioch is telling (**II 39 199; 43 84; 59 3.11**). It should not be forgotten, however, that even in Gaul there had been dicey moments.

The most damning criticism of the expedition is that it was a bad idea in itself. Ammianus (**II 50 23.5.4**) reports that Sallustius the Praetorian Prefect of Gaul wrote to Julian urging him not to embark on the campaign. Although Sallustius' objections were religious, and chime with Ammianus' warnings of doom, some modern historians have argued that the emperor should not have invaded Persia. Despite the protracted conflict with the Persians, it is observed that Constantius' efforts had yielded results. Although famous for his pursuit of a defensive policy (Warmington 1977), the emperor had contained Persia, and only the fortress of Bezabde had not been regained (Hunt

1998a: 74). In essence then, Julian embarked on an unnecessary war for his own political ends.

Thus, for diverse reasons, the emperor has been held accountable for the failure of the expedition. There are, however, certain cases for the defence. Some historians insist that Julian did have a strategy (e.g. Austin 1972: 305; Kaegi 1981: 209). It is clear that he intended Procopius and Sebastianus to play a crucial part in the campaign. Not only were they, in conjunction with Armenia, to distract Shapur, but they could rejoin Julian later, perhaps to execute a pincer movement against the Persians. Ctesiphon was indeed reached without any personal opposition from the Persian Shah. The subsequent Roman move inland can be seen as attempt to regroup with the other forces, if not just to attack other targets: it was not a retreat from the beginning. The decision to fire the ships can, in fact, be interpreted positively. Although highlighting the negative, Ammianus presents Julian's sound reasons for destroying the fleet (**II 50 24.7.4**): it saved the army transporting it, and it would not become a resource for the Persians. Libanius (**II 39 262–3**) justified the action too, noting also that the strong current of the Tigris would have made a heavy demand on manpower and that idlers would be avoided, though the latter argument seems rather forced. Modern historians can appreciate that the decision was tactically correct (e.g. Hunt 1998a: 76). Some also reject the existence of the treacherous deserter/deserters and the role ascribed to him/them (e.g. Ridley 1973: 322). Ridley (1973: 326) also argues that the fleet had been a valuable element of the expedition, and had been swift moving.

The argument that Julian was geographically ill-informed is firmly denied by Lee (1993: 87–8), who points to what he considers more convincing explanations for the failure of the expedition. These are the Persians' destruction of their own land, and the non-appearance of Procopius. The latter argument forms part of a robust defence of Julian by Ridley (1973). He asserts that the real weakness of the campaign was the army. The emperor did all he could to make the campaign a success, but he was let down by his officers and troops, who failed to support the endeavour adequately. Ridley concludes that the expedition would have been a success if Procopius had done what Julian had expected.

Finally, the view that the very undertaking of such an expedition was a mistake can be challenged. Although Constantius is renowned for pursuing a defensive policy, Blockley (1989; 1992: 12–24) has shown that the emperor's response to Persia was more varied, and that by the end of his reign he was preparing for all-out war. Thus it can be argued that Julian simply picked up where his cousin left off. Further, Kaegi

(1981) emphasises that Constantius' father Constantine the Great had also favoured the strategy of a sudden attack on Persia, and only his death had prevented him from embarking on it. In effect, then, the idea of a large-scale assault on Persia was one that was current. Julian's decision was not so extraordinary.

6. Conclusion

Many questions hang over Julian's motives for launching the Persian expedition, the objectives of the campaign, and why it was not a success. What is certain is that Julian was determined to embark on the expedition, that he followed a traditional goal in targeting Ctesiphon, and that he had envisaged the possibility of reuniting his forces with those of Procopius. It is also clear that the campaign ended in disaster for him, whether it was his own fault or not. This failure was a blot on the reputation of the last pagan emperor. Ammianus (**II 50 25.4.23**) responded by asserting that it was Constantine the Great who was responsible for stirring up the war with Persia in the first place. Ironically, however, the 'shameful treaty' which was concluded in the wake of Julian's expedition ushered in a period of peace between Rome and Persia, which was only shattered at the beginning of the sixth century.

The Elusiveness of Julian

Despite the wealth of material that exists for the study of Julian there are still difficulties in assessing his life and reign, as has been made clear by the preceding chapters. In some cases difficulties arise due to a lack of information. The year and date of Julian's birth are still debated, and the chronology of his early life and the exact course of his early education remain matters of dispute. The motivations for his conversion from Christianity to paganism are open to conjecture, as is the meaning of his bull coinage. A major impediment is, however, the polarity of opinion expressed about him by the sources. This is largely explicable in terms of the religious affiliations of the authors, and perhaps explains why those who seem to offer a more even-handed account (e.g. Ammianus Marcellinus and Socrates) prove attractive. Julian's own contribution to the documentation of his life and reign also poses problems, for he is very much aware of creating an image of himself, an image that others echoed, and one that continues to be echoed. Indeed, modern commentators are as divided in their interpretations of Julian as their ancient counterparts. This can be attributed to the difficulties of the source material, but also to personal responses to Julian and what he represents: it can be hard to remain objective about him. Central to my own view is that he was very much a man of his own day, and one that should not be taken so much at face value. Others will disagree. The reader is invited to make up their own mind. The major question presented by Julian is whether he could have succeeded in his religious aspirations for the empire (as well as his hopes for the empire generally, even if these hopes were shared by other later Roman emperors). For many, Julian was doomed to failure. However, I have no doubt that Browning was correct when he emphasised that it is not so easy to pass judgement (1975: 222). Julian reigned for too short a time for a proper assessment of his aims and achievements to be possible. And in truth, this is a major factor in the appeal of the emperor: the great 'What if?'

Like other famous figures in history – Alexander the Great, James Dean, John F. Kennedy – having his life cut short is an integral part of Julian's mystique.

Part II

Documents

Part II consists of source material of various types. To facilitate cross referencing from Part I, each source has been numbered.

1. Julian: *Panegyric on the Emperor Constantius* (*Oration* 1; c. 356)
Adapted from the translation by W. C. Wright

[4B–C] And what shall I do then? Exerting myself to praise you I appear to do so in order to curry favour, and indeed the genre of praise today has come to incur a terrible suspicion on account of its misuse, and is held to be base flattery rather than trustful testimony of the best deeds. Is it not obvious that I must put my faith in the virtue of the one I am going to praise and with full confidence devote myself to the encomium?

[6D–7A] And why is it necessary to talk about ancient history, or to recall Claudius, and to provide proofs of that man's virtue which are evident and known to all? To what end recall his battles with the barbarians across the Ister [Danube] and how piously and justly he acquired the empire, and the extreme simplicity of his lifestyle when he was emperor, which is still visible in images of him? What I might say about your grandparents is more recent, but no less splendid.

[8D–9A] Your father achieved many and noble deeds, some of which I have just recalled and others I must omit for the sake of brevity. Best of all I would say, and I think everyone else will concur, was that he begat and reared and educated you.

[16D–17A] [I]n your dealings with your brothers and your citizens and your father's friends and your armies you demonstrated justice and temperance; except that, in some cases, forced as you were by the critical times, you could not, against your own wishes, prevent others from committing errors.

[47A] Your wisdom is not at all easy to praise as it deserves, but nevertheless one must say a few words about it. But your deeds, I think, are more credible than my words.

2. Julian: *Panegyric on the Empress Eusebia* (*Oration* 3; c. 357)
Adapted from the translation by W. C. Wright

[117D–119A] So why then do I say that I have been so well treated and in return for what do I confess that I owe her a debt of gratitude for all time, that is what you are eager to hear. And I shall not conceal the facts. The emperor was kind to me almost from my infancy and he outstripped all liberality, for he rescued me from dangers so great, which not even 'a man in the strength of his youth' could easily have escaped … but lately I noticed that, I know not for what reason, he was somewhat harsh towards me. And as soon as she [Eusebia] heard the first mention not of any wrong doing, but of merely idle suspicion, she deigned to investigate it … she brought me into the sight of the emperor and brought about a dialogue; and she rejoiced when I was acquitted of every unjust charge. And when I desired to go home again, she provided a safe escort, first persuading the emperor to allow it. But when some deity … or some monstrous ill luck cut short this journey, she sent me to visit Greece, having requested this from the emperor on my behalf … for she had ascertained that I delighted in literature and she appreciated that that place was vital for culture … Indeed it had long been my great desire, as was natural, and I wanted this more than to possess much gold and silver.

[120B–C] For I am not engaging in outlandish topics if I wish to show how great were the kindnesses that she was the cause of for me because she honoured the name of philosophy. This, I know not why, has been applied to me … but I am wanting in it … and the name lacks reality. But Eusebia honoured even the name; for no other cause can I find out, nor am I able to learn from anyone else, why she thus became so eager an ally of mine …

[121B–D] [F]or when this good opinion of me was fixed in the emperor's mind she rejoiced exceedingly and chorused his song, ordering me to take courage and neither to decline through fear to accept the greatness of what was offered, nor by employing boorish and stubborn frankness lightly dishonour the vital request of one who had done me such favours. And so I harkened though it was not at all pleasing to me to submit to it, and besides I knew that to refuse it was extremely difficult … Accordingly when I agreed I had to alter my clothing and my retinue and my customary pursuits and my very house and lifestyle for what seemed full of pomp and ceremony to one whose past had naturally been so modest and humble …

[123C–124A] Do you wish therefore that I should report what else she did for me after these things, and all the good things she did for me … Shall I tell how many of my intimates she benefited, and how with the emperor she arranged my marriage? But perhaps you wish to hear also the catalogue of the gifts … one of those gifts of hers it would perhaps not be unpleasant to recollect for you, for it was one which I myself enjoyed especially. For she gave me books of the best philos-ophers and historians and many of the rhetors and poets, since I had brought hardly any with me from home, deluding myself with the hope and yearning to return home again soon, and she gave so many and all at once, that even my excessive yearning was satisfied, although I am altogether insatiable of intercourse with them, and, by means of books, she made Galatia and the country of the Celts resemble a Greek temple of the Muses.

3. Julian: *On the Deeds of the Emperor Constantius,* or *On Kingship* (*Oration* 2; c. 358)
Adapted from the translation by W. C. Wright

[51C] This is the genealogy of the house of Pelops for you, which lasted short of three generations; but the story of our family began with Claudius …

4. Julian: *Consolation to Himself on the Departure of the Excellent Salutius* (*Oration* 8; c. 358)
Adapted from the translation by W. C. Wright

[244C–D] Shall I recount how the famous Scipio, who loved Laelius and was beloved by him in return with equal yoke, as the saying goes, took pleasure in his company, but did nothing without first consulting with him and obtaining his opinion about what was to be done whence I think came the story from those who slandered Scipio because of jealousy, that Laelius was the maker of his deeds, and Africanus their actor. The same saying is applied to you and me, and not only am I not displeased about this, but I rather rejoice at it. For to be persuaded by another's good advice Zeno considered to be a mark of greater virtue than independently to decide oneself what one ought to do …

5. Julian: *Letter to Priscus* (Loeb no. 2; c. 358–9)
Adapted from the translation by W. C. Wright

Concerning a visit to me from your good self, if it is your intention, plan it now with the help of the gods and be zealous; for maybe a little later I shall not have the spare time. Seek out for me all the writings of Iamblichus to his namesake; only you can do this, for your sister's son-in-law (*gambros*) possesses a well amended version. And if I do not deceive myself, while I was writing this section, a marvellous sign appeared to me. I beseech you not to let Theodorus and his followers deafen you with their assertions that Iamblichus, that truly godlike man, and third after Pythagoras and Plato, was vainglorious … As for the collection of the works of Aristotle which you made, I will say this much to you: you have made me falsely sign myself your pupil ...

6. Julian: *Letter to Oribasius* (Loeb no. 4; c. 358–9)
Adapted from the translation by W. C. Wright

[384A–D] The divine Homer says that there are two gates of dreams, and that trust in their probable results is different in each case. But I reckon that you now, if ever before, have seen the future clearly; for I myself today also beheld such a thing. For in a certain very big room a tall tree had been planted and it was inclining towards the ground, while at its root had sprouted another, small and newly grown, and very flourishing. But I was very anxious about the little tree, lest someone should pull it up with the big one. Further, when I came near I saw that the big tree was lying at full length on the ground, while the little one was still upright, but suspended away from the ground. So when I saw this, I said in great anguish, 'Poor tree! There is a danger that not even its offshoot will be saved.' And someone who was completely unknown to me said: 'Look closely and be of good courage; for since the root remains in the ground the smaller tree will be unharmed and will be established even more firmly.' So much then for dreams. God knows what they portend.

7. Julian: *Letter to the Athenians* (autumn 361)
Adapted from the translation by W. C. Wright

[270C–271A] And that on the father's side I am descended from the same family as Constantius on his father's side is evident. For our fathers were brothers, having the same father. And although we were thus close relatives this most philanthropic emperor treated us in such a way: six of my cousins and his, and my own father, who was his uncle, plus another uncle we shared on the father's side, and my eldest brother, he killed without trial. And as for me and my other brother, he wanted to kill us, but in the end imposed exile ... he has repented, they say, and is pricked terribly, and he thinks that his unfortunate childlessness stems from these things, and his failure to do well in the Persian war he also ascribes to those things.

[271B–D] So as I asserted, they told us such things, and indeed even persuaded us, that Constantius had done such things since he was misled, and also because he submitted to the force and tumult of a disorderly and troublous army. They chanted such things to us when we had been shut up in a certain farm of those in Cappadocia, allowing no one to approach, after they had recalled him from exile in Tralles, and had removed me from the schools, when I was still just a lad. How should I describe the six years spent there? We lived as though in a stranger's property, closely observed as though we were in some Persian garrison, no stranger approached us nor was one of our old intimates permitted to visit us, we lived cut off from all serious learning and from all free converse, reared among the magnificent household and exercising with our own slaves as if they were comrades.

[272D–273A] But it was to please an androgyne, his chamberlain, who was in addition the steward of his cooks, that Constantius handed over to his bitterest enemies for execution his cousin, the Caesar, the husband of his sister, the father of his niece, whose sister he himself had married previously, to whom he owed such great rights of the gods of the family; and me he released grudgingly, after dragging me here and there for seven whole months and making a captive of me, so that, if one of the gods had not wished me to be saved and rendered the beautiful and good Eusebia favourable to me at that time, I would not have escaped his clutches then. And yet I swear by the gods that my brother had acted without even appearing to me in a dream; for I was not with him, nor did I visit him nor journey to him, and I hardly ever wrote to him, and even then only about trivial matters.

[273C–274B] And, to resume, when I was travelling homewards … a sycophant appeared near Sirmium, who concocted troubles for those there, alleging that they were contemplating a revolt … But when this affair was made known to the emperor, and Dynamius, another sycophant, suddenly reported from the land of the Celts that Silvanus was about to proclaim opposition to him, utterly terrified and afraid he at once sent to me, and he ordered me to retire to Greece for a short while then he summoned me to him from there. He had not seen me before except once in Cappadocia, and once in Italy, thanks to the efforts of Eusebia that I would be assured about my own safety. And yet I lived in the same city as him for six months, and he had even pledged to see me again. But that androgyne, his faithful chamberlain, hateful to the gods, unawares and involuntarily became my benefactor; for he did not allow me to meet with Constantius often, and perhaps the emperor did not wish it, but that man was the chief cause anyway.

[274B–D] And when I had first arrived from Greece immediately the blessed Eusebia showed me the utmost kindness through the eunuchs in her service. And a little later when her husband returned … then I was given entry to the court … and so-called Thessalian persuasion was applied to me. For when I adamantly refused intercourse with the palace, some of them, as if they had met in a barber's shop, cut off my beard, clothed me in a cloak, and fashioned me into a very laughable soldier, as they then supposed. For none of the adornments of those wretches suited me; and I walked not like those men, looking around and swaggering, but looking at the ground, as accustomed to do by the tutor who reared me.

[277A–C] And I agreed to submit. And I was quickly invested with the name and cloak of Caesar; and the subsequent slavery and the fear for my very life that hung over me each and every day, Heracles, how great it was and how awful ... I was scarcely able to bring with me to the court four of my own domestics for my more personal service, two very young, two older, of whom one alone knew of my attitude to the gods, and as far as he was able secretly joined me in their worship; I had entrusted with the custody of my books a certain doctor since he alone of my many faithful comrades and friends had gone abroad with me, and also because it was not realised that he was my friend.

[277D–278B] Giving me three hundred and sixty soldiers the emperor despatched me in the middle of winter into the nation of the Celts, which was convulsed, not as commander of the army there but rather as subordinate of the generals there. For he had written to them and commanded distinctly that they were not to watch the enemy but rather me, in case I attempt a revolt ... around the summer solstice he permitted me to join the army and to carry about his dress and image. For he had both said and written this, that he was giving the Gauls not an emperor but one supplying the image of himself to them. And, as you have heard, when the first year of campaigning finished well and good was accomplished, I returned again to winter quarters ...

[278D–279B] After that Constantius, thinking that there would be a little improvement but not such a great change in the affairs of the Celts, gave leadership of the army to me at the beginning of spring [AD 357]. And when the grain was ripe I took the field, for very many Germans had boldly settled themselves near the cities they had plundered in the land of the Celts. Indeed the number of the cities whose walls had been demolished was about forty-five, excepting the fortresses and lesser forts. And the barbarians then occupied on our side of the Rhine all the territory which extends from its sources as far as the Ocean; and those who dwelt nearest to us were three hundred stades distant from the banks of the Rhine, and there was a district three times as wide as this which had been left a desert by their pillaging, so that the Celts were not able to pasture their cattle there. And there were some cities deserted by their inhabitants, near which the barbarians were not yet dwelling. These were the conditions when I took possession of Galatia ...

[279B–C] ... I regained the city of Agrippina [Cologne] on the Rhine, which had fallen into enemy hands about ten months before, and also the nearby fort of Argentoratum [Strasbourg] ... and I contended in battle not ingloriously. Perhaps news of this battle has even reached you. Although there the gods gave me the king of the enemy as a prisoner of war, I did not begrudge Constantius the success. And yet although not allowed to celebrate a triumph, I had the right to slay my enemy, and moreover to lead him through the whole of the land of the Celts and to display him to the cities and as it were to have revelled in the misfortunes of Chnodomar.

[279D–280B] So after this came the second and third years, and all the barbarians were driven out of Galatia, most of the cities had been retaken, and very many ships had arrived from Britain. I had launched a fleet of six hundred ships, four hundred of which I had built within ten months and I introduced them all onto the Rhine, not a trivial task, on account of the barbarians dwelling nearby who were threatening us. At any rate Florentius thought this so impossible, that he pledged to pay the barbarians a fee of two thousand pounds of silver for the passage, and when Constantius learnt about this ... he commanded me to carry out the transaction, unless it appeared utterly shameful to me. But how was it not shameful, when it appeared so even to Constantius, who was too much accustomed to providing for the barbarians? Indeed nothing was given to them; instead I took the field against them, and since the gods defended me and were present, I received part of the nation of the Salians, and drove out the Chamavi, and seized many cattle and women with their children.

[280C–D] It would take too long to enumerate everything and to record every detail, so much did I achieve in four years. But the chief things are: three times did I cross the Rhine when I was still Caesar; twenty thousand people who were prisoners over the Rhine I demanded back from the barbarians; from two battles and one siege I took one thousand prisoners, and they were not of unserviceable age, but men in the prime of life; I sent to Constantius four levies of the best infantry, three others of less good infantry, and two most honoured divisions of cavalry; I have now retaken by the will of the gods all the cities, and then I had retaken a little less than forty. I call Zeus and all the gods who both protect cities and protect family as witnesses of my attitude towards Constantius and my faithfulness, that such are these towards him as I would choose a son's to be towards me.

[282B–D] But I obstructed him [Pentadius] in everything and thus he became hostile to me. Then Constantius selected and prepared another and a second and a third, Paul and Gaudentius, the renowned sycophants, engaging them to attack me, and he prepared to remove Salutius, as he was my friend, and at once Lucilianus was to be given as his successor. And a short time later Florentius also became my enemy on account of his greed, which I opposed. These men persuaded Constantius, perhaps somewhat nettled by envy of my successes also, to deprive me of all the troops. And he wrote letters filled with insults against me, and threatening destruction for the Celts; for he ordered to be led out of Galatia virtually the whole of the most effective troops without distinction, and charged this task to Lupicinus and Gintonius, while to me he announced that I would be opposed to them in nothing.

[282D–283B] But now in what manner should I relate the deeds of the gods to you … there was great uproar among all the civilians and the soldiers, and someone wrote an anonymous pamphlet to the city next to me, addressed to the Petulantes and the Celts … in which many things were written against that man and many lamentations about the betrayal of the Gauls; furthermore the author of the pamphlet lamented bitterly also my disgrace.

[284A–C] The divisions came, and I went out to meet them according to custom, and urged them to be on their way. They stayed one day, and until then I knew nothing of what they had resolved; by Zeus, Helios, Ares, Athene and all the other gods, know that such a suspicion did not cross my mind until that evening. It was already the latter part of the day, around the setting of the sun, when it was revealed to me, and at once the palace was surrounded, and they were all shouting, while I was still pondering what I ought to do and was not at all confident … I worshipped Zeus. And when the shouting became still stronger and all was in uproar in the palace, I begged the god to give me a sign and then he showed me and commanded me to submit and not oppose the desire of the army.

[285D–286A] But after this how did I behave towards Constantius? Even to this day I have not yet utilised in my letters to him the name which was given to me by the gods, but I have signed myself Caesar, and I have prevailed on the soldiers to swear to me to desire nothing else, if he would grant us for the Gauls to live without fear, and would approve what has been done … But he, instead of these, set the barbarians on us, and declared me his enemy among them, and paid them wages, so that the nation of the Gauls might be ruined …

[287A–B] … and if still now he would welcome agreement with me,

I shall keep to what I now have, but if he should intend to make war and not at all give up his former purpose, then I must suffer and do whatever is pleasing to the gods, since it would be more shameful to show myself weaker than him in unmanliness of spirit or ignorance of mind than in magnitude of power. For if he now prevails through numbers, it is not the deed of that man, but is that of the many men.

8. Julian: *Letter to Maximus the Philosopher*
(Loeb no. 8; c. November 361)
Adapted from the translation by W. C. Wright

[415C–D] I worship the gods openly, and the greater part of the army returning with me is devout. I sacrifice openly. I have offered to the gods many hecatombs as thank-offerings. The gods order me to ensure that everything is observed as it should be, and I obey them readily indeed; for they say they will grant me great rewards for my efforts as long as I am not slack. Evagrius has come to me … So come, with the help of the gods, as quickly as you can, and use two or more carriages.

9. Julian: *Letter to Themistius the Philosopher*
(late 361/early 362, or possibly 355/6)
Adapted from the translation by W. C. Wright

[253A–B] [A]nd long ago I intended to rival Alexander and Marcus and anyone else who was distinguished by virtue; but I shivered at the thought and was seized with terrible fear, lest I show myself to be utterly wanting in the courage of Alexander, and should not attain even slightly the perfect virtue of Marcus.

[259B–260B] If considering these things one is fearful to embrace so great a life, do you then show yourself to admire the Epicurean inaction and the gardens and suburbs of Athens and its myrtles and the little house of Socrates? But never have I been seen to prefer these to toil. That toil of mine I would most gladly recount for you and the terrors that hung over me from friends and relatives, at the time when I began my education under you, if you did not know them quite well enough yourself. You do not need to be told what I did before in Ionia against one who was related to me by family, but even more intimately by friendship, and that on behalf of a foreign man who was only known to me slightly, I mean the sophist. Did I not submit to go abroad for the sake of my friends? Indeed, you know how I took the part of Carterius when I went unbidden to our comrade Araxius, pleading on behalf of him. And on behalf of the property of that wonderful woman Arete and what she had suffered from her neighbours, did I not journey to Phrygia for the second time in almost two months, though I was already physically very weak on account of the ill health that had occurred because of my previous plight? Finally, before my departure to Greece occurred, when I was near the army and in extreme dangers, as most people would say, remember now what sort of letters I wrote to you, never full of lamentations or containing anything trivial or abject or excessively base. And when I departed to Greece, when everyone considered me as banished, did I not praise my fate as though it were some great festival … Thus I rejoiced at the chance that brought me to live in Greece instead of in my own house, though I possessed there no land, or garden, or a little house.

10. Julian: *Letter to the Philosopher Maximus* (Loeb no. 12; late 361 or early 362)
Adapted from the translation by W. C. Wright

[383A–B] There is a story that Alexander the Macedonian used to sleep with Homer's poems, so that by night as well as by day he would engage in military studies. But I sleep with your letters as though they were medicinal, and I do not ever stop reading them … consider that while you are away it cannot be said that I am alive, except in so far as I am able to read what you have written.

11. Julian: *Letter to Bishop Aetius* (Loeb no. 15; early 362)
Adapted from the translation by W. C. Wright

[404B–C] I have revoked banishment for all jointly who were exiled in whatever manner by the blessed Constantius on account of the folly of the Galilaeans. But in your case I do not just revoke your banishment, but also since I recall our old acquaintance and intimacy I exhort you to come to me. You will use a public carriage as far as my headquarters and one extra horse.

12. Julian: *Letter to the People of Alexandria* (Loeb no. 21; early 362)
Adapted from the translation by W. C. Wright

[379D–380C] But now by the gods though I want to praise you I am not able, on account of the breaking of the law. The people dared to rip a human being to pieces just as dogs a wolf, and then are not ashamed to proffer to the gods their hands still dripping with blood. But George deserved to suffer in this way. And I would say that he probably deserved to suffer even more extreme and severe treatment … It is a fortunate thing for you, men of Alexandria, that such an offence of yours occurred in my reign, for since I revere the god and on account of my uncle and namesake, who governed Egypt itself and your city, I preserve for you brotherly good will … I apply to you … the most gentle punishment, namely advice and arguments …

13. Julian: *Letter to Ecdicius, Prefect of Egypt*
(Loeb no. 23; early 362)
Adapted from the translation by W. C. Wright

[377D–378C] Some have a passion for horses, others for birds, yet others for wild beasts; but I since I was a little boy have been consumed by an intense desire to possess books … So grant to me this personal favour, that all George's books be sought out. For he had many on philosophy, and many on rhetoric and many also on the teachings of the impious Galilaeans; these latter I would wish to be completely obliterated except for the fact that with these more useful books may be seized, so let all these be sought out also with all due meticulousness … And I know what books George owned, and if not all of them many at least; for he lent me some of them to copy when I was in Cappadocia, and these he received back.

14. Julian: *Against the Cynic Heraclius* (*Or.* 7; spring 362)
Adapted from the translation by W. C. Wright

[227C–234C] A certain wealthy man had many flocks of sheep and herds of cattle and ranging herds of goats, and many times ten thousand horses grazed his marsh-meadows, and shepherds, both slaves and hired free men, and cowherds and goatherds and grooms for his horses, and very much property. And much of this his father had bequeathed to him, but he himself had gained many times more, wanting to enrich himself either justly or unjustly; for he cared little for the gods. And he had many wives, and sons and daughters by them, among whom that man divided his wealth then died. But he did not instruct them how to administer it … So since he reckoned that many sons would be enough to secure his wealth he took no heed how to make them zealous. But this was the initial cause of their ill treatment of one another. For each desired to have as much as his father and to have all for himself alone and turned on his neighbour ... And their relatives also shared in the folly and ignorance of the sons, since they themselves were not educated any better. Then there was a widespread glut of slaughter, as the tragic curse came to pass as the deity decreed ... the sons demolished the ancestral temples which had been despised by their father who had earlier despoiled them of the votive offerings, which had been dedicated by all and sundry, but not least by his own ancestors ... So when all was in confusion and marriages that were not marriages were being concluded and the laws of mankind were profaned together with those of the gods, pity came upon Zeus; then turning to Helios he said: 'O my son, offspring of the gods more ancient than heaven and earth, do you still resent the arrogance of that presumptuous and bold man, who by forsaking you was the cause of so many sufferings both for himself and for his race ... let us summon the Fates and see if this man is to be helped somehow.' ... Zeus began to speak to Helios: 'Regard this child there.' (And he was a relative of theirs who had been cast aside and was neglected, although he was the nephew of that wealthy man and the cousin of his heirs.) 'This child ... is your offspring. So swear by my sceptre and yours, that you will take especial care of him and cherish him and cure him of this disease. For you see how in some way he is infected with smoke and filth and fumes, and there is danger that the fire which you implanted in him will be put out, unless you will put on strength. For both I and the Fates entrust this to you.' Hearing these things king Helios was gladdened and took pleasure in the baby boy ... And father Zeus also ordered Athene, the motherless maiden, to share with Helios the rearing of the child. And when he was reared, and had become a young man ... he learned of the many evils that had befallen his relatives and his cousins, and he had wanted to throw himself into Tartarus because of the magnitude of those evils ... now everything seemed wretched to him, and for the moment there was no good anywhere. Then Hermes, who was intimate with him, appeared to him as a young man of the same age, and greeting him affectionately said, 'Come, I shall be your guide on a smoother and more level road ...' ... And when he had brought him to a great and tall mountain, he said, 'On the summit of this mountain dwells the father of all the gods. So beware! There is great danger here; you will worship him in the purest way, and ask of him whatever you would wish. You will choose, my child, the best.' ... Helios said, 'But you are young and uninitiated. Thus return to your own people, so that you can be initiated and live there safely. For you must go back and cleanse away all that impiety, and call to your aid me and Athene and the other gods.' ... 'Do you see,' said Helios, 'your cousin the heir?' ... 'How does the heir seem to you? And what of his shepherds and herdsmen?' And the young man replied 'He seems to me to slumber for most of the time and to be sunk in forgetfulness and to be devoted to pleasure, and of his shepherds a few are good, but most are wicked and savage ...' 'So what if I and Athene here,' said Helios, 'commanded by Zeus, should establish you as steward of all these instead of the heir?' ... 'But come,' said Helios, 'proceed with good hope ... we wish out of respect for your ancestors to purify your ancestral house ...'

[235A–C] For you have not been well trained nor did fate bestow on you such a guide to the poets as I had, I mean this philosopher now present. After this I came to the doors of philosophy to be perfected by that man whom I hold to surpass all the men of my own time. He used to teach me to practise virtue before all else and to consider the gods as guides to all that is good ... And although I, as you know, was furnished with external advantages, nevertheless I submitted myself to my guide and to his friends and comrades and school fellows, and I was keen to be instructed by all whom I heard praised by him, and I studied all the books that he himself approved.

15. Julian: *To the Alexandrians, an Edict* (Loeb no. 24; 362)
Adapted from the translation by W. C. Wright

[398D–399A] ... we have not, even now, consented that the Galilaeans who were banished by the blessed Constantius return to their churches, but only to their own countries. But I hear that the most daring Athanasius, elated by his accustomed impudence, has again seized what is called among them the episcopal throne, and that this is not a little displeasing to the devout people of Alexandria. Wherefore we publicly notify him to depart from the city ... But if he remains in the city we publicly notify him that he will receive a much greater and more grievous punishment.

16. Julian: *Letter to Evagrius* (Loeb no. 25; 362)
Adapted from the translation by W. C. Wright

[426D–428B] A little estate of four fields in Bithynia was gifted to me by my grandmother and I give this as a gift for your disposition towards me ... When I was still quite a young lad it seemed to me the dearest summer place, for it has also not insignificant springs and a bath which is not without beauty and a garden and trees. When I became a man I used to yearn for that old lifestyle, and came often, and our meetings there were not without literary conversations. And there is there also a small monument of my husbandry, a little vineyard, which produces a sweet-smelling and pleasant wine, which does not have to wait for time to improve it. You will see Dionysus and the Graces ... but since my mixing bowl of Dionysus is sober ... I only provided enough for myself and my friends; and few is the number of men ... I have written this letter hastily, by lamplight, so that, if I have made any mistakes, do not criticise them sharply or as one rhetor another.

17. Julian: *Letter to the Thracians* (Loeb no. 27; 362)
Adapted from the translation by W. C. Wright

For an emperor who looked to profit your request would have appeared hard to bear, and he would not have thought that he ought to damage the public resources by a private favour to anyone. But since I have not made it my object to levy the greatest possible sums from my subjects, but rather to be the cause of the greatest possible good to them, this fact shall discharge your debts for you too. But it will not discharge everything completely, but the sum shall be divided, a part for you, and the rest for the needs of the army, since from it you yourselves assuredly receive no mean benefits: peace and security. Accordingly until the third assessment I remit for you everything, all the shortfall of the preceding time. After this you will contribute in the customary way. For the amount remitted is sufficient favour for you, and for my part I must not be negligent of the public purse ... May the gods preserve you for all time.

18. Julian: *Letter to the High-priest Theodorus* (Loeb no. 20; 362)
Adapted from the translation by W. C. Wright

[452D–454A] So what is this which I say I now commit to you? It is the government of all the temples in Asia, the appointment of the priests in each city and the assignment to each of what is fitting. And what is fitting for this office is in the first place fairness, and in addition to it goodness and philanthropy towards those who deserve to receive these. For whoever is unjust to men, profanes the gods and is arrogant to all, is to be either instructed with plain speaking or punished severely. And all the things concerning all the priests must be drawn up in more detail publicly, and you and the others will know them very soon ... So when I saw that we had a great contempt for the gods, and that all piety for the ruling powers has been driven out by impure and vulgar luxury, I always lamented these things to myself. I observed that those devoted to the impious school of the Jews are thus so fired up that they would choose to die for it ... while we treat matters relating to the gods carelessly, so that we forget the customs of our forefathers ... But these Jews are in part pious, seeing that they honour a god who is truly most powerful and most good, who governs the world of sense, and who, as I well know, we worship also under other names ...

19. Julian: *To the Mother of the Gods* (*Or.* 5; March 362)
Adapted from the translation by W. C. Wright

[179D–180C] O Mother of gods and men ... grant to all men happiness, the chief of which is the knowledge of the gods, and to the people of the Romans in general, that they may rid themselves of the stain of godlessness especially, and in addition a favourable fortune in guiding their affairs of state for many thousands of years. And for myself, to have as fruit of my worship of you true knowledge in the opinions about the gods, make perfect in theurgy, and in all deeds which I undertake concerning the affairs of the state and the army grant me virtue with good fortune and the conclusion of life that is both without pain and admired, with the good hope that I journey to you.

20. Julian: *Letter to Arsacius, High-priest of Galatia* (**Loeb no. 22; 362**)
Adapted from the translation by W. C. Wright

[429C–432A] The Hellenic religion does not yet prosper according to our will, and it is the fault of those who profess it; for the worship of the gods is magnificent and great, surpassing every prayer and every hope. May Adrasteia pardon my words, for no one a short time before would have dared even to pray for such and so great a change. So why do we think that these are enough, not notice that it is their philanthropy to strangers and their care for the tombs of the dead and the sham holiness of their lives that have done most to increase godlessness? I believe that it is necessary for us truly to practise every one of these. And it is not enough for you alone to behave like this, but so must all the other priests in Galatia without exception. Either shame or persuade them to be zealous, or else remove them from their priestly office, if they do not together with their wives, children and servants, attend on the gods, but permit servants or sons or wives to show impiety to the gods, and honour godlessness more than piety. Then advise them that no priest may approach a theatre or drink in a tavern or be involved in any craft or occupation that is shameful and disgraceful. Honour those who obey you, but those who disobey expel from office. In each city set up many hostels so that strangers may profit by our philanthropy, not just our own people, but others also who are in need of money. I have lately made a plan by which you will be well provided for this ... For it is shameful that, if none of the Jews has to beg, and the impious Galilaeans support both their own and ours, it is seen that our people lack aid from us. And teach those of the Hellenic faith to contribute to such public services, and the Hellenic villages to offer their first fruits to the gods, and accustom those who love the Hellenic religion to such good works, teaching them that this was our practice long ago ... See the government officials in their homes infrequently, but write to them frequently. And when they enter the city no priest must go to meet them, but whenever they visit the temples of the gods meet them within the porch ... I am ready to help the people of Pessinus, if they make the Mother of the Gods propitious to them. But if they neglect her they are not only not blameless, but, not to speak harshly, let them take care not to enjoy my ill-will also ... Therefore persuade them, if they cleave to my protection, that all the people must become suppliants of the Mother of the Gods.

21. Julian: *Letter to Atarbius* (Loeb no. 37; 362)
Adapted from the translation by W. C. Wright

[376C–D] I swear by the gods that I do not wish the Galilaeans to be killed or beaten unjustly or suffer any other harm. However I do affirm emphatically that the god-fearing must be preferred above them; for on account of the absurdity of the Galilaeans almost everything has been overturned, but on account of the favour of the gods are we all preserved. Wherefore it is necessary to honour the gods and both god-fearing men and cities.

22. Julian: *Rescript on Christian Teachers*
(Loeb no. 36; after 17 June 362)
Adapted from the translation by W. C. Wright

[422A–424A] I reckon that true education results not in laboriously acquired graceful phrases and language, but in a healthy condition of mind, having understanding and true opinions about both good and evil things and both noble and base things. So whoever thinks one thing and teaches his pupils another, in my opinion this man fails to educate as much as he fails to be a good man too … Thus all who profess to teach anything whatever must be men of suitable character, and must not carry in their souls opinions opposed to what they profess in public … The gods were guides of all learning for Homer and Hesiod and Demosthenes and Herodotus and Thucydides and Isocrates and Lysias … I think it is absurd that men who expound the works of these writers should dishonour the gods who were honoured by them. Yet … I do not assert that they ought to change their opinions in order to instruct the young. But I give them a choice, either not to teach what they do not think is excellent, or if they wish to teach first they must persuade their pupils that neither Homer nor Hesiod nor any of these men whom they expound and have declared to be guilty of impiety, folly and error in regard to the gods, is such … but if they suppose that those writers went astray with respect to the most honoured gods, then let them go to the churches of the Galilaeans to expound Matthew and Luke … For religious and secular teachers let there be a general ordinance to this effect: any youth who wishes to go to school is not excluded; for it would not be fair to shut out from the best path boys who are still too ignorant to know which way to turn, and through fear to lead them against their will to the beliefs of their ancestors. Although it might be just to cure these, even against their will, as one cures the mad, we however concede indulgence to all for this sort of disease. For one must, I think, teach, but not punish, the insane.

23. Julian: *Letter to the Citizens of Bostra* (Loeb no. 41; 1 August 362)
Adapted from the translation by W. C. Wright

[435D–438B] I thought that the leaders of the Galilaeans would have more goodwill for me than for my predecessor in the government of the empire … For those who had been banished have had their exile remitted, and those who have had their property confiscated have been allowed by a law of mine to recover all their possessions. But they have reached such a peak of raving madness and folly that they are impelled, because they are not allowed to act like tyrants or to do what they once did to one another, and then did to the god-fearing, to move every stone and boldly to agitate the populace to be seditious, sinning against the gods, and disobeying my commands, even though these are philan-

thropic ... Thus I have decided to address all the people through this
ordinance, and to make evident, that they must not join in the sedition
of the clerics or be seduced by them to pick up stones or oppose their
officials ... I have been persuaded to issue this ordinance by the city of
Bostra in particular on account of the bishop Titus and the clerics ...
who have denounced their own people, giving the impression that they
advised them not to cause sedition ... So of your own accord banish
your accuser from the city, and you should agree with one another, and
let no one be contrary or unjust. Those of you who have wandered
should not persecute those who worship the gods correctly and justly ...
nor should those of you who worship the gods persecute, or plunder the
houses of, those who have wandered rather from ignorance than by
judgement. By reason must we persuade and educate these men, not by
blows or insolence or torture of the body.

24. Julian: *Letter to the Alexandrians* (Loeb no. 47; late 362)
Adapted from the translation by W. C. Wright

[434D] ... if you heed my advice, you lead yourselves on even a little
towards the truth. For you will not wander from the right road if you
heed one who travelled on that road of yours until his twentieth year,
and has now travelled this one with the help of the gods for twelve years.

25. Julian: *The Caesars*
(probably late 362, though possibly late 361)
Adapted from the translation by W. C. Wright

[313D] Next entered Claudius [II Gothicus], whom all the gods gazed
upon, wondering at his magnanimity, and pledged the empire to his
descendants, thinking that it was just that the family of a man who was
such a lover of his country should rule for a very long time.

[315A–B] ... and Diocletian, bringing with him the two Maximians
and my grandfather Constantius, drew near in pomp. These others held
each other by the hand, and did not walk as equals of him, but formed
a sort of chorus around him ... The gods wondered at the harmony of
the men and allowed them to sit far ahead of many of the others.

[315D] ... Licinius came as far as the doors, but since his offences
were many and disgusting Minos quickly drove him away. But Constantine came inside and sat for a long time, and then after him his sons.

[316C–D] And Silenus teased Quirinus and said, 'See if these Romans
are ever a match for this one Greek [Alexander].' 'By Zeus,' said

Quirinus, 'I think that many of them are not inferior. It is true that my descendants have admired him so much that only he of all foreign commanders is reckoned and named great. But it does not mean that they think this man greater than their own commanders, perhaps due to the sentiment of self-regard, but perhaps because it is true; we shall very soon know by examining these men.' Even when saying these things Quirinus blushed, and was clearly anxious on behalf of his descendants, lest they ended up taking second place.

[317B–318A] So Hermes called on Caesar to come forward, then Octavian, and thirdly Trajan, since they were the most warlike. Then in the silence that ensued, king Kronos looked at Zeus and said that he was astonished to see that only warlike emperors were called to the contest, and not a single philosopher. 'For me,' he said, 'such men are not lesser friends. So call Marcus in too.' And when Marcus was called he came in, looking very solemn, having his eyes and face somewhat lowered because of his labours, but he showed a natural beauty, since he kept himself simple and unadorned; for he had a very full beard, his clothes were plain and sober, and because of a deficiency of food his body was most radiant and most transparent, just like, I think, the most pure and uncorrupted light. When he too was inside the sacred enclosure, Dionysus said, 'O king Kronos and Father Zeus, can there be anything incomplete among the gods?' And when they replied that there could not, 'So let us bring in here some lover of enjoyment too.' And Zeus said, 'But it is not right that any man should enter in who does not emulate us.' Dionysus said, 'So let them be judged at the doors. And if this is agreeable let us call a man who is not unwarlike, but a slave to pleasure and enjoyment. So let Constantine come as far as the doors.'

[329C–D] And Silenus said, 'But are you not offering us gardens of Adonis as achievements, Constantine?' 'What do you mean,' he said, 'by gardens of Adonis?' 'I mean,' he said, 'those which women grow in pots for the lover of Aphrodite by heaping together garden earth. These bloom for a little while and wither forthwith.' And Constantine blushed, for he recognised that this was entirely like his own achievement.

[335C–336C] Then there was silence and the gods held a secret vote. It turned out that Marcus got most of the votes. After consulting in private with his father, Zeus arranged for Hermes to make the proclamation. And he proclaimed: 'Men who have entered this contest, such are our laws and judgements, that the victor is allowed to rejoice but the losers must not complain. Depart then,' he said, 'wherever is pleasing to each, and henceforth live under the guidance of the gods. Let each man choose for himself the guardian and guide.' After this proclamation, Alexander ran to Heracles, and Octavian to Apollo, but Marcus cleaved to both Zeus and Kronos … Trajan ran up to Alexander and sat down beside him. As for Constantine, he could not find amongst the gods the archetype of his life, but when he caught sight of Luxury who was nearby, he ran to her and she received him tenderly and embraced him, and adorning him with garments of many colours and beautifying him, she led him away to Prodigality, and there too he found Jesus who dwelt there and proclaimed to all: 'Whoever is a seducer, whoever is a murderer, whoever is sacrilegious and loathsome, let him approach with confidence. For with this water will I wash him and will make him pure at once. And even if he should be guilty of these same sins again, let him but smite his breast and beat his head and I will make him pure again.' Constantine fell in with him most gladly, when he had led his sons out of the assembly of the gods. But the avenging deities none the less afflicted both him and them for their godlessness, and exacted the penalty for the spilling of the blood of their kindred, until Zeus gave them respite on account of Claudius and Constantius. 'As for you,' Hermes said to me, 'I have given you knowledge of your father Mithras. You must keep his injunctions, and so procure for yourself a cable and firm anchorage for your life, and when you must depart from here, you can with good hope choose him as your guardian god.'

26. Julian: *To King Helios* (*Or.* 4; December 362)
Adapted from the translation by W. C. Wright

[130B–131C] [F]or I am a follower of king Helios. And of this fact I have within me more certain proofs. But I am permitted to say without blame, that from my childhood an intense longing for the rays of the god was instilled in me; and ever since I was a child my mind was so utterly captivated by the heavenly light, that not only did I long to look at it intently, but whenever I went out at night when the sky was cloudless and clear, I neglected everything else at once and gave myself up to the beauties of the heavens. No longer did I understand what anyone might say to me nor did I heed what I was doing myself. I was thought to be over-curious about these things and to be preoccupied, and already to be an astrologer when my beard had only just started to grow. And yet, by the gods, never had a book on this subject come into my hands, nor did I know what that was at that time. But why do I talk about these things, when I have more important things to say, if I should declare how I thought about the gods in those days? But let that darkness be forgotten … So I am jealous of the fortune of any man whom god has granted to receive the body compounded of sacred and prophetic seed, so that he can open the treasures of wisdom; but I do not slight the fortune which I myself was thought worthy of a share of by the god Helios, that I should be born in the imperial family that rules the world in my own time, but, I believe, if indeed one is persuaded by the wise, that this god is the common father of all mankind.

27. Julian: *Letter to a Priest* (Loeb no. 19; 362 or early 363)
Adapted from the translation by W. C. Wright

I would never have approved Pegasius so readily, unless I had been clearly convinced that even before, when he went by the title of bishop of the Galilaeans, he knew how to revere and honour the gods. I do not report this to you on hearsay … when I was called to his headquarters by blessed Constantius I journeyed by this route, and getting up and departing from Troas at the crack of dawn I came to Ilios around mid-morning. And he came to meet me, as I wished to investigate the city – for this was my pretence for visiting the temples – and he was my guide and showed me all the sights … There is a shrine to Hector, where a bronze statue of him stands in a tiny little temple. They have set up opposite this the great Achilles in the open air … And I discovered that the altars were still alight … and that the statue of Hector had been lavishly anointed with oil … And with the great readiness he took me there [the shrine of Athene of Ilios] and opened the temple, and … he showed me all the statues scrupulously preserved, and he did not act as those impious men usually do, tracing the sign [of the cross] on their impious foreheads, and that man did not hiss to himself … This same man accompanied me to the temple of Achilles too, and revealed the tomb intact; even though I had understood that this had been breached by him. But he also approached it with great reverence. I saw these things myself. And I have heard from those who now hate him that he also used to offer prayers to Helios and worship him in secret.

28. Julian: *Misopogon* (New Year 363)
Adapted from the translation by W. C. Wright

[338B–340B] Indeed I would be extremely happy to praise myself, but I have no reason to; but to criticise there are myriad reasons, and first I will begin with my face. I think nature did not make this overly beautiful or attractive or fair, but I myself due to stubbornness and bad temper have inflicted on it this thick beard … As for eating gluttonously or drinking greedily, I am not able to; for I must beware, I suppose, lest I accidentally eat up the hairs with my bread. As regards being kissed and kissing I am not troubled in the slightest ... But for me the thickness of my beard is not enough on its own, for my hair is a mess too, and I rarely have my hair and nails cut, and my fingers are usually black from using a pen ... I am not satisfied that my body is in such a state, but in addition the lifestyle that I practise is very harsh. I exclude myself from the theatres out of stupidity, and I do not allow the thymele to enter my court except on the first day of the year ... And even when I do enter the theatre I look like those who purify themselves from guilt. And I employ no one ... to lead the mimes and charioteers as my viceroy or general throughout the entire civilised world ... I hate chariot-races just as men who owe money hate the market-places. Therefore I only patronise them on the festivals of the gods; but I do not stay all day, as used to do my cousin and my uncle and my half-brother who had the same father as me ... sleepless nights on a straw mattress, and a diet free of all surfeit, make my disposition harsh and inimical to a decadent city.

[348C–D] And if these men [the Athenians] preserve in their characters an image of ancient virtue, it is quite likely that it is the same also with regard to Syrians, and Arabs and Celts and Thracians and Paeonians, and those who lie between the Thracians and Paeonians on the banks of the Ister [Danube], the Mysians, from whom indeed my own family is drawn, a people very boorish, austere, awkward, without beauty, and remaining immoveable in decisions, which are all proofs of a terrible boorishness.

[351A–352C] My character does not permit me to look languid, casting glances in all directions so I would appear beautiful to you, not at all in soul but in face ... But my tutor taught me to look at the ground when I went to school; and I did not see a theatre before my beard had more hair than my head, and even at that age it was never on my own account and according to my own desire, but three or four times, you know well, the ruler who was my kinsman and close relative, giving a gift to Patroclus, ordered me; it was when I was still a private individual. So forgive me; for I offer in my place a man whom you will hate more justly, the tutor who was fond of making enemies ... he called boorishness dignity and lack of sensuality temperance, and not submitting to desires or achieving happiness by that means manliness. Know well that the tutor said to me many times when I was still a young boy, I swear by Zeus and the Muses: 'You must never let the crowd of your mates who go to the theatres convince you to yearn for such spectacles. Do you long for chariot-races? There is one in Homer ... Take the book and go through it. Do you hear about the pantomime dancers? Renounce them! Among the Phaeacians the youths dance in a more manly manner; and you have as citharode Phemius, and as singer Demodocus. And there are in Homer many plants more delightful to hear about than those that can be seen ...' So are you eager that I should tell the name of my tutor, of what race was the man who used to say these things? By the gods and goddesses, he was a barbarian, a Scythian by race, and he had the same name as the man who persuaded Xerxes to attack Greece, and he was a eunuch, a term which twenty months ago was oft-mentioned and revered, but now is used as an insult and a reproach. He had been nurtured under the patronage of my grandfather, so as to educate my mother through the poems of Homer and Hesiod. And when she, after giving birth to me her first and only child, died a few months later, carried off by the motherless maiden from so many disasters when she was still a young girl, I was handed over to him after my seventh year. This man from that time convinced me of these things, leading me to instruction by one road; and since he himself did not want to know any other and did not permit me to walk any other he caused me to be hated by you all.

[353A–C] 'Fair enough; but why do you take it upon yourself to hear and judge cases about contracts? For surely your tutor did not teach you this also ...' But that terrible old man did persuade me ... though he too ... had been deceived by others. Names that you have met often when they are ridiculed: Plato and Socrates and Aristotle and Theophrastus. This old man was first convinced by them through folly, and then finding me when I was young and a lover of literature, he convinced me that if I should be a zealous emulator of those famous men in all things I should be better, not perhaps than other men ... but at any rate better than my former self.

[354C–D] For we are seven in number, strangers and newcomers to you, although one is a fellow-citizen of yours, a friend to Hermes and to me, a good craftsman of speeches. We do not have any business dealings with anyone, nor do we walk any other road than that which goes to the temples of the gods, and rarely, and not all of us, do we go to the theatres, since we have adopted the most shameful of deeds and the most reproachful end of life.

[355D] ... you insult your own ruler, yes even the hairs of his beard and the engravings on his coins.

[356D–357D] Whence I think it follows that you are especially happy, since you refuse all slavery, first that owed to the gods, then to the laws and thirdly to me the guardian of the laws ... know well that the gods have shared with me in the dishonour demonstrated by your city. 'The Chi,' they say, 'never wronged the city, nor did the Kappa.' What the meaning of this riddle of your wisdom is is difficult to deduce, but I happened to meet interpreters from your city and I was instructed that these are the first letters of names, and that the former signifies Christ, the latter Constantius. So bear with me, if I speak my mind. In one thing Constantius did wrong you, that when he made me Caesar he did not kill me; and as for the rest, may the gods grant you alone out of all the Romans to have experience of many Constantiuses, or rather, of the greed of that man's friends ... But since loving Christ, you have him as protector of your city in place of Zeus and the god of Daphne and Calliope ... Did the Emesenes who set fire to the tombs of the Galilaeans yearn for Christ? But what men of Emesa have I ever dis-tressed? I have however distressed many of you, I almost say all, the council, the wealthy, the people. The people for the most part, or rather all, because they have preferred godlessness ... the powerful citizens because they are hindered from selling everything for much money, but all of you because of the dancers and the theatres ...

[361A–C] ... you slandered the neighbouring cities which are holy and slaves of the gods like myself, that the compositions against me were made by them, though I know well that those cities love me more than their own sons, since they immediately restored the precincts of the gods but cast down all the tombs of the godless, subsequent to the signal which was given by me not long ago. They were so elated in mind and excited in thought that they attacked those who were offending the gods even more than I wished. And as for your actions, many of you cast down the altars which had just been raised up, and my mildness scarcely taught you to be tranquil. And when I sent away the corpse from Daphne, some of you ... handed over the precinct of the god of Daphne to those who were angry about the relics of the corpse, and the rest of you either accidentally or not caused that fire which made the strangers who were staying in the city shudder, but afforded pleasure to your people and was overlooked by the council and is still overlooked.

[361D–362B] So I raced there from the temple of Zeus Kasios, supposing that there [Daphne] especially, I should enjoy your wealth and liberality ... But when I went inside the precinct, I discovered neither incense nor a sacrificial cake nor a sacrificial victim. Instantly I was astounded and thought that I was outside the precinct and that you were awaiting the signal from me, revering me indeed as archpriest. But when I inquired what the city intended to sacrifice in celebration of the annual feast for the god, the priest said, 'I have come bringing from my own house a goose as an offering to the god, but the city this time has prepared nothing.' Thence since I love making enemies, I spoke to the council very unfair words ...

[365B] ... I have not levied gold coins nor demanded silver coins nor increased the tribute; but in addition to the arrears a fifth of the customary taxes has been remitted altogether.

[367C–368B] And previously I praised you ... thinking that you were sons of Greeks, and I myself, even if my family is Thracian, am a Greek in my customs, I assumed that we should love each other most strongly ... Then although you sent an embassy to me and it arrived not only later than the others, but later than that of the Alexandrians in Egypt, I remitted much gold coin, and much silver coin, and all the tribute for you alone apart from the other cities, and then I filled up the register of your council with two hundred councillors and spared no one; for I contemplated making your city greater and more powerful. So I gave you the chance to have the wealthiest men from those who oversee my own treasuries and who mint the coinage. But you selected from these men not the powerful ones ... Many such villainous things did you do concerning the nominations ...

[368C–369C] ... when I arrived in your city the people in the theatre, being assaulted by the wealthy, first of all emitted this phrase, 'Everything plentiful, everything expensive.' On the following day I spoke with your powerful men and attempted to persuade them that it is better to despise unjust profits and to do good for citizens and strangers. And they promised to take care of the affair, and for three months in a row while I overlooked it and waited they dealt with the affair carelessly in a way that no one would have expected ... I fixed a fair price for everything and made it known to all ... since there had been a terrible dearth because of the earlier droughts, it seemed a good idea to me to send to Chalcis and Hierapolis and cities round about, whence I imported for you four hundred thousand measures of corn. And when this had been used up also, first I disposed of five thousand, later seven thousand, then recently ten thousand bushels of corn ... all of which was my own property. And I gave to the city corn which had been imported for me from Egypt ... So what did your wealthy men do? They secretly sold the corn in the countryside for a higher price ...

[370D–371A] I think you said that three thousand lots of land were uncultivated and you requested to have them, and after you got them you all distributed them among yourselves although you did not need them. This was investigated and exposed clearly. And I took them away from those who had unjustly acquired them, and initiated no investigation about those acquired previously, which they had tax-free, though they especially should have been taxed ...

29. Inscriptions
Translated from the Greek and Latin

AE 1983: 895; Conti 2004, Nr. 54 (Thessalonica)

In the reign of the most beloved of the gods and restorer of the sacred rites, master and conqueror of every barbarian nation, Claudius Julianus, all-powerful and sole emperor of the world, Calliopius, most illustrious consular, dedicated [this altar].

AE 1991, 656; Conti 2004, Nr. 128 (Lucca, Italy)

To the liberator of the Roman world, restorer of liberty and the republic, preserver of the army and the provincials, our unconquerable lord Flavius Claudius Julianus, father of his country, ever Augustus.

CIL 2.7088; Conti 2004, Nr. 28 (Pergamum)

To our lord Flavius Claudius Julianus, lord of the whole world, master of philosophy, revered leader, most dutiful imperator, most victorious Augustus, propagator of liberty and the republic; Aelius Claudius Dulcitius, vir clarissimus, proconsul, vice sacra audiens, faithful to the divine will and majesty of the emperor.

CIL 8.18529; Conti 2004, Nr. 67 (Casae, Numidia)

To our lord Flavius Claudius Julianus, dutiful, fortunate, potent in every kind of virtue, unconquerable leader, restorer of liberty and of the Roman religion, and conqueror of the world.

30. *Theodosian Code*
Translated C. Pharr

1.9.1. Emperors Constantius Augustus and Julian Caesar
to the Secret Service (*agentes in rebus*)

All persons who are of unworthy birth status and of the worst character, and who have aspired to or have been transferred to the department of the secret service shall, upon investigation by the Most Noble count and master of offices, be removed from your society, in order that you may thus be able to enjoy the privileges which were formerly granted to you. 1. Furthermore, no person through patronage shall attain to the office of ducenarius, of centenarius, or of biarch, but each one shall arrive at it by his labor and by using the testimony of all. But he shall acquire the position as chief of office staff by his position on the office register, so that those persons shall go out as secret confidential agents and as supervisors of the public post who are called thereto by their order in the imperial service and by their labors.

...

Given and posted at Rome in the Forum of Trajan on the kalends of November in the year of the consulship of Eusebius and Hypatius. – November 1 (October 31), 359.

6.26.1. Emperor Julian Augustus to Secundus, Praetorian Prefect

Military service is of primary importance to the State. The second adornment of peace lies in the protection of letters. Therefore, We carefully consider the merits of Our bureaus, and We grant to them the second place in the matter of privileges, so that if any persons have labored fifteen years in the bureau of memorials, of arrangements, of correspondence, or of petitions, even though they are descended and trace their lineage from decurion fathers, grandfathers, and other decurion ancestors, they shall be considered exempt from all such obligations, and they shall not be called to service in municipal councils.

Given at Antioch on the seventh day before the kalends of October: September 25. Received on the fifth day before the ides of November at ... in the year of the consulship of the Most Noble Mamertinus and Nevitta. – November 9, 362.

6.27.2. Emperor Julian Augustus to Secundus, Praetorian Prefect

No person after his third year of service in the palace as a member of the secret service shall be delivered to a municipal council; nor shall any such person be thus delivered if he has been presented with his discharge in the year of My fourth consulship.

Posted at Beirut on the day before the kalends of March in the year of the fourth consulship of Julian Augustus and the consulship of Sallustius. – February 28, 363.

8.1.6. Emperor Julian Augustus to Auxonius, Governor of Tuscany

Accountants who have learned with their clever fraud to falsify the public accounts of the municipalities shall be subject to torture on the grounds of their cunning and fraud. But when they have administered the public records for five years, they shall be on the retired list for one whole year, so that in private life they may be easily available for prosecution by those who make accusations. Furthermore, in their seventh year, when it appears that said accountants have well administered the office entrusted to them, they shall be discharged with the title of honorary Most Perfect. This honor of added rank will efface the disgrace of their former low station.

Given on the sixteenth day before the kalends of February at Constantinople in the year of the consulship of Mamertinus and Nevitta. – January 17, 362.

8.5.5. The same Augustus to Musonianus, Praetorian Prefect

For some time now, orders of Our Clemency have been in existence to the effect that governors of the provinces shall be denied the right to issue post warrants, since great damage would undoubtedly be inflicted upon the public post if this license should be more widely extended. 1. Therefore We repeat the very law which We had formerly approved, and We command that said governors shall be admonished by letters issued by Your Authority, instructing them to hasten to obey Our orders.

Given on the eighth day before the kalends of August in the year of the seventh consulship of Constantius Augustus and the consulship of Constantius Caesar. – July 25, 354; 326.

8.5.12. Emperor Julian Augustus to Mamertinus, Praetorian Prefect

Since the public post has been prostrated by the immoderate presumption of certain persons and by the great number of post warrants which the authority of the vicars and the offices of the governors with the rank of praeses and consular do not cease to extend, We are compelled to undertake the supervision and the administration of this matter, and We deprive all other persons of the right to issue post warrants. 1. Therefore, no person except you shall henceforth have the right to issue any post warrant. 2. But in order that the public needs may be filled, I Myself shall grant to each vicar ten or twelve post warrants that have been written out by My own hand, and Your Sublimity shall issue to each governor two post warrants annually, by means of which said officials for necessary reasons may be able to dispatch their own apparitors to separate and remote parts of the provinces. 3. But to each of these persons Our Clemency will also grant one post warrant, that they may be able to refer matters to Us when necessity requires this to be done.

Received on the eighth day before the kalends of March at Syracuse in the year of the consulship of Mamertinus and Nevitta. – February 22, 362.

9.17.5. Emperor Julian Augustus to the People

Criminal audacity extends to the ashes of the dead and their conse-crated mounds, although our ancestors always considered it the next thing to sacrilege even to move a stone from such places or to disturb the earth or to tear up the sod. But some men even take away from the tombs ornaments for their dining rooms and porticoes. We consider the interests of such criminals first, that they may not fall into sin by defiling the sanctity of tombs, and We prohibit such deeds, restraining them by the penalty which avenges the spirits of the dead.

1. The second matter is the fact that We have learned that the corpses of the dead are being carried to burial through dense crowds of people and through the greatest throngs of bystanders. This practice, indeed, pollutes the eyes of men by its ill-omened aspect. For what day is well-omened by a funeral? Or how can one come to the gods and temples from a funeral? Therefore, since grief loves privacy in its obsequies and since it makes no difference to those who have finished their days whether they are carried to their tombs by night or by day, the sight of all the people must be freed from this spectacle. Thus grief may appear to be associated with funerals, but not pompous obsequies and ostentation.

Given on the day before the ides of February at Antioch in the year of the fourth consulship of Julian Augustus and the consulship of Sallustius. – February 12, 363.

10.3.1. Emperor Julian Augustus to Secundus, Praetorian Prefect

(After other matters.) We command that their public landholdings shall be restored to the municipalities, so that they may be leased at fair rates, in order that provision may be made for the reconstruction of all the municipalities.

Posted on the ides of March at Constantinople in the year of the consulship of Mamertinus and Nevitta. – March 15 (13), 362.

11.16.10. Emperor Julian Augustus to Secundus, Praetorian Prefect

It is right that no tax levy shall be made upon the provincials without Our knowledge, and that from tax levies which have been made, no remissions shall be granted. Therefore, all landholders shall be com-pelled on equal terms to fulfill all tax obligations that are specified by custom or by Our regulation, that is, payments for the public post, transportation, care of the highways, and all such similar requirements. (Etc.)

Posted on the third day before the ides of March at Constantinople in the year of the consulship of Mamertinus and Nevitta. – March 13, 362.

12.1.48. The same Augustus to the Senate

If by chance any decurions should refuse their compulsory services and should betake themselves to the association of Our Senate, they shall be removed from the official list of the Senate and delivered to their own cities. If any persons should have performed the office of praetor, they shall remain in the Senate, but they must restore what they took away from the accounts of the fisc or from the vitals of their cities. Thus hereafter opportunity for obtaining this honor shall be barred to all.

Given on the fifth day before the nones of May in the year of the consulship of Taurus and Florentius. – May 3, 361.

12.1.50. Emperor Julian Augustus to Secundus, Praetorian Prefect

(After other matters.) Decurions who evade their compulsory public services on the ground that they are Christians shall be recalled.

1. The municipal councils shall be exempt from the tax payable in gold and silver which is levied upon the tradesmen, unless perchance it should appear that a decurion is engaged in merchandising to any extent. Thus the senates of the municipalities shall be exempt from the arrears of such burdens, as We have already said.

…

Posted on the third day before the ides of March at Constantinople in the year of the consulship of Mamertinus and Nevitta. – March 13, 362.

12.1.52. The same Augustus to Julianus, Governor of Phoenicia

The fact that a person who is claimed as a resident is said to be a decurion elsewhere shall not bar a petition of the decurions of his place of residence. For the aforesaid person can be detained by the decurions also in his place of residence if his property permits and if he has been unwilling to renounce his residence before he is sued. Reasons of equity do not permit the aforesaid person to be burdened because of the bare possession of property, if he has not established his lares, although he is said to have purchased the property of a decurion. Of course, he must be held by the right of residence in this instance, if he has neither borne arms nor been in charge of a military expedition nor been made Senator by the recommendation of having held an administrative office.

Given on the third day before the nones of September at Antioch. – September 3. Received on the ides of October at Tyre in the year of the consulship of Mamertinus and Nevitta. – October 15, 362.

12.1.53. The same Augustus to Sallustius, Praetorian Prefect

Since, from a few instances, We suspect, not without reason, that very many misdeeds have been committed, We revoke as invalid all nominations whatever that were made by the municipal councils after the kalends of September, except those that were made in the customary manner. You shall immediately institute a legal investigation about all preceding nominations.

…

Given on the fourteenth day before the kalends of October at Antioch in the year of the consulship of Mamertinus and Nevitta. – September 18, 362.

12.13.1. Emperor Julian Augustus to Sallustius, Praetorian Prefect

Crown gold is a voluntary service which not only must not be levied on Senators but not even on other persons. It is permissible that it should be required by a certain necessity of levy, but such matters must be reserved for Our judgement.

Given on the third day before the kalends of May in the year of the consulship of Mamertinus and Nevitta. – April 29, 362.

13.3.5. The same Augustus

Masters of studies and teachers must excel first in character, then in eloquence. But since I cannot be present in person in all the municipalities, I command that if any man should wish to teach, he shall not leap forth suddenly and rashly to this task, but he shall be approved by the judgement of the municipal senate and shall obtain the decree of the decurions with the consent and agreement of the best citizens. For this decree shall be referred to Me for consideration, in order that such teachers may enter upon their pursuits in the municipalities with a certain higher honor because of Our judgement.

Given on the fifteenth day before the kalends of July. – June 17. Received on the fourth day before the kalends of August at Spoleto in the year of the consulship of Mamertinus and Nevitta. – July 29, 362.

15.1.3. The same Augustus to Secundus, Praetorian Prefect

We direct that judges of the provinces shall be admonished that they must know that they shall not arrange for any new work until they have completed those works which were commenced by their predecessors, excepting only the reconstruction of temples.

Given on the third day before the kalends of July in the year of the seventh consulship of Constantine Augustus and the consulship of Constantius Caesar. June 29, 326; 362.

16.2.3. The same Augustus to Bassus, Praetorian Prefect

A constitution was issued which directs that thenceforth no decurion or descendant of a decurion or even any person provided with adequate resources and suitable to undertake compulsory public services shall take refuge in the name and the service of the clergy, but that in the place of deceased clerics thereafter only those persons shall be chosen as substitutes who have slender fortunes and who are not held bound to such compulsory municipal services. But We have learned that those persons also are being disturbed who became associated with the clergy before the promulgation of the aforesaid law. We command, therefore, that the latter shall be freed from all annoyance, and that the former, who in evasion of public duties have taken refuge in the number of the clergy after the issuance of the law, shall be completely separated from that body, shall be restored to their orders and to the municipal councils, and shall perform their municipal duties.

Posted on the fifteenth day before the kalends of August in the year of the sixth consulship of Constantine Augustus and the consulship of Constantius Caesar. – July 18, 320; 329.

16.10.6. The same Augustus and Julian Caesar

If any persons should be proved to devote their attention to sacrifices or to worship images, We command that they shall be subjected to capital punishment.

Given on the eleventh day before the kalends of March at Milan in the year of the eighth consulship of Constantius Augustus and the consulship of Julian Caesar. – February 20, 356.

31. Sextus Aurelius Victor: *De Caesaribus* (c. 361)
Translated H. W. Bird

[42.16] When he [Silvanus] had climbed still higher from that rank [Master of Infantry] through fear or madness, he was slaughtered on about the twenty-eighth day during a mutiny of the legions from which he had hoped for protection. [17] For this reason, so that there might be no rebellion among the Gauls, who are headstrong by nature, especially because the Germans were ravaging most of those districts, Constantius appointed Julian as Caesar in command of the Transalpine regions since he was acceptable to him by virtue of their family relationship, and the latter quickly subdued (those) fierce nations and captured their famous kings. [18] Although these exploits were accomplished by his vigour, they nevertheless came about through the good fortune and planning of the emperor.

32. Claudius Mamertinus: *Speech of Thanks to Julian*
(1 January 362)
Translated M. M. Morgan

[3.1] Shall I now proceed to recall, as though they were something new and previously unheard of, the reconquest, by means of your valour, of the Gallic provinces, the subjection of the whole barbarian race, when these triumphs have, in this part of the Roman Empire, been hailed as most deserving of glory by the laudatory voice of popular acclaim, to such an extent as to merit the envy of your cousin the Emperor? For what else alienated the goodwill of your associate in government, if not the brilliance of your renown?

[6.2] So it was that, once he had put down the rebellious Alamanni, caught in the midst of their preparations for war, this prince of ours, who had but lately traversed, at the head of a victorious army, regions, mountains and rivers of unknown name, passing through kingdoms at the ends of the earth and inhabited by savage tribes, flying over the heads of rulers and spurning them beneath his feet, appeared suddenly and unexpectedly in the very midst of Illyria. [3] Those of us who were fortunate enough to accompany the prince on this expedition witnessed how the astonished inhabitants of the cities were unable to credit what their eyes told them. [4] … Young girls, youths, women, trembling old crones, tottering old men, looked on in fright and stupefaction as the emperor, burdened with heavy armour, burned up miles of his long journey, his breath shortened by haste yet without inducing exhaustion, rivulets of sweat trickling over his strong neck, and through the furring dust which covered his hair and beard, his eyes brilliant and glinting like stars.

[9.1] And what a marvellous thing it was to behold, that whilst still navigating the Danube you were, at the same time, extending your munificence as far as the Adriatic, as far as the Tyrrhenian Sea, as far, even, as the Egyptian Sea … [4] … But it would take too long to list all the cities restored to life at the intervention of the Emperor: it is sufficient only to note that all the cities of Macedonia, Illyria and the Peloponnesus, thanks to one or two letters from the hand of our all powerful emperor, enjoyed a sudden resurgence of youth …

[11.1] Up to now one might have assumed that the sole reward of power is that the emperor may be distinguished from all other citizens not by the valour of his actions nor by the splendour of his glory but by the enormity of his expenses. [2] For instance, quite apart from the colossal and unnecessary construction work involved in building their accommodation, the expense of keeping up the immense court and all its hangers-on easily exceeded the cost of maintaining the legions. [3] Furthermore, the State was well aware of the extravagant elaboration of their lunches and dinners, for their gourmet foods were valued not so much for savour as for rarity, unusual birds, fish from far-away oceans, fruit out of season, snow in summer and roses in winter! All these excesses the emperor's soul rejected, victorious over such sensual gratifications. [4] Nor had he any need to acquire paintings, marble inlays, panelled ceilings decorated with solid gold, he who was accustomed, during the greater part of the year, to sleep on the bare ground and with only the sky for shelter; nor had he any use for a host of contractors ready to minister to his pleasures, he who had need of so little; nor had he any time for banquets, he who, more often than not, took his meal standing up and then only as much as was necessary for the maintenance of life, content with the rations of an ordinary soldier, served by the attendant at hand and accompanied by whatever drink available.

[13.3] Suppose one of the gods were to restore them [power-mad would-be usurpers] briefly to life and address them as follows, 'You for instance, Nepotianus and Silvanus, you sought the supreme power, even at the risk of drawn swords and the ever present threat of death. Today the throne is offered to you spontaneously on condition that you rule in the same spirit as Julian: you shall be vigilant day and night for the peace of all and, despite your title of Master, you shall labour to serve the liberty of the citizen, you shall go to war more often than to table, you shall be indebted to none and ready, furthermore, with largesse for all, you shall grant privilege to none, offer violence to none, in all the lands of the earth you shall not harm the reputation of any maiden, for your bed shall be free even from permitted and legitimate pleasures being more chaste than the couches of the Vestals, bareheaded you shall endure in summer the dust of the Alamanni, in winter the frosts of Thrace.' Assuredly their delicate ears would not be able to sustain the impact of the very words ...

[27.3] Let us see, now, whether, puffed up by his success, he has changed in any way the gentleness and simplicity of his former life. Yes indeed, he has quite unmistakably changed. His moderation is even more marked and has assuaged the envy of his success. [4] To whom has he not given a proof of his calmness of temperament, even at that very time when, on seeing the State delivered from the fear of a disastrous war, we were all giving way to wild transports of joy? [5] For our emperor, although he realised that the safety of the State was maintained only by divine assistance, yet took pity on human frailty and pardoning all offences, took on the true role of a brother: the very man whom he knew to be taking up arms against himself was that same man he surrounded with honours on his death and afterwards himself paid his last respects in person. Equally remarkable in the acts of remembering and forgetting, he forgot his enmity and remembered only his obligation as his heir.

[28.1] But why do I search so far to find evidence of his courteous and gentle nature? Today, this very day, I repeat, has given sufficiently clear proof of his moderation. [2] My colleague and I were afraid lest our noble emperor should go too far in his desire to demonstrate his courtesy. [3] So we make our way to the palace at the crack of dawn. Our arrival is announced to the prince just at the moment when he is receiving the salutations of his courtiers. Instantly, as though he had anticipated us, he started down from his throne with a troubled and anxious expression, just such as I should have worn if I had arrived late to present myself to the prince. [4] With difficulty he cleared a way through the great throng of people who had preceded us, thus causing himself to walk as far as possible to meet us. And then, O holy divinity, amidst universal rejoicing, with what expression and with what voice he said 'May you fare well, eminent consul!' He deigned to honour us with a kiss from those lips hallowed by connexion with the gods and offered us his right hand, that hand, immortal pledge of virtue and loyalty …
[29.4] After the initial greetings and good wishes he enquired what action we proposed to take as a result of our consular power, whether, on the completion of our senatorial duties, we saw fit to go before the tribunal, or to summon the assembly or to mount the rostrum. But it was to the Curia that the decrees of the Senate directed us, following the established practice of our times. [5] What is more he offered to accompany us himself and so, flanked on either side by his consuls wearing the toga praetextata, he proceeded forth, not easily distinguished from his magistrates by the nature and colour of his robes. [30.1] Perhaps it may appear superfluous to recall events which you yourselves have witnessed … yet it is essential to commit to writing, to record in histories, to hand on to future generations the marvels which those of centuries to come will scarcely be able to credit. [2] He was on the verge of ordering the consular chairs to be carried within the very doors of the palace, and, when, obedient to a sentiment of respect and veneration for his person, we refused that seat reserved for the highest dignity, he forced us, almost

with his own hands, to take our places and then, hemmed about by the crowd of citizens in togas, he set out to precede us on foot, adjusting his pace more or less to the beckoning of the lictor and the orders of the summoner. [3] Will anyone believe such a thing possible, who has beheld so recently the haughtiness of those who wore the purple? Who for that very reason heaped such honours on their own courtiers in order not to have to despise them as men without honours. Will anyone believe that after such a long period of time, the old freedom of ancient days has been restored to the State? Even the consulate of Lucius Brutus and Publius Valerius, who, after the expulsion of the kings, were the first to govern the city with an annual authority, ought not, in my judgement to be ranked above ours. [4] … In the year of their consulate liberty was born, in ours it is restored.

33. Libanius: *Letter to Julian* (Loeb no. 30; early 358)
Adapted from the translation by A. F. Norman

[1] You have won a double victory, one in arms, the other in words, and your trophies are set up, one over the barbarians, the other over me your friend … [6] So now that you exhort me to be expansive, I shall submit. First, I congratulate you upon the fact that, although you have your hands full with weapons, you have not terminated your zeal for words, but you fight as if that were your sole object and yet spend your life among books as if discharged from battle. Next, I congratulate you that you have given your colleague in empire no cause to repent of his gift of it, but regard him alike as your cousin, co-ruler, lord, and teacher, and by your actions you increase his fame, and say to his opponents as they fall, 'What would you suffer if the emperor were present?' [7] I praise all these, as well as the fact that you have not changed your mind along with your attire nor cast off the remembrance of your friends on account of your position of power …

34. Libanius: *Address to Julian* (*Or.* 13; July 362)
Adapted from the translation by A. F. Norman

[11] But this [being sent to Nicomedia to remove him from the public eye] was the origin of the greatest blessings both for him and for the world. For there was hidden there a spark of divination that had barely escaped the hands of the impious. Hence as you first began to track down hidden lore, you were tamed by its utterances and checked your violent hatred against the gods.

[25] At this point of the speech, a Homer would have said, 'Speak to me now, you Muses who live in Olympian dwellings.' I, however, would beg you to tell how everything came to pass [in Gaul]. But there is no need for you to speak about these things, it will suffice to provide the history that you composed about your own campaigns, a general turned historian.

35. Libanius: *To Julian on behalf of Aristophanes* (*Or.* 14; autumn 362)
Adapted from the translation by A. F. Norman

[29] Remind yourself, emperor, of the letter you sent to the Corinthians after embarking upon the war against your will … In it you explicitly call the Corinthians your benefactors. I must cite the very part of your letter … [30] 'I have an hereditary friendship with you,' you wrote, 'for my father lived among you and departed thence, just like Odysseus from the Phaeacians, after resting from his long wanderings.' Then, after a few words about his wicked stepmother [Helena], you went on, 'Here my father rested.'

36. Libanius: *Address to the Emperor Julian as Consul* (*Or.* 12; 1 January 363)
Adapted from the translation by A. F. Norman

[33] Fastening upon philosophy, after a glimpse of her meadow, it was not possible for him to hold false notions about the divine. Immediately he cleansed the stain and … acknowledged the real gods instead of the false one. [34] That day I call the beginning of freedom for the world, and I bless the place where this change occurred and the healer of his mind, who personally undertook this noble hazard, carried conviction with him and, in company with his pupil, sailed through the Cyanean rocks.

37. Libanius: *The Embassy to Julian* (*Or.* 15; March 363)
Adapted from the translation by A. F. Norman

[27] … [W]hen you were nearing manhood, you had no huntsman to take you in hand and instruct you how to hit beasts … Your instructor was a Spartan man [Nicocles], a priest of righteousness, a leader in learning, who knew, if anyone did, the secrets of the mind of Homer and of all of Homer's school.

38. Libanius: *Letter to Aristophanes*
(Loeb no. 109; spring/summer 363)
Adapted from the translation by A. F. Norman

[1] I think that Rumour has done what she did long ago and taught the Greeks of the misfortune of the barbarians … [2] For as the emperor invaded as soon as it was spring which they did not anticipate, the Assyrians were taken at once – many villages and a few cities; for there are not many. Then the Persians being woken up were frightened out of their wits and fled, while the emperor pursued and captured everything without a fight, or rather he captured the greater part without a fight, but he killed 6,000 of them who had come out on reconnaissance and also for any action that might occur. [3] These things are reported by those who come on winged camels … and we expect the emperor to come leading the present leader [Shapur], after the latter has handed over the kingdom to the fugitive [Hormisdas].

39. Libanius: *Funeral Oration for Julian* (*Or.* 18; 365)
Adapted from the translation by A. F. Norman

[10] When Constantine fell ill and died, the sword fell on almost all the family, fathers and sons alike. This man and his elder brother escaped the prevalent slaughter, one [Gallus] preserved by an illness, the other [Julian] by his youthfulness … [11] … Julian's tutelary deity impelled him to the love of learning, and he busied himself with this in the greatest city after Rome, going to school … An excellent eunuch was the guardian of his temperance and another tutor who was not without his share of learning … [12] … A wicked sophist [Hecebolius] had the young man as a reward for speaking ill of the gods, and he was being brought up with such notions concerning the gods and was suffering the incompetence in rhetoric because of the war waged against the altars by his teacher. [13] He was already approaching manhood, and his imperial nature was revealed by many great proofs. These did not allow Constantius to be at ease, and so … he sent him to the city of Nicomedia … He did not attend my lectures … but by buying copies of my speeches he was not deprived of association with me. [14] The reason for the fact that he delighted in my speeches but fled their father was that marvellous teacher of his. He had bound him with many terrible oaths never to be or to be called my pupil and never to be registered on the list of my students [15] … He arranged for someone to convey to him my lectures each day, by means of great gifts …

Whence, I think, in the speeches later composed by him there is some kinship with mine and he was considered to be one of those who associated with me.

[19] Despite the alteration in his beliefs, he pretended that he held the same views as before, since to reveal them was not possible ... [20] His fame being carried in all directions, devotees of the Muses and of the other gods too, journeyed by land and sea, eager to see him and to make his acquaintance, to speak with him themselves and to hear what he said ... [21] ... On the lips of every right-thinking man was the prayer that the young man should become lord of earthly affairs and that the destruction of the civilised world be checked, and that there be put in charge one who knew how to heal such ills. [22] I would not say that that man objected to these prayers ... but that he wished this too, and that he wished it from a longing not for luxury, or power or the imperial purple, but for the restoration by his own efforts of the other things and not least the worship of the gods to the nations from which they had been expelled. [23] ... thus he desired not power but to treat the cities well.

[113] The letters sent by the cowardly and treacherous man [Constantius] to the barbarians were of the greatest help to him [Julian], for as he sailed or marched along [the Danube], he read these to the cities and to the garrisons, comparing his own toils with such fine letters as these. These excited the hearers to hostility against the man, and they allied with the other even though his army was but a fraction of Constantius'.

[120] Nothing was stronger than his nature. His first question was about the dead man and where his body was and if it was honoured in the customary way ... And he did not limit his mourning for the deceased there, but he went down to the harbour of the great city, assembled all the people, and began mourning while the body was still being transported by sea. He cast away all symbols of imperial status except his cloak, and with his hands grasped the coffin, not deigning to blame the dead for the plots he had contrived in his lifetime.

[126] So first of all ... he restored piety as if a fugitive. Some temples he built new, others he repaired, while he introduced statues into others. Those who had built houses for themselves with the stones of the temples began to contribute money. One might have seen pillars transported by boat or by waggon for the despoiled gods, and everywhere there were altars and fire and blood and fat and smoke ... [127] ... a temple to the god who rules the day was built in the middle of the palace ...

[130] ... turning his attention to the imperial service he beheld a useless crowd of people maintained to no purpose. There were a thousand cooks, as many barbers, and even more cup-bearers, swarms of waiters, eunuchs more in number than flies around the flocks in spring, and a multitude of drones of every sort and kind ... [131] He also got rid of the many secretaries ... [135] A third group of wicked staff he ejected from the palace doors, thieves and robbers who would say and do anything for greed of gain. These were the people who had deprived their own native land of their services, who had run away from the town councils and the customary public services, and had been enrolled among the messengers and had purchased the position of investigator. On the face of it they were guards, so that the emperor would not remain in ignorance of what was being contrived against him, but in fact they were rogues ... [141] So people were drained dry one after another and, as the cities were reduced to poverty, these racketeers became rich. Our emperor had long been disgusted by this and he swore that if he was able to he would stop it ... he disbanded that whole tribe, took away their rank and title ... and used his own men for the despatching of letters ... [143] So the mules used in the public post died of continuous toil and were starved to death by the afore-mentioned people, and these by starving them procured Sybaris ... [144] ... And I forbear to mention the similar abuse of horses and, which was much more terrible, of asses ... [145] At any rate Julian halted this excessive behaviour. He halted the journeys that were not truly necessary and declared both the grant and receipt of such favours to be equally punishable, instructing his officials either to buy or to hire their animals. And there was seen an unbelievable thing, muleteers exercising their mules, and grooms their horses.

[146] He displayed the same concern also about the councils in the cities. Formerly they had flourished both in the numbers and wealth of their members, but thereafter they did not, for their members, except for a very few, had melted away to serve either in the army or in the great council [senate] ... [147] Yet who does not know that a strong council is the soul of a city ... [148] But at last the councils also were to regain their strength. For that praiseworthy letter, that every man must be called to a council and be enrolled unless he had valid reason for exemption, so rectified the situation that the council chambers proved to be too small to contain the multitude of entrants. [149] For there was no secretary or eunuch to exempt them for a price ...

[154] He entered the senate house also and seated around him the great council which had long been deprived of this honour. For

previously it had been summoned to the palace to stand and listen to trivial things, and the emperor did not come to sit with it, for since he was not a good speaker he fled a place that required a rhetor. Julian however … sought out such meetings, allowing whosoever wished to speak freely to him and participating himself … [155] And once when he was speaking … it was announced that his teacher [Maximus], an Ionian, the philosopher whom he had summoned from Ionia, was coming, he leapt up from the midst of the elders and dashed to the doors, affected just as Chaerephon was by Socrates, but while he was just a Chaerephon in the wrestling school of Taureas, Julian was ruler of all and in the great senate demonstrating to all and heralding by his deeds that wisdom was more honoured than imperial status and that whatever was noble in him this was a gift of philosophy. [156] So he embraced him and greeted him in the customary way that private citizens do or emperors one another. Then he led him in although he was not a member of the council, for he thought not that the man was honoured by the place, but the place by the man. And he asserted how much he had been affected by that man and departed holding his hand.

[164] … A letter from Persia reached him [at Antioch], asking him to receive an embassy and to resolve differences through discussion. So all the rest of us leapt up, applauded, shouted to accept the offer, but he ordered the letter to be rejected as a disgrace, and he said it was appalling to converse with them while the cities lay in ruins. He sent back the response that there was no need of ambassadors as the Persian would see him soon enough.

[190] And this expression ['My friend'] applied to everyone, not to rhetors alone, was now for the first time used by the ruler towards his subjects, and it was more productive of good will than any magic charm. For he did not believe that it increased his majesty for them to be frightened and silent, to fold their hands, to prostrate themselves to the ground and to look at his shoe-toe rather than his face, and in all their words and deeds to be seen as slaves rather than free men. But he believed that all those who associated with him should be able to revere him for himself instead of all that. [191] And when he wore the purple cloak that had to be worn by an emperor, he wore it as if it were nothing out of the ordinary.

[195] … [S]uddenly there was in the hippodrome [in Antioch] the cry of a famished populace, that the land had suffered from a bad season, and the city from the well off, who did not offer their long-hoarded stocks to the public but increased the price of corn. He summoned together the farmers and the manufacturers and retailers … and

compelled them by law to be moderate and he himself was the first to bring his own wheat to market in obedience to the law ... he perceived the council actively opposing the law and using his contributions while hiding away its own ...

[199] But although he was loathe to shed blood, ten soldiers [at Antioch] hatched another plot to kill him and they waited for the day of the practice of manoeuvres. But fortunately drink forestalled the critical moment and everything was undone, and what was concealed for so long became visible.

[213] This [Julian's strategy against Persia] was as follows: knowing the great importance of secrecy ... he revealed neither the time of the invasion, nor its route, nor the tactics to be used. In fact, he disclosed nothing of what he planned, for he knew that as soon as everything is divulged it is in the ears of spies.

[214] ... [at Carrhae] he detached from his force twenty thousand soldiers and sent them to the Tigris to watch the area, should any danger arise there, and to join forces with him if he summoned them in due course. [215] It was also arranged that Armenia do something similar ...

[255] And if they [the Roman troops who had crossed over the Tigris at night] had not delayed around the dead in desire for spoil but had immediately stormed the gates and pulled them up or torn them down, they would have occupied celebrated Ctesiphon.

[257] ... but he [Shapur] ... after the events I have narrated sent someone entreating that the war be stopped at once and that the victor desist from further hostilities and that their empire be had as a friend and ally. [258] And the individual sent on this mission ... came to the brother [Hormisdas] of the one who had sent him, for that man was with us ... But Julian ordered Hormisdas to be silent and to send the envoy away in silence ... He decided not to abandon the war ... [259] ... but he ... advanced against the walls and summoned the besieged to battle ...

[262] The boats had been consigned to fire, for it was better than to the enemy ... For breaking upon their bows swift and strong the Tigris made the ships need many men to handle them and more than half the army would have been needed to haul them ... [263] In addition the fire had done away with any inclination towards laxity. For all the slackers would lie sleeping on board pretending to be sick ... if those adversely affected must denounce the fire, it would be the Persian who naturally had reason for complaint.

[268] ... the emperor so as to mend the break made haste with

only one attendant, when a cavalryman's spear struck him when he was without armour, for he was I think confident that he would prevail and did not protect himself, and the spear went through his arm and entered his side … [272] You would know his virtue even from his last words. For when all those standing round him gave themselves up to lamentation and not even the philosophers were able to hold out he reproved both the former and especially the latter … His tent was like the prison which imprisoned Socrates, the company like the company there, the wound the poison, his words those words … [274] So who killed him you are anxious to hear. I do not know his name, but that his murderer was not of the enemy is plainly indicated by the fact that none of the enemy was rewarded for the blow … [275] … those fellows, who found his living disadvantageous to themselves, and whose way of life was contrary to the laws, plotted against him for a long time and then getting the chance they acted …

40. Libanius: *Upon Avenging Julian* (*Or.* 24; c. 379)
Adapted from the translation by A. F. Norman

[6] That man Julian received the wound in his side … The assailant who wounded him was a Taiene, discharging their leader's injunction. This action, indeed, would probably bring the leader a reward from those people who were keen to kill that man [i.e. Christians].

41. Libanius: *Autobiography* (379 onwards)
Adapted from the translation by A. F. Norman

[129] … I was the last to enter the fray, for the emperor himself had so contrived it that there would be the largest audience, and people asserted that Hermes … stirred each member of the audience with his wand, so that no single expression of mine should depart without its share of wonder. The emperor contributed to this, first by the pleasure which he declared at my style, then by being on the point of leaping up, until finally when he could no longer restrain himself … he sprang up from his throne and, with outstretched arms, opened wide his cloak. Some of our boors would say that being carried away he forgot dignity, but anyone who knows well what makes kingship solemn would maintain that he remained within the bounds of what is seemly. For what is more imperial than that the soul of the emperor should be raised up to the beauty of eloquence?

42. Salutius: *Concerning the Gods and the Universe* (c. 363)
Translated A. D. Nock

[16] I think it worth while to add a few words about sacrifices. In the first place, since everything we have comes from the gods, and it is just to offer to the givers first fruits of what is given, we offer first fruits of our possessions in the form of votive offerings, of our bodies in the form of hair, of our life in the form of sacrifices. Secondly, prayers divorced from sacrifices are only words, prayers with sacrifices are animated words, the word giving power to the life and the life animation to the word. Furthermore, the happiness of anything lies in its appropriate perfection, and the appropriate perfection of each object is union with its cause. For this reason also we pray that we may have union with the gods. So, since though the highest life is that of the gods, yet man's life also is life of some sort, and this life wishes to have union with that, it needs an intermediary (for objects most widely separated are never united without a middle term), and the intermediary ought to be like the objects being united. Accordingly, the intermediary between life and life should be life, and for this reason living animals are sacrificed by the blessed among men to-day and were sacrificed by all the men of old, not in a uniform manner, but to every god the fitting victims, with much other reverence. Concerning this subject I have said enough.

43. Gregory of Nazianzus: *Against Julian* 1
(*Or.* 4; shortly after Julian's death)
Translated C. W. King (with some slight alterations)

[4] … For not merely are thanksgivings in words most suitable unto that 'Word', Who, of all the names whereby He is called, especially delights in *this* appellation, and in such a sense of the title, but also a fitting judgement is it for that man to be punished by means of words for his transgressions against *words*, which, though the common property of all rational beings, he begrudged to the Christians, as though they were his own exclusively; devising as he did a most irrational thing with respect to words; although, in his own opinion, the most rational of men. [5] In the first place, because he wickedly transferred the appellation to a *pretence*, as though the Greek speech belonged to religious worship exclusively, and not to the tongue; and for this reason he debarred us from the use of words as though we were stealing other people's goods … and in the next place, because he fancied he should escape our notice, not in his attempt to rob us of a

benefit of the first class ... but in his apprehensions of our refutation of his impiety, just as though our force lay in the elegance of diction, and not in the knowledge of truth and in arguments, from which it is more impossible to preclude us than to hinder us from acknowledging God as long as we have a tongue.

[21] First and foremost then, this man having been saved by the great Constantius, immediately on his succession to his father, when the army rose against those in power (making a revolution through their apprehension of revolution), and settled the government under new sovereigns; being saved together with his brother (a salvation beyond belief and all expectation), he neither felt gratitude to God for his escape nor to the emperor through whose means he had been preserved, but showed himself wicked towards both, by conceiving apostacy from the one and rebellion against the other. [22] But to come to what is necessary for me to state in the beginning – they were honoured with an imperial maintenance and upbringing in one of the imperial estates, being treasured up for imperial power by this most humane emperor, as the sole relics of his family: who thus, at the same time, made his excuse for the revolution that had taken place upon his accession on the plea that it had been audaciously done and not with his consent; and equally seeking to display his own magnanimity by the sharing of the empire with them; and thirdly, to establish his power on more solid foundations by means of these props – a thing that showed he planned more kindly than wisely. [23] Whilst they were here enjoying complete leisure ... they had masters in all branches of learning, their uncle [sic] and sovereign causing them to be instructed in the complete and regular course of education; they studied also, and still more extensively, our own kind of philosophy, that which deals not with words alone, but which conveys piety by means of moral training: living in intercourse with the most zealous of men, and in the exercise of the most pleasant of occupations, and which offers a great field for the display of virtue: for both brothers offered and enrolled themselves amongst the clergy; reading aloud the sacred books to the people ... [24] By most sumptuous monuments to Martyrs, by emulation in their offerings, by all the other marks by which the fear of God is characterised, did they make known their love of wisdom and their love of Christ: the one of them being sincerely pious; for although too hasty in temper, nevertheless he was genuine in piety: the other awaiting his opportunity, and concealing under a mask of goodness his evil disposition. A proof of this ... was the miracle which then occurred [story of the building of shrines to the Martyrs: 25–6].

[30] But when, as the two advanced to man's estate, they began to handle the doctrines of philosophy (which I wish they had never done), and were deriving that power from words which to the good is the weapon of virtue, but to the more villainous the incentive to vice, this man was no longer able to restrain his disease in every part, nor to plan within himself alone the plot of his impiety in all its completeness ... he conceal[ed] the most part of his impiety, by reason of the times and the superintendence of the ruler (for as yet it was not safe to be impious); still, in some points he exposed the secrets of his thoughts; and to the more sharp-sighted, his impiety rather than his intelligence, by exerting himself in advocacy of the Hellenes, in his disputations against his brother, to a greater degree than was becoming ... [31] But when the kindness of the emperor appoints his brother ruler, and puts into his hands no small part of the civilised world, this youth obtained opportunity to hold intercourse, in all freedom and security, with teachers and opinions of the freest kind. Asia was his school of impiety; whatever works wonders as regards astronomy, nativities, the show of knowledge of the Future, and all the sorcery that goes along with them.

[55] He had descended into one of those sanctuaries, inaccessible to the multitude, and feared by all ... in company with the man that was as bad as many sanctuaries put together, the wise in such things, or sophist more rightly to be called; for this is a kind of divination amongst them to confer with darkness, as it were, and the subterranean demons concerning future events ... But when, as my fine fellow proceeded to the rites, the frightful things assailed him, unearthly noises, as they say, and unpleasant odours, and fiery apparitions ... being terror-struck at the novelty ... he flies for help to the Cross, his old remedy, and makes the sign thereof against his terrors ... [56] ... The celebrant is at hand, explaining away the truth ... and by dint of talking he persuades, and by persuading he leads his disciple into the pit of perdition ... [57] But when the birth-pains were growing strong ... he became aware of something ... that to carry on the war openly, and to preside in person over the impious attempt, besides being both rash and crude, was in all respects most damaging to his object; for that we should become the more obstinate when oppressed, and would oppose to tyranny our zeal in the cause of religion ... but if he carried on the war with artifice, and coloured violence with persuasion, and like covering round a hook with the bait, so covered his tyranny with wheedling, his enterprise would become at once ingenious and likely to be successful. [58] For ... he begrudged the honour of martyrdom to our combatants, and for this reason he contrives now to use compulsion, and yet not seem to do so

... [61] ... he attacks our religion in a very rascally and ungenerous way, and introduces into his persecution the traps and snares concealed in *arguments* ... (and what was yet more inhuman, he made over the exercise of his tyranny to mobs and to cities, of whom the frenzy is less open to blame on account of their want of reason, and inconsiderate impetuosity in everything; and this he did, not by means of a public order, but by not repressing their outbreaks, making their will and pleasure an unwritten law).

[71] ... thou most philosophical and high-minded of men, admiring the Epaminondases and Scipios of old in the article of the endurance of hardship; thou that marchest on foot along with thy troops, and eatest whatever food is at hand, and praisest that kind of generalship which does everything for itself.

[74] ... Before settling any other of the affairs of state he rushes upon the Christians, and these two objects engrossed his whole attention, namely the 'Galilaeans' (as he insultingly used to call us), and the Persians ... but now that the Word of Salvation was spread abroad, and prevailed the most in our parts of the world, the attempt to change or upset the *status* of the Christians was no other than to toss about the Roman empire ...

[75] The public post administered with moderation, the lowering of the taxes, the judicious choice of magistrates, the punishment of peculators, and all the other marks of a transient and momentary prosperity and illusion were, forsooth, likely to produce great benefit to the public, and our ears must by dinned with their praises; but populations and cities torn by faction, families torn asunder, households set at variance, marriages dissolved, and all else that it was natural should follow that mischievous step ... were these things conducive either to that man's glory, or to the benefit of the public?

[81] Like those who mix poison with food, he mixes his impiety (idolatry) with the customary honours of the sovereign ... he associates his own portraits with the figures of his demons, pretending that they were some other sort of customary representations. He exposes these figures to peoples and to cities, and above all to those in government of nations, so that he could not miss being in one way or another mischievous: for either by the honour paid to the sovereign that to idols was also insinuated, or else by the shunning of the latter the sovereign himself was insulted, the worship of the two being mixed up together.

[83] There was placed before him gold, there was placed before him incense; the fire at hand; the masters of the ceremonies close by. And the pretext how plausible! that this was the regular formality of the imperial

Soldiers were forced to be pagans

donative [to soldiers] ... What next? Each was obliged to throw incense upon the fire, and so to receive gold from the emperor, pay for perdition, small price for so dear a thing – for entire souls of men, and for sin against God ... A whole army to be purchased for one trick ... [84] ... they [some Christian soldiers] ... exhorted the rest to understand the fraud, to recover from their intoxication, to make excuse to Christ with their blood [i.e. become martyrs]. The Emperor was exasperated at this, but avoided putting them to death openly, that he might not make martyrs out of them ... he sentenced them to banishment ...

[86] To pass over his edicts against the sacred edifices ... his confiscation of offerings and revenues ... his robbery of consecrated vessels ... and the archers running through towns and villages, yet more cruel and more fierce than he who had commanded this ... to say nothing of all this, who does not know of the cruelty of the Alexandrians ... Who is ignorant of the tumult of the Heliopolitans? Who, of the mad behaviour of the people of Gaza – those that were admired and honoured by that man because they had properly appreciated his magnificence? Who has not heard of the insanity of the Arethusians ... [87] They [the Heliopolitans] are said – for I must relate one fact out of many, a thing to cause a shudder even in those without God! – to have seized consecrated virgins ... and brought them out into their midst, stripping them of their clothes in order to abase them first by the exposure, then ripping them up and cutting them open ... [88] But as to the affair of Marcus ... and of the Arethusians, who is there so much out of our world as to be ignorant of it ... [89] The aged priest was led in triumph through the city, a voluntary champion of the faith ... [91] Are these things then evidences of good nature and clemency, or the reverse, marks of audacity and cruelty? Let these tell us who admire the philosopher king. For my part I fancy no one in the world will be at a loss for the proper and true answer, and I have not yet added that amongst those who saved the villain when his whole family was in danger, and carried him off by stealth, this Marcus was one ...

[93] But who is ignorant of the story how that when a certain mob was running mad against the Christians, and had already committed great slaughter, and was threatening a great deal more, the governor of that province [Palestine], steering a middle course between the temper of the times and the law ... he executed many of the Christians, but punished a very few of the Hellenes. Thereupon, being summoned before the emperor ... he was cashiered, arrested, and tried on this charge. He put forward in his defence the laws in accordance with which

he had been entrusted with the administration of justice – he narrowly escaped being sentenced to death ... And how admirable and humane was the judgement, when that *upright judge*, that *non-persecutor* of the Christians, said: 'What great matter is it if a single Grecian hand has despatched ten Galiliaeans!'

[96] ... [Julian was planning] to deprive the Christians of all freedom of speech, to exclude them from all meetings, markets, and public assemblies, nay, even from the law-courts; for that no one should be allowed to participate in all these who did not first burn incense upon altars set there for the purpose ...

[111] He ... was intending to establish schools in every town, with pulpits and higher and lower rows of benches, for lectures and expositions of the Hellenic doctrines, both of such as give rules of morality and those that treat of abstruse subjects, also a form of prayer alternately pronounced, and penance for those that sinned proportionate to the offence, initiation also, and completion, and other things that evidently belong to our constitution. He was purposing also to build inns and hospices for pilgrims, monasteries for men, convents for virgins, places for meditation, and to establish a system of charity for the relief of the needy, and also that which is conducted by means of letters of recommendation by which we forward such as require it from one nation to another – things which he had especially admired in our institutions.

44. Gregory of Nazianzus: *Against Julian* 2
(*Or.* 5; shortly after Julian's death)
Translated C. W. King (with some slight alterations)

[3] ... [H]e stirred up against us the nation of the Jews, making his accomplice in his machinations their well-known credulity, as well as that hatred for us which has smouldered in them from the very beginning; prophesying to them out of their own books and mysteries that *now* was the appointed time come for them to return into their own land, and to rebuild the Temple, and restore the reign of their hereditary institutions – thus hiding his true purpose under the mark of benevolence.

[9] ... All the land of the Assyrians that the Euphrates flows through, and skirting Persia there unites itself with the Tigris, all this he took and ravaged, and captured some of the fortresses, in the total absence of anyone to hinder him, whether that he had taken the Persians unaware by the rapidity of his advance, or whether he was out-generalled by

them and drawn on by degrees further and further into the interior (for
both stories are told); at any rate, advancing in this way, with his army
marching along the river's bank and his flotilla upon the river supplying
provisions and carrying the baggage, after a considerable interval he
touches Ctesiphon, a place which, even to be near, was thought by him
half the victory, by reason of his longing for it. [10] From this point,
however, like sand slipping from beneath the feet, or a great wave
bursting upon a ship, things began to go back with him; for Ctesiphon
is a strong fortress, hard to take, and very well secured by a wall of burnt
brick, a deep ditch, and the swamps coming from the river … he leaves
the place in his rear … [11] … [A] man, one of no little consideration
amongst the Persians … on the pretence that he had some quarrel, or
rather a very great one and for a very great cause, with his king, and, on
that account very hostile to the Persian cause, and well disposed towards
the Romans, thus addresses the emperor: … But if you will listen to
me, you will burn this flotilla: what a relief to this fine army will be the
result! and yourself will take another route, better supplied and safer
than this; along which I will be your guide … and will cause you to enter
into the heart of the enemy's country, where you can obtain whatever
you please … [12] And … everything that was dreadful happened at
once; the boats were the prey of the flames, there was no bread, the
ridicule of the enemy came to fill up the measure, the fatal blow was
inflicted by his own hand, even hope had well nigh vanished, the guide
had disappeared along with his promises, round about him the enemy,
swelling up round him the war, the advance not easy, provisions not
procurable, the army in despair and discontented with their commander … [13] Up to this point, such is the universal account; but
thenceforward, one and the same story is not told by all, but different
accounts are reported and made up by different people, both of those
present at the battle, and those not present … At any rate, he receives a
wound truly seasonable (or mortal) and salutary for the whole world …
but what surprises me, is how the vain man that fancied he learnt the
future from that means [sacrifice and reading of entrails], knew nothing
of the wound about to be inflicted on his own entrails … [14] One
action of this person deserves not to be passed over in silence … He was
lying upon the bank of the river, and in a very bad way from his wound,
when, remembering that many of those before his time who had aimed
at glory, in order that they might be thought something higher than
mortals, had … disappeared from amongst men, and thereby got themselves accounted gods; so he … endeavours to *throw his body* into the
river … And had not one of the imperial eunuchs perceived what was

[margin, handwritten:] tricked by Zosimo

going on ... another new god ... would have manifested himself to the stupid!

[17] ... And when the corpse [of Constantius II] drew near to the great imperial city, what needs it to mention the *cortège* of the whole army and the escort under arms that attended as upon the living emperor, or the crowd that poured forth from the splendid city ... Nay, even that audacious and bold person [Julian], decorated with the still new purple ... himself forms a part of the funereal honour paid his predecessor, paying and receiving the same honour, partly out of constraint, partly (they say) of his own free will, for the whole army, even though they submitted to the existing authority, nevertheless paid more respect to the deceased ... so they persuade, nay, *compel*, the rebel to go to meet the corpse in befitting form, that is, stripping his brow of the diadem, and with head bent before his sovereign ... thus to escort the corpse ... to the tomb and to the famous Church of the Apostles ...

[21] That part, too, is certainly to be commended in the training of our philosopher, that he was so very *free from anger*, and superior to all the passions, after the model of the emperors of any period who were impassive and motionless and would not turn their faces round, whatever should happen, or betray any trace of feeling! so that when sitting in judgement he used to fill the whole palace with his cries and exclamations, as though it were *he* that was being ill-treated and punished ... [22] But the puffings and blowings of the fire ... when he was kindling the sacrificial flame, in what part of our discourse shall we place *them*? How fine a thing to behold the cheeks of the emperor of the Romans thus distorted, and occasioning laughter, not merely to the outside world, but to the very people whom he thought to please by acting thus ... [23] This character of his was made known by experience to others, and by his coming to the throne which gave him free scope to display it. But I had witnessed it in some way long before, ever since I lived with this person at Athens ... At that time ... I remember that I became no bad judge of his character ... what made me a true guesser was the inconsistency of his behaviour and his extreme excitability ... A sign of no good seemed to me to be his neck unsteady, his shoulders quaking and shaking, his eye rolling and glancing from side to side with a certain insane expression, his feet unsteady and stumbling, his nostrils breathing insolence and disdain, the gestures of his face ridiculous and expressing the same feelings, his bursts of laughter unrestrained and gusty, his nods of assent and dissent without any reason, his speech stopping short and interrupted by his taking breath, his questions without any order and unintelligent, his answers not a whit better

than his questions, following one on top of the other, and not definite, nor returned in the regular order of instruction.

45. Ephrem the Syrian: *Hymns against Julian* (shortly after Julian's death)
Translated J. M. Lieu

[1.16] The (Jewish) People raged and raved and sounded the trumpets;
they rejoiced because he [Julian] was a diviner, they were overjoyed
because he was a Chaldaean
The circumcised saw the image which unexpectedly had become a bull;
on his coins they saw the bull, a thing of shame,
and they began celebrating it with cymbals and trumpets
because they saw in that bull their calf of former times.

[17] The bull of paganism which was engraved in his heart,
he imprinted on that (coin) face that image for the People who loved it.

...

[18] ...
The king, the king of Greece [Julian], suddenly became a bull
and butted the churches and had to be led away.

...

[20] ...
The king, the king of Greece, was rebuked
because he provoked God to anger and rejected Daniel
and there, near Babel, he was judged and found guilty.

[2.5] ...
He was for them [the pagans] he-goat and priest
and for (the thing of) shame he grew his beard long like a Nazirite
and he bowed down so that the incense of the smoke of sacrifice might ascend through it.

[3.1] A fortuitous wonder! There met me near the city [Nisibis] the corpse of that accursed one [Julian] which passed by the wall;

the banner which was sent from the East wind
the Magian took and fastened on the tower
so that a flag might point out for spectators
that the city was the slave of the lords [Persians] of that
  banner.
RESPONSE: Praise to him who clothed his corpse in shame.
[2]   I was amazed as to how it was that there met and were present
the body and the standard, both at the same time.
And I knew that it was a wonderful preparation of justice
that while the corpse of the fallen one was passing,
there went up and was placed that fearsome banner so that it
  might proclaim that
the injustice of his diviners had delivered that city.
      ...
[4]   ...
I went and came, my brethren, to the bier of the defiled one
and I stood over it and I derided his paganism,
I said: Is this he who exalted himself
against the living name and who forgot that he is dust?
(God) has returned him to within his dust that he might know
  that he is dust.
      ...
[7]   That the Cross when it had set out had not conquered
          everything
was not because it was not able to conquer, for it is victorious,
but, so that a pit might be dug for the wicked man,
who set out with his diviners to the East,
when he set out and was wounded, it was seen by the
          discerning
that the war had waited for him so that through it he might be
  put to shame.
      ...
[14]   Because he dishonoured him who had removed the spear of
          Paradise,
the spear of justice passed through his belly.
They tore open that which was pregnant with the oracle of the
  diviners,
and (God) scourged (him) and he groaned and remembered
what he wrote and published that he would do to the
  churches.
The finger of justice had blotted out his memory.

[15] The king saw that the sons of the East had come and deceived him,
the unlearned (had deceived) the wise man, the simple the soothsayer.
They whom he had called, wrapped up in his robe,
had, through unlearned men, mastered his wisdom.
He commanded and burned his victorious ships,
and his idols and diviners were bound through the one deceit.

[16] When he saw that his gods were refuted and exposed,
and that he was unable to conquer and unable to escape,
he was prostrated and torn between fear and shame.
Death he chose so that he might escape in Sheol [hell]
and cunningly he took off his armour in order to be wounded
so that he might die without the Galilaeans seeing his shame.

[17] When he mocked and nicknamed the brethren 'Galilaeans'
behold in the air the wheels [of the chariot] of the Galilaean King!

[4.3] He [Julian] indeed saw his kindred in that relative [Julian's maternal uncle]
who while alive swarmed and was destroyed by worms.
…

[4] He was his blood and his flesh; in him was prefigured his whole self,
and with the one visible name both of them were imprinted
just as they were possessed by the one secret demon.
…

[9] …
He worshipped the sun and it turned round and insulted him,
because he had set out to kill its worshippers and attendants [the Persians].
This is the party of Satan which is totally deceitful and divided.

[10] For if he set out by the power of the sun to conquer those
who for a long time had been making offerings to the sun,
then he was convicting himself.
…

[16] He [Constantius II] was a cedar who at his time quietly bowed
and fell upon his bed and, at rest, he died in peace.
And there grew and came up from their sweet root
a young plant of paganism which seemed
to be long (and) wearying mountains with its shade.

[handwritten margin note: was tricked despite wisdom]

In a night it sprung forth and in a night it shrivelled.

...

[18]   At that time terrible events were stirred up to reprove (men);
    (God) proclaimed the truth to souls in the world,   ⚹
    in that cities were overthrown, to the reproach of paganism.
    Jerusalem condemned particularly
    the accursed and the crucifiers who presumptuously
        threatened and even entered
    in order to rebuild the desolation which they had caused by
        their sins.

...

Jerusalem trembled when she saw   Jews
that her destroyers again entered her and disturbed her
    tranquillity.
She complained of them to the Most High and she was heard.
[20]   He ordered the winds and they blew, he beckoned earthquakes
        and they came,
    lightning and it caused turmoil, the air and it became dark,
    walls and they were overthrown, gates and they opened
        themselves;
    fire came forth and consumed the scribes
    who had read in Daniel that it would be desolate for ever;
    and because they had read but did not learn, they were
        violently
    smitten and then they learned!

46. Eutropius: *Breviarium* (c. 369)
Translated H. W. Bird

[10.14] Subsequently he sent Julian, his cousin and the brother of
Gallus, to the Gallic provinces as Caesar, after giving him his sister in
marriage, since the barbarians had stormed many towns, had besieged
others, there was dreadful devastation everywhere and the Roman
empire was already tottering to certain disaster. Julian, with only a
modest force, overwhelmed vast numbers of Alamanni at Strasbourg,
a city in Gaul, captured their most distinguished king and restored
the Gallic provinces. Afterwards this same Julian performed many outstanding exploits against the barbarians, the Germans were driven back
beyond the Rhine, and the Roman empire was restored to its original
boundaries. [15] Not long after, when the German armies were with-
drawing from the defence of the Gallic provinces, Julian was made

Augustus with the consent of the soldiers and, after a year had elapsed, set out to seize possession of Illyricum while Constantius was occupied with campaigns against the Parthians. The latter, after learning of this, turned back to take up the civil war but died on the way between Cilicia and Cappadocia in the thirty-eighth year of his reign, the forty-fifth of his life, and was deservedly enrolled among the gods … [16] Accordingly Julian took possession of the state and after vast preparations waged war against the Parthians. I was also a member of this expedition. He accepted the surrender of or forcibly seized several of their towns and fortresses, devastated Assyria, and for a time established a permanent camp at Ctesiphon. As he was returning victorious and mingling too rashly in the battles he was killed by the hand of an enemy on the twenty-sixth of June in the seventh year of his reign and the thirty-second of his life and was enrolled among the gods. He was an outstanding man and would have governed the state remarkably well if the fates had allowed. He was highly accomplished in the liberal disciplines, but more learned in Greek literature to such an extent that his erudition in Latin was by no means comparable to his knowledge in Greek. He possessed a remarkable and quick eloquence, a most tenacious memory and in certain respects was more like a philosopher. Towards his friends he was generous, but less discriminating than befitted such a great emperor, for there were some who damaged his reputation. To the provincials he was extremely just and he reduced their taxes as much as he could. He was gracious to all, was only moderately concerned with the public treasury, was eager for glory and in this regard was generally disposed to be excessive. He persecuted the Christian religion too much, but nevertheless in such a manner that he abstained from bloodshed, and he was not unlike Marcus Aurelius, whom he even took pains to emulate.

47. Festus: *Breviarium* (c. 370)
Translated T. M. Banchich and J. A. Meka,
Canisius College Translated Texts series

[XXVIII] To *Princeps* Julian, of proven good fortune against external enemies, due measure against Persia was lacking. For he, with immense provision, in as much as he was sovereign of the entire world, set hostile standards against the Parthians, and sailed through the Euphrates a fleet furnished with supplies. Relentless in his advance, he either took control of the Persians' cities and bases which had surrendered or took them by force. [2] When he had made camp opposite Ctesiphon on the banks of the confluence of the Tigris and Euphrates and was holding daily competitions in order to reduce the enemy's attentiveness, in the middle of the night he rapidly transferred to the opposite bank soldiers who had been loaded on ships. These, distinguishing themselves through hardships which would have been difficult to surmount even in daylight and with no opposition, threw the Persians into confusion by means of unexpected fright and, when the units of the entire race had been turned about, the victorious soldiery would have entered the open gates of Ctesiphon, if the opportunity for plunder had not been greater than the concern for victory. [3] Having obtained such great glory, when he was warned by his staff concerning his return, he gave his own plan more credence and, after the ships had been burnt, when, having been led on a route toward Madenea by a deserter who had delivered himself for the purpose of deceiving him, he pursued shortcuts, again traversing a route along the right bank of the Tigris, with his soldiers' flank exposed, when he wandered too incautiously through the formations and when his own men's sight had been snatched away as a result [of] dust that had been stirred up, he was wounded, pierced through the abdomen near the groin with a lance by a cavalryman of the enemy who had encountered him. Amidst an effusion of much blood, after he, though injured, had restored the ranks of his men, having said many things to his friends, he breathed out his lingering soul.

48. John Chrysostom: *Homily on St Babylas* (late 370s)
Translated M. M. Morgan

[XV/80] Now Julian was a constant visitor to Daphne, his hands full of offerings and accompanied by a multitude of sacrificial victims: and after having them slaughtered in a horrific welter of blood he would importune the god [Apollo], demanding in return a reply from the oracle and an answer to the problems that were on his mind. But that noble one ... was nevertheless restrained from stating clearly and explicitly that it was the holy Babylas and the force which resided in the neighbourhood that had curbed his speech, and prevented him from uttering his oracles, for he was afraid of becoming a laughing stock amongst his devotees.

[XVI ... 90] The sarcophagus of the martyred Babylas was carried away on its long journey and the saint returned, like a victorious athlete wearing a second crown, to his own city, whence he bore away the first one ... [XVII ... 93 ...] For what happened next? Behold the miracle which reveals not only the power of God but his inexpressible love of men. The holy martyr was reposing once more within the sacred precincts where he had been lain previously, before he was removed to Daphne. But the unhappy god soon realised that his wily artifices had been in vain and that the struggle was not with a dead body but with a living and moving spirit, triumphant not only over Apollo himself but over all the gods. For Babylas prayed that God would send down fire upon the temple of Daphne: whereupon fire indeed destroyed the whole of the roof and consumed the idol right down to its feet, leaving nothing but a heap of dust and ashes: and of the whole temple only the walls were left standing.

[96] ... the holy martyr had so shaken Julian to the core with terror that he did not dare to pursue his impious ways any further. He would not, on account of the (loss of the) roof, have so ill-treated the priest of Apollo, whom he had previously held in such honour, he would not have torn him to shreds like some ravaging beast, even to flaying the flesh from his bones, if the matter had not been universally recognised as a crime of exceptional magnitude.

[XIX/103] ... For one would have thought that Julian reigned for this purpose only, namely to get rid of all the animals of the world, so lavish was the massacre of sheep and cattle on the altars of the temple! Indeed he carried it to such frenzy that a great many of those among them who still appeared to be philosophers came up with crude nicknames for him, such as 'cook' and 'butcher' and so on.

[107] It behoved him [Apollo], if nothing else, to take pity on his own priest, so unjustly tortured, by clearly identifying the guilty author of the fire. Indeed, if the arsonist managed to escape from the scene at the very time when the unfortunate priest was being suspended from hooks and having the flesh flayed from his back, and not even so being able, when interrogated, to name the culprit, (Apollo) ought to have revealed his hiding-place. But in fact this ungrateful and inconsiderate god cared nothing for his priest so unreasonably tortured, nothing for the emperor made a laughing stock after he had made so many offerings of sacrifices! The whole world mocked at Julian and held him to be crazy and out of his mind for venting his rage on that unhappy priest.

49. Jerome: *Chronicon* (c. 380–1)
Translated R. Pearse, The Tertullian Project

283rd Olympiad …

18 …
   a Julian, brother of Gallus, is named Caesar at Milan.
…

285th Olympiad
23 *b* Constantius II dies at Mopsocrene, between Cilicia and
Cappadocia, in the forty-fifth year of his life.

36th [emperor] of the Romans, Julian reigned for 1 year and 8 months

1   *c* As Julian had been converted to the worship of idols, there was a
mild persecution, more swaying than compelling people to have to
sacrifice, in which many of our people fell by their own will.

d After George, who had been ordained bishop in place of
Athanasius by the Arians, had been burned to death because of a
revolt of the people, Athanasius is returned to Alexandria.

e Eusebius and Lucifer are returned from exile, from where Lucifer,
having adopted two other confessors, makes Paulinus, the presbyter
of bishop Eustathius and who had never polluted himself in the
communion of the heretics, bishop in the Catholic part of Antioch.

2   *f* When the law had been given that Christians could not be teachers
of the liberal arts, Proheresius the Athenian sophist spontaneously
gave up his school, although Julian had specially conceded that he
might teach despite being a Christian.

a Aemilianus is burned by the vicarius because he had overturned
the altars at Dorostorum.

b The church at Antioch was shut and a most serious storm of
imminent persecution was quieted by the will of God. For Julian
had proceeded into Persia and vowed our blood after a victory to
the gods. There he was led into the desert by a certain pretended
deserter, when he had lost his apostate army by hunger and thirst

and had unadvisedly strayed from the ranks of his own men, he was by chance stabbed in the groin with a lance by a hostile horseman of the enemy and perished in the 32nd year of his life. After which, the following day, Jovian the primicerius of the household troops was made emperor.

50. Ammianus Marcellinus: *Res Gestae* (c. 395)
Translated J. C. Rolfe

[15.2.7] But then the artillery of slander was turned against Julian … lately brought to account, and he was involved, as was unjustly held, in a two-fold accusation: first, that he had moved from the estate of Macellum … into the province of Asia, in his desire for a liberal education; and, second, that he had visited his brother Gallus as he passed through Constantinople. [8] And although he cleared himself of these implications and showed that he had done neither of these things without warrant, yet he would have perished at the instigation of the accursed crew of flatterers, had not, through the favour of divine power, Queen Eusebia befriended him …

[15.8.1] … Constantius was disquieted by frequent messages reporting that Gaul was in desperate case … he at length hit upon the right plan and thought of associating with himself in a share of the empire his cousin Julian, who not so very long before had been summoned from the district of Achaia and still wore his student's cloak … [3] To them [the intimates of Constantius] in their obstinate resistance the queen alone opposed herself, whether she dreaded journeying to a far country or with her native intelligence took counsel for the common good …

[15.8.17] Finally, he [Julian] was taken up to sit with the emperor in his carriage and conducted to the palace, whispering this verse from the Homeric song: 'By purple death I'm seized and fate supreme.'

[16.1.1] … Julian Caesar at Vienne was admitted by Augustus … into the fellowship of the consular fasti. Urged on by his native energy, he dreamed of the din of battle and the slaughter of savages, already preparing to gather up the broken fragments of the province, if only fortune should at last aid him with her favouring breeze. [2] Accordingly, since the great deeds that he had the courage and good fortune to perform in Gaul surpass many valiant achievements of the ancients,

I shall describe them one by one in progressive order ... [3] Now whatever I shall tell ... will almost belong to the domain of the panegyric. [4] For some law of a higher life seems to have attended this youth from his noble cradle even to his last breath. For with rapid strides he grew so conspicuous at home and abroad that in his foresight he was esteemed a second Titus ... in the glorious progress of his wars as very like Trajan, mild as Antoninus Pius, and in searching out the true and perfect reason of things in harmony with Marcus Aurelius, in emulation of whom he moulded his conduct and character.

[16.2.5] And to avoid any delay, he took only the cuirassiers and the crossbowmen, who were far from suitable to defend a general, and traversing the same road [as Silvanus the Master of Infantry had], he came to Auxerre.

[16.5.3] Lastly, though he constantly read the booklet which Constantius, as if sending a stepson to the university, had written with his own hand, making lavish provision for what should be spent on Caesar's table, he forbade the ordering and serving of pheasants and of sow's matrix and udders, contenting himself with the coarse and ordinary rations of a common soldier.

[16.5.10] ... [T]his philosopher, being a prince, was forced to practise the rudiments of military training and learn the art of marching rhythmically in pyrrhic measure to the harmony of the pipes ...

[16.5.14] ... [W]hat good he did to Gaul, labouring as it was in utmost destitution, appears most clearly from this fact: when he first entered those parts, he found that twenty-five pieces of gold were demanded by way of tribute from every one as a poll- and land-tax; but when he left, seven only for full satisfaction of all duties.

[16.7.1] At that time Constantius, apprised by approaching rumour that when Caesar was blockaded at Sens, Marcellus had not brought aid, discharged the latter from the army and commanded him to depart to his home. Whereupon Marcellus ... began to contrive a plot against Julian, presuming on Augustus, whose ears were open to every slander. [2] And so, when Marcellus was on his way, Eutherius, the head chamberlain, was sent immediately after him, to confute him in case he should trump up anything. But Marcellus, unaware of this, presently came to Milan, blustering and making trouble ... and when admitted to the council, he charged Julian with being arrogant and already fitting himself with stronger pinions, so as to soar up higher ...

[16.10.9] Accordingly, being saluted as Augustus with favouring shouts, while hills and shores thundered out the roar, he never stirred, but showed himself as calm and imperturbable as he was commonly seen in the provinces. [10] For he both stooped when passing through lofty gates (although he was very short), and, as if his neck were in a vice, he kept the gaze of his eyes straight ahead ... neither did he nod when the wheel jolted nor was he ever seen to spit, or to wipe or rub his face or nose, or move his hands about.

[16.10.18] Meanwhile Constantius' sister Helena, wife of Julian Caesar, had been brought to Rome under pretence of affection, but the reigning queen, Eusebia, was plotting against her; she herself had been childless all her life, and by her wiles coaxed Helena to drink a rare potion, so that as often as she was with child she should have a miscarriage. [19] For once before, in Gaul, when she had borne a baby boy, she lost it through this machination: a mid-wife had been bribed with a sum of money, and as soon as the child was born cut the umbilical cord more than was right, and so killed it; such great pains and so much thought were taken that this most valiant man might have no heir.

[16.11.1] But Julianus Caesar, after having passed a troubled winter at Sens ... with the threats of the Germans thundering on every side, stirred by favourable omens hastened to Rheims. He felt the greater eagerness and pleasure because Severus was commanding the army, a man neither insubordinate nor overbearing but well known for his long excellent record in the army ... [2] From another direction Barbatio ... came from Italy at the emperor's order with twenty-five thousand soldiers to Augst. [3] For it was planned and carefully arranged before-hand that the Alamanni ... should be driven into straits as if with a pair of pliers by twin forces of our soldiers, and cut to pieces.

[16.11.13] However, it was current rumour everywhere, that Julian was not chosen to relieve the distress of Gaul, but that he might meet his death in the cruellest of wars, being even then (as it was thought) inexperienced and one who could not stand even the clash of arms.

[16.12.13] The soldiers did not allow him to finish what he was saying, but gnashed and ground their teeth and showed their eagerness for battle by striking their spears and shields together, and besought him that they might be led against an enemy who was already in sight ... [14] To add to this eagerness there was the full approval of the high command and especially of Florentius, the praetorian prefect ...

[16.12.29] And since to address them all at once was impossible, both on account of the wide extent of the field and the great numbers of the multitude that had been brought together ... without thought of his own safety he flew past the enemy's weapons and by these and similar speeches animated the soldiers, strangers as well as acquaintances, to deeds of valour.

[16.12.64] Thereupon, since Julian was a man of greater mark than his position, and more powerful in his deserts than in his command, he was hailed as Augustus by the unanimous acclamation of the entire army; but he rebuked the soldiers for their thoughtless action, and declared with an oath that he neither expected nor desired to attain that honour.

[16.12.67] On the successful outcome of these exploits ... some of the courtiers in Constantius' palace found fault with Julian, in order to please the emperor himself. Or facetiously called him Victorinus, on the ground that, although he was modest in making reports whenever he led the army in battle, he often mentioned defeats of the Germans ... [70] ... When this battle was fought near Strasburg, although he [Constantius] was distant forty days' march, in his description of the fight he falsely asserts that he arranged the order of battle, and stood among the standard-bearers, and drove the barbarians headlong, and that Chonodomarius was brought to him, saying nothing (Oh, shameful indignity!) of the glorious deeds of Julian ...

[17.1.14] In this memorable war ... Caesar took pride as a fortunate and successful general. And one might well believe his detractors, who pretended that he had acted so courageously on all occasions because he chose rather to perish fighting gloriously than to be put to death like a condemned criminal (as he expected), after the manner of his brother Gallus – had he not with equal resolution, even after Constantius' death, increased his renown by marvellous exploits.

[17.3.2] And whereas Florentius, the praetorian prefect, after having reviewed the whole matter (as he asserted) stated that whatever was lacking in the poll-tax and land-tax accounts he supplied out of special levies, Julian, knowing about such measures, declared that he would rather lose his life than allow it to be done ... [5] But when long afterwards an increase in taxation was nevertheless proposed to him, he could not bring himself to read it or sign it, but threw it on the ground. And when he was advised by a letter of Augustus, after the prefect's report, not to act so meticulously as to seem to discredit Florentius, he wrote back that it would be a cause for rejoicing if the provincials ... might at least have to furnish only the prescribed taxes, not the additional amounts ... And so it came to pass then and thereafter, that through the resolution of one courageous spirit no one tried to extort from the Gauls anything beyond the normal tax. [6] Finally, contrary to precedent, Caesar by entreaty had obtained this favour from the prefect, that he should be entrusted with the administration of the province of Second Belgium, which was overwhelmed by many kinds of calamities, and indeed with the proviso that no agent either of the prefect or of the governor should force anyone to pay the tax. So every one whom he had taken under his charge was relieved by this comforting news, and without being dunned they brought in their dues before the appointed date.

[17.9.3] ... [T]he crops were not yet ripe, and the soldiers, after using up what they carried, could find no food anywhere; and resorting to outrageous threats, they assailed Julian with foul names and opprobrious language, calling him an Asiatic, a Greekling and a deceiver, and a fool with a show of wisdom ... [6] And they had good reason for their complaints. For ... the soldiers, though worn out by their labours in Gaul, had received neither donative nor pay from the very day that Julian was sent there, for the reason that he himself had no funds available anywhere from which to give, nor did Constantius allow any to be expended in the usual manner.

[17.11.1] ... [A]ll those who had the chief influence in the palace ... turned Julian's well-devised and successful achievements into mere mockery by endless silly jests of this sort: 'This fellow, a nanny-goat and no man, is getting insufferable with his victories,' jibing at him for being hairy, and calling him a 'chattering mole' and 'an ape in purple', and 'a Greek pedant', and other names like these ...

[20.4.1] When Constantius was hastening to lend aid to the Orient ... he was tormented by the valorous deeds of Julian ... [2] Excited by these and similar exploits, and fearing that their fame would grow greater, urged on besides, as was reported, by the prefect Florentius, he sent Decentius, the tribune and secretary, at once to take from Julian his auxiliaries, namely the Aeruli and Batavi and the Celts and Petulantes, as well as three hundred picked men from each of the other divisions of the army; and he ordered him to hasten their march under the pretext that they might be able to be on hand for an attack on the Parthians early in the spring.

[20.4.13] And in order to treat with greater honour those who were going far away, he invited their officers to dinner and bade them make any request that was in their minds. And since they were so liberally entertained, they departed anxious and filled with twofold sorrow: because an unkindly fortune was depriving them both of a mild ruler and of the lands of their birth. But though possessed by this sorrow, they were apparently consoled and remained quiet in their quarters. [14] But no sooner had night come on than they broke out in open revolt ...

[20.8.18] Along with this letter he sent another of a more private nature to be delivered to Constantius secretly, which was written in a more reproachful and bitter tone; the content of this it was not possible for me to examine, nor if it had been, would it have been fitting for me to make it public. [19] To perform this mission two men of importance were chosen, Pentadius, the court marshal, and Eutherius, who was then head chamberlain.

[21.1.4] Therefore, making light of the letter that Constantius had sent through Leonas [the quaestor], and recognising the authority of none of those whom his rival had promoted except Nebridius [made praetorian prefect in place of Florentius], being now an Augustus he celebrated quinquennial games [at Vienne]; and he wore a magnificent diadem ... whereas at the beginning of his principate he had assumed and worn a cheap crown ... [5] While these games were going on he had sent to Rome the remains of his deceased wife Helena, to be laid to rest in his villa near the city on the via Nomentana, where also her sister Constantina, formerly the wife of Gallus, was buried.

[21.2.4] And in order to win the favour of all men and have opposition from none, he pretended to be an adherent of the Christian religion, from which he had long since secretly revolted; and making a few men sharers in his secrets, he was given up to soothsaying and auguries, and to other practises which the worshippers of the pagan gods have always followed. [5] And in order temporarily to conceal this, on the day of the festival which the Christians celebrate in the month of January and call the Epiphany, he went to their church, and departed after offering a prayer to their deity in the usual manner.

[21.3.4] ... Constantius, thinking that Vadomarius would be loyal to him, made him the secret and efficient executor of his plots (if rumour alone is to be trusted), and wrote to him that he should pretend to break the treaty of peace from time to time and attack the districts bordering on his domain; to the end that Julian, in fear of this, should nowhere abandon the defence of Gaul.

[21.6.4] At that same time Constantius took to wife Faustina, having long since lost Eusebia, sister of the ex-consuls Eusebius and Hypatius, a lady distinguished before many others for beauty of person and of character, and kindly in spite of her lofty station, through whose well-deserved favour (as I have shown) Julian was saved from dangers and declared Caesar.

[21.10.7] And now, lifting himself higher and believing that Constantius could never be brought into harmony with him, he wrote to the senate a sharp oration full of invective, in which he specifically charged Constantius with disgraceful acts and faults. When these were read in the House, while Tertullus was still acting as prefect, the striking independence of the nobles was manifest as well as their grateful affection; for with complete agreement they one and all shouted: 'We demand reverence for your own creator.'

[21.11.2] Two of Constantius' legions, which with one cohort of bowmen he had found at Sirmium, being not yet sure of their loyalty he had sent to Gaul under colour of urgent necessity. These ... were planning a rebellion, aided and abetted by Nigrinus, a native of Mesopotamia and commander of a troop of horsemen. Having arranged the plot by secret conferences and added to its strength by profound silence, on arriving at Aquileia ... with hostile intent they suddenly closed its gates, supported in this revolt by the native population, because of the dread which was even then connected with the name of Constantius.

[21.16.15] Now, although this emperor [Constantius] in foreign wars met with loss and disaster, yet he was elated by his success in civil conflicts ...

[21.16.18] ... And since throngs of bishops hastened hither and thither on the public post-horses to the various synods, as they call them, while he [Constantius] sought to make the whole ritual conform to his own will, he cut the sinews of the courier-service.

[22.3.1] Shortly after this Salutius Secundus was raised to the rank of praetorian prefect, and given, as a trustworthy official, the chief oversight of the inquisitions that were to be set on foot; and with him were associated Mamertinus, Arbitio, Agilo, and Nevitta, and also Jovinus ... [2] These crossed all to Chalcedon, and in the presence of the generals and tribunes of the Joviani and the Herculiani examined the cases with more passion than was just and right with the exception of a few, in which the evidence showed that the accused were most guilty ... [7] ... [F]or the death of Ursulus, count of the sacred largesses, Justice herself seems to me to have wept, and to have accused the emperor of ingratitude. For when Julian was sent as Caesar to the western regions, to be treated with extreme niggardliness, being granted no power of making any donative to the soldiers ... this very Ursulus wrote to the man in charge of the Gallic treasury, ordering that whatever the Caesar asked for should be given him without hesitation. [8] After Ursulus' death Julian found himself the object of the reproaches and curses of many men, and thinking that he could excuse himself for the unpardonable crime, he declared that the man had been put to death without his knowledge, alleging that his taking off was due to the anger of the soldiers, who remembered his words ... when he saw the ruins of Amida. [9] From this it was clear that Julian was timorous, or that he did not know what was fitting, when he put Arbitio, who was always untrustworthy and excessively haughty, in charge of these inquisitions ... for Arbitio was a man whom he knew above all others to be a threat to his own safety, as was to be expected of one who had taken a valiant part in the victories of the civil wars.

[22.4.9] It happened at that same time that a barber who had been summoned to trim the emperor's hair, appeared in splendid attire. On seeing him, Julian was amazed, and said: 'I sent for a barber, not a fiscal agent.' However, he asked the man what his trade brought him in; to which the barber replied twenty daily allowances of bread, and the same amount of fodder for pack-animals ... as well as a heavy annual salary, not to mention many rich perquisites. [10] Incensed by this, Julian discharged all attendants of that kind (as being not necessary to him), as well as cooks and other similar servants ...

[22.5.1] Although Julian from the earliest days of his childhood had been more inclined towards the worship of the pagan gods, and as he gradually grew up burned with longing to practise it, yet because of his many reasons for anxiety he observed certain of its rites with the greatest possible secrecy. [2] But when his fears were ended, and he saw that the time had come when he could do as he wished, he revealed the secrets of his heart and by plain and formal decrees ordered the temples to be opened, victims brought to the altars, and the worship of the gods restored. [3] And in order to add to the effectiveness of these ordinances, he summoned to the palace the bishops of the Christians, who were of conflicting opinions, and the people, who were also at variance, and politely advised them to lay aside their differences, and each fearlessly and without opposition to observe his own beliefs. [4] On this he took a firm stand, to the end that, as this freedom increased their dissension, he might afterwards have no fear of a united populace, knowing as he did from experience that no wild beasts are such enemies to mankind as are most Christians in their deadly hatred of one another.

[22.7.1] And so the first of January came, when the consular annals took on the names of Mamertinus and Nevitta; and the emperor showed himself especially condescending by going on foot to their inauguration in company with other high officials, an action which some commended but others criticised as affected and cheap. [2] Then, when Mamertinus gave games in the Circus and the slaves that were to be manumitted were led in by the assistant master of ceremonies, the emperor himself with too great haste, pronounced the usual formula, that it be done according to the law; and on being reminded that the jurisdiction that day belonged to another, he fined himself ten pounds of gold, as guilty of an oversight. [3] Meanwhile, he came frequently into the senate house to give attention to various matters with which the many changes in the state burdened him. And when one day, as he was sitting in judgement there, and it was announced that the philosopher Maximus had come from Asia, he started up in an undignified manner, so far forgetting himself that he ran at full speed to a distance from the vestibule, and after having kissed the philosopher and received him with reverence, brought him back with him. This unseemly ostentation made him appear to be an excessive seeker for empty fame ...

[22.7.8] ... [H]is intimates tried to persuade him to attack the neighbouring Goths, who were often deceitful and treacherous; but he replied that he was looking for a better enemy; that for the Goths the Galatian traders were enough, by whom they were offered for sale everywhere without distinction of rank.

[22.9.4] When he saw that [Nicomedia's] walls had sunk into a pitiful heap of ashes, showing his distress by silent tears he went with lagging step to the palace: and in particular he wept over the wretched state of the city because the senate and the people … met him in mourning garb. And certain of them he recognised, since he had been brought up there under the bishop Eusebius, whose distant relative he was.

[22.9.12] … [I]t was … hard and censurable that under his rule anyone who was sought by the *curiales*, even though protected by special privileges, by length of service in the army, or by proof that he was wholly ineligible by birth for such a position, could with difficulty obtain full justice; so that many of them through fear bought immunity from annoyance by secret and heavy bribes.

[22.10.6] And these and similar instances led to the belief, as he himself constantly affirmed, that the old goddess of Justice … had returned to earth during his reign, were it not that sometimes Julian followed his own inclination rather than the demands of the laws, and by occasionally erring clouded the many glories of his career. [7] For after many other things, he also corrected some of the laws … But this one thing was inhumane, and ought to be buried in eternal silence, namely, that he forbade teachers of rhetoric and literature to practise their profession, if they were followers of the Christian religion.

[22.12.1] Meanwhile, Julian was preparing a campaign against the Persians, which he had long before planned with lofty strength of mind, being exceedingly aroused to punish their misdeeds in the past … [2] He was inflamed besides with a two-fold longing for war, first, because he was tired of inactivity and dreamed of clarions and battle; and then, exposed as he had been in the first flower of his youth to warfare with savage nations, while his ears were still warm with the prayers of kings and princes who (as it was believed) could more easily be vanquished than led to hold out their hands as suppliants, he burned to add to the tokens of his glorious victories the surname Parthicus.

[22.12.6] … [H]e drenched the altars with the blood of an excessive number of victims, sometimes offering up a hundred oxen at once, with countless flocks of various other animals, and with white birds hunted out by land and sea; to such a degree that almost every day his soldiers, who gorged themselves on the abundance of meat, living boorishly and corrupted by their eagerness for drink, were carried through the squares [of Antioch] to their lodgings on the shoulders of passers-by from the public temples, where they indulged in banquets that deserved punishment rather than indulgence; especially the Petulantes and the Celts, whose wilfulness at that time had passed all bounds. [7] Moreover, the ceremonial rites were excessively increased, with an expenditure of money hitherto unusual and burdensome.

[22.13.3] It was said, however, though on very slight evidence, that the cause of the burning of the temple [of Apollo at Daphne] was this: the philosopher Asclepiades ... when he had come to that suburb from abroad to visit Julian, placed before the lofty feet of the statue a little silver image of the Dea Caelestis ... and after lighting some wax tapers as usual, went away. From these tapers after midnight ... some flying sparks alighted on the woodwork ... and the fire, fed by the dry fuel, mounted and burned whatever it could reach ...

[22.14.1] ... [I]t did seem superfluous, that with no satisfactory reason for such a measure, but merely from a desire for popularity, he wished to lower the price of commodities ... [2] And, although the senate at Antioch clearly pointed out that this could not be done at the time when he ordered it, he in no wise gave up his plan ... Therefore raging against them one by one as recalcitrant and stubborn, he composed an invective, which he entitled *The Antiochian* or *Misopogon*, in which he enumerated in a hostile spirit the faults of the city, including more than were justified. After this, finding that he was the object of many jests, he was forced at the time to disregard them, but was filled with suppressed wrath. [3] For he was ridiculed as a Cecrops, as a dwarf, spreading his narrow shoulders and displaying a billy-goat's beard, taking mighty strides as if he was the brother of Otus and Ephialtes, whose height Homer describes as enormous. He was also called by many a slaughterer instead of high-priest, in jesting allusion to his many offerings ...

[23.1.2] ... [E]ager to extend the memory of his reign by great works, he planned at vast cost to restore the once splendid temple at Jerusalem ... He had entrusted the speedy performance of this work to Alypius of Antioch ... [3] But, though this Alypius pushed the work on with vigour, aided by the governor of the province, terrifying balls of flame kept bursting forth near the foundations of the temple, and made the place inaccessible to the workmen, some of whom were burned to death; and since in this way the element persistently repelled them, the enterprise halted.

[23.1.5] ... [H]e was alarmed by an omen which, as the result showed, was most trustworthy. For when Felix, head of the public treasury, had suddenly died of a haemorrhage, and Count Julian had followed him to the grave, the people as they looked at the public inscriptions, uttered the names as Felix, Julianus and Augustus.

[23.2.3] ... He himself, when on the point of leaving Antioch, appointed as governor of Syria a certain Alexander of Heliopolis, who was hot-tempered and cruel; and he said that the man did not deserve the post, but was the kind of judge proper for the avaricious and rebellious people of Antioch.

[23.3.5] ... Julian (as he had previously planned) ... put 30,000 picked men under the command of ... Procopius, and joined to him with equal powers Sebastianus ... with orders to keep for the present on this side of the Tigris and to watch carefully everywhere and see that nothing unexpected should happen on the unprotected side ... And he gave the order that (if it could be done to greater advantage) they should join King Arsaces, march with him through Corduene and Moxoëne, lay waste in passing by Chiliocomum, a fruitful region of Media, and other places, and meet him while he was still in Assyria, so as to aid him in cases of necessity.

[23.5.4] But while Julian was lingering at Circesium ... he received a sorrowful letter from Sallustius, prefect of Gaul, begging that the campaign against the Parthians might be put off, and that Julian should not thus prematurely, without having yet prayed for the protection of the gods, expose himself to inevitable destruction. [5] But the emperor ... pushed confidently on, since no human power or virtue has ever been great enough to turn aside what the decrees of fate had ordained.

[24.3.1] The day after these events the serious news came to the emperor, while he was quietly at table, that the Persian leader called the Surena had unexpectedly attacked three squadrons of our scouting cavalry, had killed a very few of them, including one of their tribunes, and carried off a standard. [2] At once roused to furious anger, Julian hurried forth with an armed force ... and routed the marauders in shameful confusion; he cashiered the two surviving tribunes as inefficient and cowardly, and following the ancient laws, discharged and put to death ten of the soldiers who had fled from the field. [3] Then, after the city [Pirisabora] was burned … Julian mounted a tribunal erected for the purpose and thanked the assembled army, urging them all to act in the same way in the future, and promised each man a hundred pieces of silver. But when he perceived that the smallness of the promised sum excited a mutinous uproar, he was roused to deep indignation and spoke as follows … [8] By this address of an emperor self-contained amid prosperity and adversity the soldiers were quieted for the time, and, gaining confidence through the anticipation of better days, they promised to be obedient and compliant.

[24.6.1] Then we came to an artificial river, by name Naarmalcha, meaning 'the kings' river', which at that time was dried up. Here in days gone by Trajan, and after him Severus, had with immense effort caused the accumulated earth to be dug out, and had made a great canal in order to let in the water from the Euphrates and give boats and ships access to the Tigris. [2] It seemed to Julian in all respects safest to clean out that same canal … As soon as the canal was cleared, the dams were swept away by the great flow of water, and the fleet in safety covered thirty stadia and was carried into the channel of the Tigris … [4] Since thus far everything had resulted as he desired, the Augustus now with greater confidence strode on to meet all dangers, hoping for so much from a fortune which had never failed him that he often dared many enterprises bordering upon rashness. He unloaded the stronger ships of those which carried provisions and artillery, and manned them each with eight hundred armed soldiers; then keeping by him the stronger part of the fleet, which he had formed into three divisions, in the first quiet of night he sent one part under Count Victor with orders speedily to cross the river and take possession of the enemy's side of the stream. [5] His generals in great alarm with unanimous entreaties tried to prevent him from taking this step, but could not shake the emperor's determination. The flag was raised according to his orders, and five ships immediately vanished from sight. But no sooner had they reached the opposite bank than they were assailed so persistently with firebrands and every kind of inflammable material, that ships and soldiers would have been consumed, had not the emperor, carried away by the keen vigour of his spirit, cried out that our soldiers had, as directed, raised the signal that they were already in possession of the shore, and ordered the entire fleet to hasten to the spot with all speed of their oars. [6] The result was that the ships were saved uninjured, and the surviving soldiers … after a fierce struggle scaled the high, precipitous banks and held their position unyieldingly.

[24.6.17] Fully convinced that similar successes would follow these, he prepared to offer many victims to Mars the Avenger; but of ten fine bulls that were brought for this purpose nine, even before they were brought to the altar, of their own accord sank in sadness to the ground; but the tenth broke his bonds and escaped, and after he had been with difficulty brought back and sacrificed, showed ominous signs. Upon seeing these, Julian in deep indignation cried out, and called Jove to witness, that he would make no more offerings to Mars; and he did not sacrifice again, since he was carried off by a speedy death.

[24.7.1] Having held council with his most distinguished generals about the siege of Ctesiphon, the opinion of some was adopted, who felt sure that the undertaking was rash and untimely, since the city, impregnable by its situation alone, was well defended; and, besides, it was believed that the king would soon appear with a formidable force. [2] So the better opinion prevailed … [3] But Julian, ever driven on by his eager ambitions, made light words of warning, and upbraiding his generals for urging him through cowardice and love of ease to loose his hold on the Persian kingdom, which he had already all but won; with the river on his left and with ill-omened guides leading the way, resolved to march rapidly into the interior. [4] And it seemed as if Bellona herself lighted the fire with fatal torch, when he gave orders that all the ships should be burned, with the exception of twelve of the smaller ones, which he decided to transport on wagons as helpful for making bridges. And he thought that this plan had the advantage that the fleet, if abandoned, could not be used by the enemy, or at any rate, that nearly 20,000 soldiers would not be employed in transporting and guiding the ships, as had been the case since the beginning of the campaign. [5] Then, as every man murmured, in fear for his life … and as the deserters, on being put to the torture, openly confessed that they had used deceit, orders were given to use the greatest efforts of the army to put out the flames. But the frightful spread of fire had already consumed the greater number of the ships … [6] By this disaster the fleet was needlessly lost, but Julian, trusting to his united army … advanced into the interior, where the fruitful country furnished an abundance of supplies.

[25.3.3] Excited by the misfortune, he forgot his coat-of-mail, and merely caught up a shield in the confusion ... [6] Julian, careless of his own safety ... rushed boldly into the fight. His guards, who had scattered in their alarm, were crying to him from all sides to get clear of the mass of fugitives ... when suddenly – no one knows whence – a cavalryman's spear grazed the skin of his arm, pierced his ribs, and lodged in the lower lobe of his liver. [7] While he was trying to pluck this out with his right hand, he felt that the sinews of his fingers were cut through on both sides by the sharp steel. Then he fell from his horse, all present hastened to the spot, and he was taken to camp and given medical treatment.

[25.3.22] Meanwhile, all who were present wept, whereupon even then maintaining his authority, he chided them, saying that it was unworthy to mourn for a prince who was called to union with heaven and the stars. [23] As this made them all silent, he himself engaged with the philosophers Maximus and Priscus in an intricate discussion about the nobility of the soul. Suddenly the wound in his pierced side opened wide, the pressure of blood checked his breath, and after a draught of cold water for which he had asked, in the gloom of midnight he passed quietly away in the thirty-second year of his age.

[25.4.4] ... [I]n time of peace the frugality of his living and his table excited the wonder of those who could judge aright, as if he intended soon to resume the philosopher's cloak. And on his various campaigns, he was often seen partaking of common and scanty food, sometimes standing up like a common soldier.

[25.4.15] There are many undoubted tokens of his generosity. Among these are his very light imposition of tribute, his remission of crown-money, the cancellation of many debts made great by long standing, the impartial treatment of disputes between the privy purse and private persons, the restoration of revenues from taxes to various states along with their lands ... furthermore, that he was never eager to increase his wealth, which he thought was better secured in the hands of its possessors; and he often remarked that Alexander the Great, when asked where his treasures were, gave the kindly answer, 'in the hands of my friends'.

[25.4.18] He delighted in the applause of the mob, and desired beyond measure praise for the slightest matters, and the desire for popularity often led him to converse with unworthy men.

[25.4.22] The figure and proportion of his body were as follows. He was of medium stature. His hair lay smooth as if it had been combed, his beard was shaggy and trimmed so as to end in a point, his eyes were fine and full of fire, an indication of the acuteness of his mind. His eyebrows were handsome, his nose very straight, his mouth somewhat large with a pendulous lower lip. His neck was thick and somewhat bent, his shoulders large and broad. Moreover, right from top to toe he was a man of straight well-proportioned bodily frame and as a result was strong and a good runner.

[25.4.23] And since his detractors alleged that he had stirred up the storms of war anew, to the ruin of his country, they should know … that it was not Julian, but Constantine, who kindled the Parthian fires, when he confided too greedily in the lies of Metrodorus, as I explained fully some time ago.

[25.6.6] … [T]he enemy from the wooded heights assailed us with weapons of all kinds and with insulting language, as traitors and murderers of an excellent prince. For they also had heard from the mouths of deserters, in consequence of an unfounded rumour, that Julian had been killed by a Roman weapon.

[25.9.12] … Then Procopius was sent with the remains of Julian, in order to inter him, as he had directed when still alive, in the suburb of Tarsus.

51. Eunapius: *History* (late fourth century; revised early fifth century)

Translated R. C. Blockley. The *History* has been lost, but fragments survive in other sources, notably the themed collections of excerpts compiled under the Byzantine emperor Constantine VII (913–59), such as the *Excerpta de Sententiis* and the *Excerpta de Legationibus*.

[Fragment 15 (Blockley); from Constantine VII, *Exc. de Sent.* 5] … Henceforth my narrative centres upon the one who was its object from the beginning, and, feeling the love that I do for him [Julian], I am compelled to turn my attention to his achievements. Of course, I never saw him or personally knew him; for when he was Emperor, the writer of this History was just a child … Oribasius of Pergamum, the most intimate of Julian's companions … declared openly that I should be committing a sin if I did not write my History. Furthermore, he composed for my use in writing a detailed memorandum of the deeds of the Emperor; for he was familiar with all, having been present at them.

[Fragment 17 (Blockley); from Constantine VII, *Exc. de Sent.* 7] ... the most noble Emperor Julian, enthused by his own achievements, adequately described in his own words these events [the battle of Strasbourg] in a pamphlet which he dedicated to the battle ...

[Fragment 24 (Blockley); from Constantine VII, *Exc. de Leg. Gent.* 3] After Julian had been proclaimed Augustus embassies came to him from everywhere, and many golden crowns were brought to him from the provinces. On that occasion the inhabitants of Ionia had all their requests granted both large or small, and the Lydians achieved more than they had sought.

[Fragment 28.1 (Blockley); from Constantine VII, *Exc. de Sent.* 24] ... [Julian] became Emperor not because he really lusted after kingship but because he observed that mankind needed a ruler; and he was exceedingly solicitous for his soldiers not because he sought common popularity but because he knew that this was to the advantage of the state.

52. Eunapius: *Lives of the Sophists* (c. 396)
Translated W. C. Wright

[473] ... Maximus was one of those who had been saturated with the wisdom of Aedesius; moreover he received the honour of being the teacher of the Emperor Julian. After all his relatives had been put to death by Constantius, as I have recorded with more details in my account of Julian, and the whole family had been stripped bare, Julian alone was left alive, being despised on the score of his tender years and his mild disposition. Nevertheless, eunuchs from the palace took charge of him, and were assigned to keep watch so that he might not waver from the Christian faith. But even in the face of these difficulties he displayed the greatness of his genius. For he had their books so thoroughly by heart that they fretted at the scantiness of their erudition, since there was nothing that they could teach the boy. Now since they had nothing to teach him and Julian had nothing to learn from them, he begged his cousin's permission to attend the schools of the sophists and lectures on philosophy. He, as the gods so willed, permitted this, because he wished Julian to browse among books and to have leisure for them, rather than leave him to reflect on his own family and his claim to empire. After he had obtained this permission, since ample and

abundant wealth from many sources was at his disposal, he used to travel about [474] accompanied by the emperor's suspicions and a bodyguard, and went where he pleased. Thus it was that he came to Pergamon, following on the report of the wisdom of Aedesius. But the latter was by this time far on in years, and his bodily strength was failing. First and foremost of all his students were Maximus ..., Chrysanthius of Sardis, Priscus the Thesprotian or Molossian, and Eusebius who came from Myndus, a city of Caria. On being allowed to study under Aedesius, Julian, who was old for his boyish years, in amazement and admiration of his vigour and the divine qualities of his soul, refused to leave him, but like those who had been bitten by the snake in the story he longed to drink down learning open-mouthed and at a gulp, and to win his end used to send Aedesius gifts worthy of an emperor. [However, Aedesius does not accept these, and orders Julian to study with Eusebius and Chrysanthius.]

On hearing this, Julian did not even leave the philosopher, but for the greater part of his time he devoted his attention to Eusebius and Chrysanthius. Now Chrysanthius had a soul akin to that of Maximus, and like him was passionately absorbed in working marvels, and he withdrew himself in the study of the science of divination, and in other respects also had a very similar character. But Eusebius, at least when Maximus was present, used to avoid precise and exact divisions of a disputation and dialectical devices and subtleties; though when Maximus was not there he would shine out like a bright star, with a light like the sun's; such was the facility and charm that flowered in his discourses ... At the close of his exposition Eusebius would add that these [i.e. dialectical discussions] are the only true realities, whereas the impostures of witchcraft and magic that cheat the senses are the work of conjurors who are insane men led astray into the exercise of earthly and material powers. The sainted Julian frequently heard the closing words, and at last took Chrysanthius aside, and said: 'If the truth is in you, dear Chrysanthius, tell me plainly what is the meaning of this epilogue that follows his exposition?' Having reflected deeply and with prudence, he said: 'The wise thing for you to do will be to inquire this not of me but of himself.' ... [475] ... Then when the next lecture took place, Eusebius ended with the same words as before, and Julian boldly asked him what was the meaning of the epilogue that he perpetually recited. Thereupon Eusebius ... said: 'Maximus is one of the older and more learned students, who, because of his lofty genius and super-abundant eloquence scorned all logical proof in these subjects and impetuously resorted to the acts of a madman. Not long since, he invited us to the temple of Hecate and produced many witnesses of his folly. When we had arrived there and had saluted the goddess: "Be seated," said he, "my well-beloved friends, and observe what shall come to pass, and how greatly I surpass the common herd." When he had said this, and we had all sat down, he burned a grain of incense and recited to himself the whole of some hymn or other, and was so highly successful in his demonstration that the image of the goddess first began to smile, then even seemed to laugh aloud. We were all much disturbed by this sight, but he said: "Let none of you be terrified by these things, for presently even the torches which the goddess holds in her hands shall kindle into flame." And before he could finish speaking the torches burst into a blaze of light. Now for the moment we came away astounded by that theatrical miracle-worker. But you must not marvel at any of these things, even as I marvel not, but rather believe that the thing of the highest importance is that purification of the soul which is attained by reason.' However, when the sainted Julian heard this, he said: 'Nay, farewell and devote yourself to your books. You have shown me the man I was in search of.' After saying this he kissed the head of Chrysanthius and started for Ephesus. There he had converse with Maximus, and hung on to him and laid fast hold on all that he had to teach. Maximus persuaded him to summon thither the divine Chrysanthius also, and when this had been done the two of them barely sufficed to satisfy the boy's great capacity for acquiring this kind of lore.

Now when his studies with them were prospering, he heard that there was a higher wisdom in Greece, possessed by the hierophant of the goddesses [i.e. Demeter and Persephone worshipped at Eleusis], and hastened to him with all speed ... [476] ... Julian had no sooner become intimate with the most holy of hierophants and greedily absorbed his wisdom, than he was forcibly removed by Constantius to be his consort in the Empire and elevated to the rank of Caesar ... Thus did Julian obtain what he did not desire, but had thrust upon him. As Caesar he was despatched to Gaul, not so much to rule there as with the intention that he should perish by violent means, while holding his imperial office; but contrary to all expectation, by the providence of the gods he emerged alive, concealing from all men his pious devotion to the gods, but overcoming all men by reason of that devotion. He crossed the Rhine and defeated and subjugated all the barbarian tribes beyond that river, and this in spite of numerous plots and schemes that were woven against him, as I have related in full in his *Life*. Then he summoned the hierophant from Greece, and having with his aid performed certain rites known to them alone, he mustered up courage to abolish the tyranny of Constantius. His accomplices were Oribasius of Pergamon and a certain Euhemerus, a native of Libya ... But all this has been described in fuller detail in my work on Julian ... [477–8] [Once emperor Julian summons Maximus and Chrysanthius to his court. Following ill-omens Chrysanthius refuses, but Maximus goes and becomes puffed up due to his influence at court. Priscus is also summoned to court] ... The emperor was suspicious about the refusal of his invitation, but he appointed Chrysanthius high priest of Lydia, along with his wife [a cousin of Eunapius], and entrusted to them the selection of other priests. Meanwhile he himself was setting out in haste for the war against Persia. Both Maximus and Priscus accompanied him, and certain other sophists joined the expedition, so that they amounted to a considerable number; they were, in fact, a mob who sang their own praises and were inflated with pride because the emperor said that he had associated with them. But when the enterprise which began with such great and splendid hopes had fallen with a crash to a vague and shapeless ruin and slipped through his fingers, as I have described more fully in my *Life* of Julian, Jovian was made emperor ...

[493] ... In the reign of the Emperor Julian, Prohaeresius was shut out of the field of education because he was reputed to be a Christian ...

[494] ... Himerius was a native of Bithynia, yet the author never knew him, though he lived in the same period. He travelled to the court of the Emperor Julian to declaim before him, in the hope that he would be regarded with favour on account of the emperor's dislike of Prohaeresius; and when Julian left this world, Himerius spent his time abroad.

[497] ... Nymphidianus was a native of Smyrna, whose own brother was Maximus the philosopher ... He was a man who, though he never shared in the education and training enjoyed at Athens, nevertheless in the art of rhetoric proved himself worthy of the reputation of the sophists. The Emperor Julian entrusted him with the task of expressing the imperial utterances, and made him Imperial Secretary for such letters as were composed in the Greek tongue.

[498] ... Oribasius came of a good family on both sides, and from his boyhood he was distinguished because he acquired every kind of learning that conduces to virtue and perfects it. When he reached early manhood he became a pupil of the great Zeno ... and he lost no time in attaining the first rank in medicine ... Since he won fame even from his earliest youth, Julian, when he was promoted to the rank of Caesar, carried him away with him to practise his art; but he so excelled in every other excellence that he actually made Julian emperor. However, these

matters have been more fully described in my account of Julian's reign.

[501] ... Chrysanthius having been appointed high priest of the whole country [Lydia], since he knew clearly what was about to happen, was not oppressive in the exercise of his office. He built no temples, as all other men in their hot haste and perfervid zeal hastened to do, nor was he excessively harsh to any of the Christians. But such was the mildness of his character that throughout Lydia the restoration of the temples almost escaped notice.

53. Anonymous: *Epitome De Caesaribus* (late fourth century)
Translated T. M. Banchich, Canisius College Translated Texts series

[43.1] Then Julian, the care of the Roman world having been returned to one man, himself, excessively desirous of glory, marched toward Persia. [2] There, led by a certain deserter into an ambush, when the Parthians were pressing upon him from different directions, he rushed from a just-established camp with a hastily snatched shield. [3] And when, with unthinking ardor, he attempted to order the ranks for battle, he was struck with a pike by a single man, from the enemy and, in fact, in flight. [4] And borne back to his tent and having emerged once again to encourage his men, gradually drained of blood, he died at just about midnight, having said beforehand, when consulted about *imperium*, that he recommended no one, lest, as is customary in a multitude with discrepant inclinations, † he produce danger for a friend from envy and for the state as a result of the discord of the army. [5] There had been in him immense knowledge of literature and of affairs, he had equaled the philosophers and the wisest of the Greeks. [6] He was very disposed toward exercise of the body, in which he was strong indeed, but he was short. [7] A disregard of due measure in certain matters diminished these things. His desire of praise was excessive; his worship of the gods superstitious; he was more daring than befits an *imperator*, by whom personal safety always must be maintained for the security of all, <but> in war most of all. [8] The desire of glory had so violently overwhelmed him that neither by the movement of the earth nor by the very numerous presages through which he was forbidden to attack Persia was he led to put an end to his ardor, and not even a massive sphere observed by night to fall from heaven before the day of battle kept him cautious.

† Suspected corruption.
< > Editorial addition.

54. Rufinus: *Church History* (c. 402/403)
Translated P. R. Amidon

[10.28] After him [Constantius] Julian as sole ruler received as a legitimate sovereignty what he had presumed to take. At first, as though critical of what Constantius had done, he bade the bishops be released from exile, but afterwards he rose against our people with every hurtful stratagem.

[10.33] Now Julian, once he had come into the East to drive out the Persians by war and began to be carried away by an unconcealed craze for idolatry which earlier he had kept secret, showed himself more astute than the others as a persecutor in that he ruined almost more people by rewards, honors, flattery and persuasion, than if he had proceeded by way of force, cruelty, and torture. Forbidding Christians access to the study of pagan authors, he decreed that elementary schools should be open only to those who worshipped the gods and goddesses. He ordered that posts in the armed and civil services should be given only to those who sacrificed. He decreed that the government of provinces and the administration of justice should not be entrusted to Christians, since their own law forbade them to use the sword. And he progressed daily in seeking out such laws as embodied all sorts of ingenious and cunning policies, although they did not appear particularly cruel.

[10.36] … He became so furious [subsequent to the transfer of the body of St Babylas] that the next day he ordered Christians to be arrested at random, thrust into prison, and subjected to torture. [37] Salutius, his prefect, did not approve of this, although he was a pagan, but he followed his order and tortured a youth named Theodore… We ourselves later saw Theodore in Antioch, and when we asked him if he had felt the pain fully, he said that while he had felt some slight pain, a youth had stood by him wiping away his perspiration with the purest white cloth while he was sweating and had kept applying cool water to him, and he had enjoyed it so much that he was unhappy when he was ordered off the rack. The emperor, then, threatening to do a better job of subduing the Christians after his victory over the Persians, set out but never returned. Wounded either by his own men or by the enemy, we do not know which, he brought to an end there his reign as Augustus, upon which he had presumed to enter, after a year and eight months.

[10.38] Now such was his refined cunning in deception that he even deluded the unhappy Jews, enticing them with the sort of vain hopes that he himself entertained. First of all, summoning them to him he

asked why they did not sacrifice, when their law included command-
ments for them about sacrifices. Thinking an opportunity had come
their way, they answered, 'We cannot do so except in the temple in
Jerusalem. For thus the law ordains.' And having received from him
permission to repair the temple, they grew so arrogant that it was as
though some prophet had come back to them.

55. Orosius: *History against the Pagans* (c. 417)
Translated from the Latin

[7.30.1] In the 1116th year since the founding of the city [Rome],
Julian, having been Caesar for a while, became the 36th emperor since
Augustus, only holding supreme power for one year and eight months.
[2] Assailing the Christian religion with skill rather than authority, so as
to negate the faith of Christ and promote the cult of idols, he aimed
rather to appeal with honours than to force with tortures. [3] However
he ordered openly in an edict that no Christian was to be a teacher of
the liberal arts; but nevertheless, as in fact we have learnt from our
elders, everyone almost everywhere affected by the conditions of the
precept preferred to forsake their office rather than their faith. [4] But
Julian, readying for war against the Parthians with Roman forces drawn
from everywhere, dragged to destined ruin with him, vowed the blood
of the Christians to his gods, to persecute the church openly if he
secured victory. [5] For he ordered an amphitheatre to be built in
Jerusalem in which, on returning from Parthia, he would throw to
beasts made more savage by artifice bishops, monks and all the holymen
of that place, and watch them being torn to pieces. [6] And so after
striking camp at Ctesiphon, led into the desert by the guile of some
deserter, the army perished worn out by the degree of thirst and the heat
of the sun and the demands of the sands besides, and the emperor,
troubled by such great dangers while recklessly crossing the vast desert,
died when struck by the pike of some enemy cavalryman he encountered: thus merciful God destroyed impious plans by the death of the
impious man.

56. Philostorgius: *Church History* (c. 439)
Translated E. Walford. The full history has been lost, but there
survives an epitome made in the ninth century by the
Byzantine intellectual and churchman Photius.

[2.16] He says that Constantine, having entered upon the thirty-second
year of his reign, was poisoned by his brothers at Nicomedia. And that
when his end drew near, and the plot was discovered, he drew up a
testament enjoining that the authors of his death should be punished,
and ordering that whichever of his sons should first arrive, should
proceed to take measures against them, lest his children too should be
destroyed by a like conspiracy. He further adds, that the document itself
… was intrusted to Eusebius, bishop of Nicomedia … [Constantius]
was the first of the brothers to arrive.

[3.27] … Aetius [an Arian teacher] … went to the court of Gallus
and was reckoned amongst his friends. He was also repeatedly sent to
Julian, especially at the time when Gallus had taught [sic; read instead
'discovered'] his brother to lean rather to the side of heathenism. He was
sent, however, with the design of recalling Julian from his impiety.

impiety

[4.7] Constantius, when his wife Eusebia, whom he dearly loved,
was afflicted with a disease of the womb, found it necessary to recall
Theophilus [the Indian] from exile, for the latter was celebrated for
his divine skill in healing diseases. Accordingly Constantius implored
his pardon for all the injuries which he had inflicted upon him,
and earnestly entreated him to cure his wife. And his request, as
Philostorgius testifies, was not made in vain, for as soon as Theophilus
had laid his healing hands upon the empress, she was set free from her
malady.

[7.3] … During the reign of Julian … the heathen who inhabited
Paneas [Caesarea Philippi in Phoenicia] were excited by an impious
frenzy to pull down this statue [of Christ] from its pediment, and to
drag it through the midst of the streets with ropes fastened round
its feet; afterwards they broke in pieces the rest of the body, while
some persons, indignant at the whole proceeding, secretly obtained
possession of the head, which had become detached from the neck as it
was dragged along, and they preserved it as far as was possible. This
transaction Philostorgius declared that he witnessed with his own eyes.

allowed destruction of Christian property

[7.15] … [A] certain old man, who had long since been discharged
from the Persian service, contrived by fraud and treachery to insnare the
Apostate as he was making war in Persia. And when he had brought the
Romans into the greatest straits by leading them into a pathless desert,

in which a very great portion of the army perished, he gave the enemy, like the prey of a hunter, into the hands of his countrymen. For the Persians rushed upon the Romans, having joined to their forces as allies some Saracenic horsemen who were armed with spears. One of them hurled a spear against Julian, which struck him on the thigh near the groin; and when the spear was drawn out, it was followed by a quantity of dung and blood also. One of the body-guard of the emperor immediately attacked the Saracen who had wounded the king, and cut off his head: while the Romans immediately placed Julian, thus mortally wounded, on a shield, and carried him off into a tent. Many even thought that the fatal blow was struck by Julian's own friends, so sudden and unexpected was it, and so much at a loss were they to know whence it proceeded. But the wretched Julian took up in his hands the blood which flowed from his wounds, and cast it up towards the sun, exclaiming, 'Take thy fill'; and he added curses upon the other gods as villains and destroyers. In his train was a most distinguished physician, one Oribasius, a native of the Lydian city, Sardis. But the wound was far beyond all medical art, and carried Julian off after three days of suffering, after he had enjoyed the dignity of Caesar for five years, and the imperial throne two years and a half from the death of Constantius. Philostorgius in this passage writes, that Julian sprinkled his blood towards the sun and cursed his gods. But most historians write that he used this act as an expression of hatred against our Lord and only true God, Jesus Christ.

57. Socrates: *Church History* (c. 439–43)
Translated A. C. Zenos

[3.1.9] ... And Julian, when he was grown up, pursued his studies at Constantinople, going constantly to the palace, where the schools were, in plain clothes, under the superintendence of the eunuch Mardonius. [10] In grammar Nicocles the Lacaedemonian was his instructor; and Hecebolius the Sophist, who was at that time a Christian, taught him rhetoric ... [12] His proficiency in literature soon became so remarkable, that it began to be said that he was capable of governing the Roman empire; and this popular rumour becoming generally diffused, [13] greatly disquieted the emperor's mind, so that he had him removed from the Great City to Nicomedia, forbidding him at the same time to frequent the school of Libanius ... nevertheless he privately procured his orations ... [16] As he was becoming very expert in the rhetorical art, Maximus the philosopher arrived in Nicomedia ... [18] From him

Julian received, in addition to the principles of philosophy, his own religious sentiments, and a desire to possess the empire. [19] When these things reached the ears of the emperor, Julian, between hope and fear, became very anxious to lull the suspicions which had been awakened, and therefore began to assume the external semblance of what he once was in reality. He was shaved to the very skin, and pretended to live a monastic life: [20] and while in private he pursued his philosophical studies, in public he read the sacred writings of the Christians, and moreover was constituted a reader in the church of Nicomedia.

[3.1.50] The body of Constantius he honored with an imperial funeral, but expelled the eunuchs, barbers and cooks from the palace. The eunuchs he dispensed with, because they were unnecessary in consequence of his wife's decease, as he had resolved not to marry again; the cooks, because he maintained a very simple table; and the barbers, because he said one was sufficient for a great many persons ... he also reduced the majority of the secretaries to their former condition ... [52] The mode of public travelling and conveyance of necessaries he also reformed ... [53] These various retrenchments were highly lauded by some few, but strongly reprobated by all others, as tending to bring the imperial dignity into contempt, by stripping it of those appendages of pomp and magnificence which exercise so powerful an influence over the minds of the vulgar. [54] Not only so, but at night he was accustomed to sit up composing orations which he afterwards delivered in the senate: though in fact he was the first and only emperor since the time of Julius Caesar who made speeches in that assembly.

[3.17.1] ... The emperor having extorted immense sums of money from the Christians, hastening his expedition against the Persians, arrived at Antioch in Syria. [2] There, desiring to show the citizens how much he affected glory, he unduly depressed the prices of commodities; neither taking into account the circumstances of that time, nor reflecting how much the presence of an army inconveniences the population of the provinces, and of necessity lessens the supply of provisions to the cities. [3] The merchants and retailers therefore left off trading, being unable to sustain the losses which the imperial edict entailed upon them. [4] The Antiochians not bearing the insult ... instantly broke forth into invectives against Julian; caricaturing his beard also, which was a very long one, and saying that it ought to be cut off and manufactured into ropes. They added that the bull which was impressed upon his coin, was a symbol of his having desolated the world. [5] For the emperor, being excessively superstitious, was continually sacrificing bulls on the altars of his idols; and had ordered the impression of a bull and altar to be made on his coin.

[3.21.4] Having invested the great city Ctesiphon, he reduced the king of the Persians to such straits that the latter sent repeated embassies to the emperor, offering to surrender a portion of his dominions, on condition of his quitting the country, and putting an end to the war. [5] But Julian was unaffected by these submissions ... [6] Giving credit to the divinations of the philosopher Maximus ... he was deluded into the belief that his exploits would not only equal, but exceed those of Alexander of Macedon; so that he spurned with contempt the entreaties of the Persian monarch. [7] He even supposed in accordance with the teachings of Pythagoras and Plato on 'the transmission of souls', that he himself was Alexander in another body ... [13] ... Some say that a certain Persian hurled the javelin, and then fled; others assert that one of his own men was the author of the deed, which indeed is the best corroborated and most current report. [14] But Callistus, one of his body-guards, who celebrated this emperor's deeds in heroic verse, says in narrating the particulars of this war, that the wound of which he died was inflicted by a demon.

58. Sozomen: *Church History* (c. 443–50)
Translated C. D. Hartranft

[5.2.9] ... After this wonderful preservation, a residence was assigned to the two brothers in a palace called Macellum, situated in Cappadocia; this imperial post was near Mount Argeus, and not far from Caesarea; it contained a magnificent palace and was adorned with baths, gardens, and perennial fountains ... [12] It is said that they undertook to deposit the tomb of St. Mammas the martyr in a large edifice, and to divide the labour between themselves ... [13] The part of the edifice upon which Gallus laboured advanced rapidly and according to wish, but of the section upon which Julian laboured, a part fell into ruin; another was projected upward from the earth; a third immediately on its touching the foundation could not be held upright, but was hurled backward as if some resistant and strong force from beneath were pushing against it. This was universally regarded as a prodigy.

[5.3.5] ... When the inhabitants of Nisibis sent to implore his aid against the Persians ... he refused to assist them because they were wholly Christianised, and would neither reopen their temples, nor resort to the sacred places ... [6] He likewise accused the inhabitants of Constantia in Palestine, of attachment to Christianity, and rendered their city tributary to that of Gaza ... a city addicted to pagan rites.

[5.4.1] About the same time, the emperor erased Caesarea, the large and wealthy metropolis of Cappadocia ... from the catalogue of cities, and even deprived it of the name of Caesarea ... [2] He had long regarded the inhabitants of this city with extreme aversion, because they were zealously attached to Christianity, and had formerly destroyed the temple of the ancestral Apollo and that of Jupiter, the tutelar deity of the city. The temple dedicated to Fortune, the only one remaining in the city, was overturned by the Christians after his accession; and on hearing of the deed, he hated the entire city intensely and could scarce endure it. [3] He also blamed the pagans, who were few in number, but who ought, he said, to have hastened to the temple, and, if necessary, to have suffered cheerfully for Fortune.

[5.5.6] ... It may be concluded from what has been said, that if Julian shed less blood than preceding persecutors of the Church, and that if he devised fewer punishments for the torture of the body, yet that he was severer in other respects; for he appears as inflicting evil upon it in every way, except that he recalled the priests who had been condemned to banishment by the Emperor Constantius; [7] but it is said he issued this order in their behalf, not out of mercy, but that through contention among themselves, the churches might be involved in fraternal strife, and might fail of her own rights, or because he wanted to asperse Constantius.

[5.9.12] ... Julian, far from evincing as much anger against them [the people of Gaza, who had killed the Christians Eusebius, Nestabus and Zeno] as he had manifested against the Alexandrians on the murder of George, did not even write to rebuke the people of Gaza. [13] On the contrary, he deposed the governor of the province, and held him as a suspect, and represented that clemency alone prevented his being put to death. The crime imputed to him was, that of having arrested some of the inhabitants of Gaza, who were reported to have begun the sedition and murders, and of having imprisoned them until judgement could be passed upon them in accordance with the laws. 'For what right had he,' asked the emperor, 'to arrest the citizens merely for retaliating on a few Galileans the injuries that had been inflicted on them and their gods?'

[5.15.13] ... [A]lthough not absolutely persecuted by the emperor, the Christians were obliged to flee from city to city and village to village. [14] My grandfather and many of my ancestors were compelled to flee in this manner. My grandfather was of pagan parentage; and, with his own family and that of Alaphion, had been the first to embrace Christianity in Bethelia, a populous town near Gaza, in which there are

temples highly reverenced by the people of the country, on account of
their antiquity and structural excellence.

[5.19.2] ... [The Antiochenes'] resentment found vent in ridiculing
the length of his beard, and the bulls which he had stamped upon his
coins; and they satirically remarked, that he upset the world in the same
way that his priests, when offering sacrifice, threw down the victims.

[6.2.1] In the document above quoted, Libanius clearly states that the
emperor fell by the hand of a Christian; and this, probably, was the truth
... [2] ... Beyond this I know nothing accurately concerning the men
who committed this murder besides what I have narrated. All men,
however, concur in receiving the account which has been handed down
to us, and which evidences his death to have been the result of Divine
wrath. A proof of this is the divine vision which one of his friends had,
which I will now proceed to relate. [3] He had ... travelled into Persia,
with the intention of joining the emperor. While on the road, he found
himself so far from any habitation that he was obliged, on one night,
to sleep in a church. He saw, during that night, either in a dream or a
vision, all the apostles and prophets assembled together, and com-
plaining of the injuries which the emperor had inflicted on the Church,
and consulting concerning the best measures to be adopted. [4] After
much deliberation and embarrassment two individuals arose in the
midst of the assembly, desired the others to be of good cheer, and left the
company hastily, as if to deprive Julian of imperial power [5] ... [they]
suddenly returned and announced his death to the others. [6] On the
same day a vision was sent to Didymus, an ecclesiastical philosopher,
who dwelt at Alexandria ... [10] ... it is said, when he [Julian] was
wounded, he took some of the blood that flowed from the wound, and
threw it up into the air, as if he had seen Jesus Christ appearing, and
intended to throw it at him, in order to reproach him with his slaughter.
[11] Others say that he was angry with the sun because it had favoured
the Persians ... and that it was to express his indignation against this
luminary that he took blood in his hand and flung it upwards in the air.

59. Theodoret of Cyrrhus: *Church History* (late 440s)
Translated B. Jackson (it should be noted that the chapter divisions
in the translation differ from those in editions of the text)

[3.3] ... To tell all the deeds dared by the slaves of idolatrous deceit at
that time would require a history of these crimes alone, but out of the
vast numbers of them I shall select a few instances. At Askalon and at
Gaza, cities of Palestine, men of priestly rank and women who had lived

all their lives in virginity were disembowelled, filled with barley, and given for food to swine. At Sebaste, which belongs to the same people, the coffin of John the Baptist was opened, his bones burnt, and the ashes scattered abroad. Who too could tell without a tear the vile deed done in Phoenicia [at Heliopolis] … At the neighbouring city of Emesa they dedicated to Dionysus … the newly erected church, and set up in it his ridiculous androgynous image. At Dorystolum, a famous city of Thrace, the victorious athlete Aemilianus was thrown upon a flaming pyre, by Capitolinus, governor of all Thrace. To relate the tragic fate of Marcus, however, bishop of Arethusa, with true dramatic dignity, would require the eloquence of an Aeschylus or a Sophocles.

[3.8] … Of the great church [in Antioch] which Constantine had built he nailed up the doors and declared it closed to the worshippers wont to assemble there. At this time it was in possession of the Arians. In company with Julianus the prefect of the East, Felix the imperial treasurer, and Elpidius, who had charge of the emperor's private purse and property … made their way into the sacred edifice. Both Felix and Elpidius, it is said, were Christians, but to please the impious emperor apostatised from the true religion. Julianus committed an act of gross indecency on the Holy Table and, when Euzoius [the bishop] endeavoured to prevent him, gave him a blow on the face, and told him, so the story goes, that it is the fate of the fortunes of the Christians to have no protection from the gods. But Felix, as he gazed upon the magnificence of the sacred vessels, furnished with splendour by the munificence of Constantine and Constantius, 'Behold,' said he, 'with what vessels Mary's son is served.' But it was not long before they paid the penalty of these deeds of mad and impious daring.

[3.11] Now Julian … began to arm himself against true religion, wearing indeed a mask of moderation, but all the while preparing gins and traps which caught all who were deceived by them in the destruction of iniquity. He began by polluting with foul sacrifices the wells in the city and in Daphne, that every man who used the fountain might be partaker of abomination. Then he thoroughly polluted the things exposed in the Forum, for bread and meat and fruit and vegetables and every kind of food were aspersed … Two officers in the army, who were shield bearers in the imperial suite, at a certain banquet lamented in somewhat warm language the abomination of what was being done … One of the guests gave information of this, and the emperor arrested these right worthy men and endeavoured to ascertain by questioning them what was the language they had used. They accepted the imperial enquiry as an opportunity for open speech, and with noble enthusiasm replied ⌐Sir we were brought up in true religion; we were obedient to most excellent laws, the laws of Constantine and of his sons; now we see the world full of pollution, meats and drinks alike defiled with abominable sacrifices, and we lament. We bewail these things at home, and now before thy face we express our grief, for this is the one thing in thy reign which we take ill.' No sooner did he whom sympathetic courtiers called most mild and most philosophic hear these words than he took off his mask of moderation, and exposed the countenance of impiety. He ordered cruel and painful scourgings to be inflicted on them and deprived them of their lives … He pretended indeed that punishment was inflicted upon them not for the true religion … but because of their insolence, for he gave out that he had punished them for insulting the emperor ⌐ … The name of one was Juventinus; of the other Maximinus. The city of Antioch honoured them as defenders of true religion, and deposited them in a magnificent tomb, and up to this day they are honoured by a yearly festival.

[3.15] … He … now armed the Jews too against the believers in Christ. He began by enquiring of some whom he got together why, though their law imposed on them the duty of sacrifices, they offered none. On their reply that their worship was limited to one particular spot, this enemy of God immediately gave directions for the re-erection of the destroyed temple, supposing in his vanity that he could falsify the prediction of the Lord, of which, in reality, he exhibited the truth.

[3.19] A man who in the body imitated the lives of the bodiless, namely Julianus, surnamed in Syrian Sabbas, whose life I have written in my 'Religious History', continued all the more zealously to offer his prayers to the God of all, when he heard of the impious tyrant's threats. On the very day on which Julian was slain, he heard of the event while at his prayers, although the Monastery was distant more than twenty stages from the army. It is related that while he was invoking the Lord with loud cries and supplicating his merciful Master, he suddenly checked his tears, broke into an ecstasy of delight, while his countenance was lighted up and thus signified the joy that possessed his soul.

[3.20] … The best generals are wont to fill their troops with enthusiasm, and, if they see them growing discouraged, to cheer them and raise their hopes; but Julian by burning the bridge of retreat cut off all good hope. A further proof of his incompetence was his failure to fulfil the duty of foraging in all directions and providing his troops with supplies … The name of the man who dealt that righteous stroke no one knows to this day. Some say that he was wounded by an invisible being, others by one of the Nomads who were called Ishmaelites;

others by a trooper who could not endure the pains of famine in the
wilderness. But whether it were man or angel who plied the steel,
without doubt the doer of the deed was the minister of the will of God.

60. Zosimus: *New History* (late fifth/early sixth century)
Translated R. T. Ridley

[2.29.2] Without any consideration for natural law he killed his son
Crispus ... on suspicion of having had intercourse with his step-
mother, Fausta. And when Constantine's mother, Helena, was saddened
by this atrocity and was inconsolable at the young man's death,
Constantine as if to comfort her, applied a remedy worse than the
disease: he ordered a bath to be over-heated, and shut Fausta up in
it until she was dead. [3] Since he was himself aware of his guilt and of
his disregard for oaths as well, he approached the priests seeking
absolution, but they said that there was no kind of purge known which
could absolve him of such impieties. A certain Egyptian, who had come
from Spain to Rome and was intimate with the ladies of the court, met
Constantine and assured him that the Christian religion was able to
absolve him from guilt and that it promised every wicked man who was
converted to it immediate release from all sin. [4] Constantine readily
believed what he was told and, abandoning his ancestral religion,
embraced the one which the Egyptian offered him.

[2.40.1] After this division of the empire, Constantius, as if purposely
anxious not to fall short of his father in impiety, decided to prove his
manhood to everyone by beginning at home with his relatives' blood.
[2] First he managed to have his uncle, Constantius, murdered by
the soldiers, then he devised a similar plot for Delmatius Caesar
and Optatus ... [3] Also put to death at that time was Ablabius, the
praetorian prefect ... Proceeding as it were against all his relatives, he
also killed Hannibalianus, urging the soldiers to cry out that they would
suffer no other rulers but Constantine's sons.

[3.1.1] After treating Gallus Caesar in this way, Constantius left
Pannonia for Italy. Everywhere he saw the Roman empire being dis-
membered by barbarian incursions: the Franks, Alamanni and Saxons
had already taken forty cities on the Rhine and left them in ruins
by carrying off countless numbers of their inhabitants and untold
spoils; the Quadi and Sarmatians had very boldly overrun Pannonia
and Upper Moesia; and the Persians were continually harassing the East
whereas previously they had been inactive for fear of being attacked by
Gallus Caesar. In the face of all this he was at a loss what to do, because

although he did not consider himself able to cope with these troubles alone, yet he was not confident enough to elect a colleague because of his excessive love of power, and his suspicion of everyone made him think he had no friends at all. [2] While he was overcome by utter helplessness and the empire was in the gravest danger, Eusebia, his wife, who was extremely well educated and wiser than women usually are, suggested that he appoint Julian, half-brother of Gallus and grandson of that Constantius [I] who was made Caesar by Diocletian, as Caesar in the provinces beyond the Alps. As Eusebia knew that the emperor Constantius suspected all his relatives, she brought him round by saying [3] that 'he is a young man of simple character, who has spent his whole life as a student, and his complete lack of experience in worldly matters will make him more suitable than anyone else; for either he will be lucky and his successes will be ascribed to the emperor, or he will make a mistake and get killed and Constantius will be free of any imperial successors.' [3.2.1] After patiently listening to her, Constantius sent for Julian from Athens, where he was a pupil of the philosophers and excelled his teachers in every kind of learning. When he came in answer to this summons from Greece to Italy, Constantius declared him Caesar, married his sister, Helena, to him, and sent him to the provinces beyond the Alps. [2] Being distrustful by nature and not at all confident of Julian's affection for himself or his trustworthiness, he sent Marcellus and Salustius with him and entrusted the government there to them instead of Julian.

[3.5.3] … Seeing the soldiers' affection for him on account of the simplicity of his private life, his courage in war, and his self-control with regard to wealth, and other virtues in which he excelled virtually all his contemporaries, Constantius was smitten with envy at Julian's achievements. Thinking that the shrewdness of Salustius … was the cause of Julian's considerable reputation in military and administrative affairs, he sent for him on the pretext of making him Prefect of the East. [4] And although Julian readily let him go, resolving to obey Constantius' every order, everything under his care prospered almost daily: the army's strength and discipline improved together, and the cities enjoyed the fruits of peace.

[3.8.3] When now the East seemed quiet and everyone was talking about Caesar's achievements, Constantius became terribly depressed with jealousy, and stung by the prosperity in Gaul and Spain, he invented excuses gradually and imperceptibly to reduce Julian's forces and deprive him of his rank. So he sent him an order to despatch two legions of the soldiers in Gaul, ostensibly because he needed their help.

[4] Julian, oblivious of his plan and anxious not to antagonise him, immediately obeyed ... Then Constantius demanded that the Caesar send more legions, and when this request was granted, not long after requisitioned four troops of cavalry, which Caesar signalled to prepare to depart immediately. [3.9.1] Julian was at this time staying at Parisium ... The soldiers, ready to march, were supping late at night near the imperial quarters. They were totally unaware of the plot against the Caesar until certain military tribunes discovered the truth about the designs against him and unobtrusively distributed anonymous notes among the troops ... [2] When some of the soldiers read the notes and informed the rest of what was happening, all were inflamed with rage. Thereupon they rose from their drinking in uproar, and going to the imperial quarters with the cups still in their hands, they burst open the doors without ceremony and led Caesar forth. Raising him aloft on a shield they declared him Imperator Augustus and forced a crown onto his head.

[3.10.3] ... When not long after [Julian had reached Sirmium] the army that had followed him from Gaul arrived, he wrote to the Senate and armies in Italy that the cities would be safe now that he was emperor. [4] ... He also wrote to the Athenians, Lacedaemonians and Corinthians, explaining the reasons for his coming.

[3.11.2] ... Accepting what the gods had bestowed on him, Julian advanced on his journey. When he came to Byzantium, everyone received him with joyful acclamations, calling him fellow citizen and darling, since he was born and reared in this city ... [3] He attended to civil and military matters: he allowed the city to have a senate just as at Rome; built a large harbour as a protection for ships exposed to the south wind, and a curved stoa leading to the harbour; and established a library in the imperial stoa, where he deposited all his books. Then ... he prepared for the Persian war ... he went on to Antioch.

[3.26.1] The next day the emperor very confidently sent his army across the river Tigris, and the third day after the battle he himself crossed with his guard. Coming to a place which the Persians called Abuzathia, he stayed there five days. [2] Reviewing the march ahead, he decided, rather than continuing to send his army along the river, to go inland, since there was now no reason for them to rely on their ships. With these considerations in mind, he informed the army of his plan and bade them burn the fleet, [3] which they did, except eighteen Roman ships and four Persian, which were carried along on wagons to be used as the need arose.

[3.28.3] ... At this juncture, the Persian army appeared and joined battle, but the Romans were much superior and killed many Persians. [4] A little before noon the next day, after organising themselves into a large force, the Persians unexpectedly attacked the rear of the Roman army. The Romans, though disorganised and confused by the suddenness of the attack, fought back vigorously, with the emperor, as usual, going about encouraging the troops. [3.29.1] During the hand to hand engagement, he at one moment visited the tribunes and centurions, at another mixed with the common soldiers. And at the very height of the battle he was wounded by a sword, and being laid on his shield was hurried to his tent, where he lasted till midnight. At the time of his death, he had almost entirely destroyed the Persian empire.

[3.34.3] Jovian marched quickly through the cities, which were so overcome with grief and gloom that they could not bring themselves to offer any cheer of pleasure, contrary to their usual practice. Accompanying the emperor to Antioch was the imperial guard, while the whole army attended Julian's body, which was taken to Cilicia and buried in a royal tomb in a suburb of Tarsus. And this inscription was written on the tomb:

> 'Having left the swift-flowing Tigris, Julian lies here,
> both a noble king and a valiant spearman.'

[4.37.1] Such was the end of Gratian's reign. Maximus, believing his power secure, sent an embassy to Theodosius, not to ask pardon for what he had done to Gratian, but making arrogant demands. [2] The man sent for this purpose was the imperial chamberlain, who was not a eunuch but an old man who had attended Maximus since his youth. Maximus would not allow eunuchs to be in charge of his court.

61. Malalas: *Chronicle* (c. 565)
Translated E. Jeffreys, M. Jeffreys and R. Scott et al.

[13.19] … He made a speech about the Antiochenes, attacking them as rebels. He displayed the speech he had delivered against them outside the palace in the city on what is known as Tetrapylon of the Elephants, near the Regia.

[13.21] As the emperor Julian was marching out against Sapor, emperor of the Persians, he arrived at Hierapolis. He sent and had boats built at Samosata, a city in Euphratesia, some made of wood and some made of skins, as the very learned chronicler Magnus of Carrhae, who accompanied the emperor Julian, wrote … The emperor Julian was victorious and camped on the plain of the city of Ktesiphon, desiring with the support of his senate to go on as far as Babylon and take control of affairs there. [22] … Deceived by the oaths which they [Persian 'deserters'] swore, the emperor Julian followed them with his army … [23] About the second hour of that day the emperor Julian, while moving among the army and urging them not to behave in an undisciplined way, was mysteriously wounded. He went into his tent and died during the night, as Magnus, whom we referred to above, stated. But the Cappadocian chronicler Eutychianos, a soldier and *vicarius* of his *numerus*, the Primoarmeniaci, also took part in the war himself, and he wrote that the emperor Julian … occupied the country as far as the city known as Ktesiphon … Julian wanted to set off the next day with the senate and army as far as Babylon, and to capture it during the night. While he slept, he saw in a dream a full-grown man wearing a cuirass approaching him in his tent in a city known as Asia near the city of Ktesiphon; the man struck him with a spear. The emperor was frightened and woke up with a cry. The eunuch *cubicularii* and *spatharii* and the soldiers guarding the tent got up and went in to him with imperial lamps. The emperor Julian, observing that he had been fatally wounded in the armpit, asked them, 'What is the name of the town where my tent is?' They told him that it was called Asia. Immediately he cried out, 'O Helios, you have destroyed Julian'. And, bleeding profusely, he breathed his last at the fifth hour of the night … [25] That same night Basil, the most holy bishop of Caesarea in Cappadocia, saw in a dream the heavens opened and the Saviour Christ seated on a throne and saying loudly, 'Mercurius, go and kill the emperor Julian, who is against the Christians.' St Mercurius, standing before the Lord, wore a gleaming iron breast-plate. Hearing the command, he disappeared, and then he re-appeared, standing before the Lord, and cried out, 'The emperor Julian has been fatally wounded and has died, as you commanded, Lord.'

62. Zonaras: *Chronicle* (twelfth century)
Translated from the Greek

[13.10.2–3] It is said that when his mother was pregnant Julian appeared to her in a dream and she thought she gave birth to Achilles. And waking up she related the dream to her husband, and gave birth to her son with hardly any labour pains, before she realised that she was going to give birth.

[13.12.17–23] And on becoming emperor and securing the realm for himself he at once broke out into blatant paganism. For earlier, as was related, he foreswore Christianity, but he certainly did not dare to let the birth of the impiety break out into the open. For it is said that whilst nurturing a desire for the empire and concealing this as under ashes in his soul he approached seers and wizards, asking if he was going to obtain power, and he was corrupted by them and was converted to paganism. And on obtaining power by the incomprehensible judgements of God he created many martyrs; and so he raved against the Christians, even forbidding them from partaking of Hellenic learning, saying that it was not right that those who both called and slandered this as myth should profit from it and through it be armed against it. So when the children of those bearing the name of Christ were prevented from approaching the poets, Apollinarios is said to have hastened to the paraphrase of the *Book of Psalms* and Gregory, great in theology, to the making of verses, so that the youths learning these instead of the Hellenic culture should both be Hellenised in tongue and instructed in the metres.

[13.13.19–25] And it is said that when a violent blast then blew, a dense mist spread over the air there; for the throngs of the companies stirred up a great dust cloud, so that they did not know where they were or what to do; and it is unknown from where the spear which struck him was thrown, whether from an enemy or from one of his men or from a more divine power; for these are also credited. Wherefore they say that he filled the hollow of his hand with blood flowing from the wound and scattering this upon the air he said 'Have you fill, Nazarene.' And after living so impiously he disgorged his soul violently, having ruled for two years. And the army after carrying away his body to Tarsus in Cilicia entombed it in a suburb of the city; and on his tomb this inscription was inscribed:

> By the silvery Kydnos far from the streams of the Euphrates
> out of the land of Persia after an unaccomplished task
> moving his army Julian acquired this grave,
> both a good emperor and a mighty warrior.

And later it was brought back to the Queen of Cities.

63. Medallion of Julian as Caesar of Constantius II
(Kent 1981: 298, Nr. 464)

64. Coin of Julian as Augustus before the death of Constantius II
(Kent 1981: 226, Nr. 284)

65. Julian's Bull Coinage
(Kent 1981: 462, Nr. 162)

66. Statue of Julian, Louvre

67.   Edward Armitage: *Julian the Apostate Presiding at a Conference of Sectarians* (1874), Walker Art Gallery

Chronology

331/332	Julian born in Constantinople
22 May 337	Death of Constantine the Great
338/339	Mardonius becomes Julian's tutor
c. 342–348(?)	Julian and Gallus at Macellum in Cappadocia
350	Death of Constans and usurpation of Magnentius
c. 351	Conversion of Julian
March 351	Gallus proclaimed Caesar
September 351	Magnentius defeated at the battle of Mursa
354	Execution of Gallus; Julian summoned to Milan
355	Usurpation of Silvanus
Summer 355	Julian in Athens
6 November 355	Julian proclaimed Caesar
1 December 355	Julian despatched to Gaul
356	Julian recovers Cologne
April 357	Constantius II visits Rome
August 357	Battle of Strasbourg
October 359	Fall of Amida to the Persians
359/360	Death of Eusebia
February 360	Julian proclaimed Augustus at Paris
Spring 360	Death of Helena
October 360	Julian celebrates his *quinquennalia* at Vienne
6 January 361	Julian celebrates the Feast of Epiphany at Vienne
May 361	Julian at Sirmium
June 361	Julian at Naissus
3 November 361	Constantius II dies of a fever at Mopsucrenae in Cilicia
11 December 361	Julian enters Constantinople

17 June 362	Julian issues edict against Christian teachers
18 July 362	Julian enters Antioch
22 October 362	The temple of Apollo at Daphne burns down
January 363	Julian posts his *Misopogon*
5 March 363	Julian departs Antioch for Persia
18 March 363	Julian at Carrhae
27 March 363	Julian at Callinicum
4 April 363	Julian passes Zaitha
26 June 363	Death of Julian

Further Reading

Part I Debates

Introduction

The subject of Julian is a perennial favourite with historians, and thus there is no shortage of books about his life and reign. Key examples are Bidez (1930), Browning (1975) and Bowersock (1978), and more recently there is Murdoch (2003). A useful short account is supplied by Hunt (1998a). Some historians eschew the more traditional narrative approach to Julian, and focus instead on his intellectual and ideological profile. Examples of this treatment of Julian are provided by Athanassiadi (1992) and Renucci (2000), and a particularly rewarding case is that of Smith (1995), which challenged many of the accepted truths that had developed concerning the emperor. Given the increasing popularity of Late Antiquity as a field of study, a number of introductions and guides to the period are freely available. A useful example is Cameron (1993). For more detailed treatment see the *Cambridge Ancient History* vols 12 and 13 (Bowman, Garnsey and Cameron 2005; Cameron and Garnsey 1998). The groundbreaking study of Jones (1964) is still valuable.

The rich seam of sources relating to Julian has produced a wealth of study, though some authors have received more attention than others. Undoubtedly the most studied historian of late antiquity is Ammianus Marcellinus (see especially Thompson 1947; Matthews 1989; den Boeft, den Hengst and Teitler 1992; Barnes 1998; Drijvers and Hunt 1999). A good introduction to Eunapius and his lost history is Blockley (1981: 1–26) (and on his *Lives of the Sophists* see the introduction to Wright's translation (1921: 319–41) and Penella 1990: esp. 1–38). As is well known, Zosimus drew upon Eunapius' lost history for his *New History*, on which see Ridley (1982) and also Paschoud (1979–2000). For Malalas see Jeffreys, Jeffreys and Scott (1986: esp. xi–xxiii), and for Zonaras see DiMaio (esp. 1977). The more summary historians have also received study. For Sextus Aurelius Victor and Eutropius see the introductions of Bird's translations (1993, 1994); for Festus see Eadie (1967: esp. 1–20); on Jerome's *Chronicon* see for example Donalson (1996: 1–38); and for Orosius see Arnaud-Lindet (1990–1: vol. 1, ix–cxix). Of the church historians Socrates has received particular attention (see for example Urbainczyk 1997), but see also

Amidon (1997: vii–xix) on Rufinus, and in general see Penella (1993) and Trompf (2000: esp. 213–52). Of the more contemporary sources for Julian, his own works are of especial interest. These are discussed in the general studies of his life and reign, and Smith (1995) is particularly helpful. More focused studies also exist, such as treatments of his *The Caesars* (e.g. Baldwin 1978; Bowersock 1982) and the *Misopogon* (e.g. Gleason 1986). The panegyric of Claudius Mamertinus is discussed in the invaluable volume on Julian in the Liverpool University Press series Translated Texts for Historians (Lieu 1989: esp. 3–12; but see also Blockley 1972b, and Nixon and Rodgers 1994: esp. 386–92). Also introduced in the TTH volume are Ephrem's hymns against Julian (Lieu 1989: 89–104; but see also Griffith 1987) and John Chrysostom's *Homily on St Babylas* (Lieu 1989: 41–58). For Libanius see especially Norman's prefatory chapters to his volume on the Julianic orations (1969: ix–lx), whilst for Gregory of Nazianzus see Bernardi's introduction to his edition and French translation of the orations against Julian (1983: 11–83) (and for Cyril of Alexandria's refutation of Julian see Wilken 1999). For discussion of Salutius' pagan tract see the chapters accompanying Nock's edition and translation (1926: xvii–cxxiii). Finally, Braun and Richer (1978–81) provide a useful collection of analyses of treatments of Julian across history.

Chapter 1: Family

Constantine the Great is even more written about than his nephew Julian. Amongst the huge range of literature on him a key treatment is Barnes (1981). Unfortunately his father Constantius I is rather more neglected, despite his crucial role in establishing the imperial credentials of the family. Constantius II is also somewhat overlooked, in spite of maintaining the legacy of his father (though see for instance Blockley 1972a, 1980 and 1989, and Barnes 1993). He also tends to have a negative reputation, since he was reviled by supporters of Julian as well as by Nicene Christians. On the image of Constantius see for instance Blockley (1980), Teitler (1992), Tougher (1999) and Whitby (1999). For the role of Constantius' wife Eusebia in the life of Julian, and interpretations of her actions, see for instance Aujoulat (1983) and Tougher (1998a and 1998b). On empresses in general in the later Roman and early Byzantine empire see James (2001).

Chapter 2: Conversion

Particular attention is devoted to Julian's educational and religious development in Athanassiadi (1992), Smith (1995) and Renucci (2000). Also extremely useful on Julian's intellectual life is Bouffartigue (1992). On Julian's relationship with Themistius see especially Brauch (1993b), who argues against the traditional view that there was a breakdown in relations between the two men when Julian became emperor. For Neoplatonism see for instance Wallis (1995) and Smith (2004), and on theurgy see especially Dodds (1947) and Shaw (1985).

Chapter 3: Gaul

On the Germans see in general Todd (1992, 1998: esp. 461–71). For a challenge to the accepted truth of the major German threat on the Rhine frontier in the middle decades of the fourth century see Drinkwater (1996). A detailed examination of the Rhine frontier during the reigns of the sons of Constantine would be welcome. The treatment of Julian's authority and military activities in Gaul by Bowersock (1978: 33–45) is particularly rewarding (though see also Blockley 1972a). On Julian's imperial panegyrics see especially Athanassiadi (1992: esp. 61–6), Curta (1995) and Tougher (1998a).The question of whether Julian set out to usurp the position of Augustus has much occupied historians: see for example Müller-Seidel (1955), Drinkwater (1983: 370–83), Matthews (1989: 93–9) and Buck (1993). For Oribasius see for instance Baldwin (1975).

Chapter 4: Imperial Style and Reform

On imperial style in late antiquity see for example MacCormack (1981). On the question of whether Julian was influenced by the model of Marcus Aurelius see Hunt (1995). On Julian the reformer see especially Kolb (1998), which focuses on the *cursus publicus* but has more general points to make about the extent to which the emperor was innovatory and had a programme of reform. For eunuchs at the later Roman court see in particular Hopkins (1963 and 1978: 172–96), but also Cameron (1965), Stevenson (1995) and Tougher (1999). For Julian in Antioch see for example Gleason (1986).

Chapter 5: Religion

On paganism and Christianity in late antiquity see for instance the useful sourcebook of Lee (2000). On the place of Mithras in Julian's religious identity and ambitions see especially Athanassiadi (1992) and Smith (1995), and on the question of Julian's pagan 'church' see Nicholson (1994). On Julian and sacrifice see for example Bradbury (1995). On the bull coinage and its meaning there is a large literature: see for instance Kent (1954), Gilliard (1964), Vanderspoel (1998), Woods (2000) and Tougher (2004). On the image of Julian as an undeclared persecutor of Christians see for example Penella (1993). On the teaching edict see especially Banchich (1993). On Julian and the rebuilding of the Temple of Jerusalem see for example Blanchetière (1980) and Drijvers (1992).

Chapter 6: Persia

For Rome and Sasanid Persia see for example Dodgeon and Lieu (1991) and Blockley (1992). For the dealings of Constantius II with Persia see especially Warmington (1977) and Blockley (1989). On the question of the influence of the model of Alexander the Great on Julian see for instance Baynes (1912), Athanassiadi (1992: esp. 193 and 224–5) and Lane Fox (1997). On the objectives and course of Julian's Persian campaign see for example Austin (1972), Ridley (1973), Kaegi (1981), Fornara (1991) and Seager (1997).

Part II Documents

Translations of texts are available as follows:

Ammianus Marcellinus: *Res Gestae* – Rolfe (3 vols 1950–2 rev. ed.); abridged version, Hamilton (1986)

Claudius Mamertinus: *Speech of Thanks to Julian* – Lieu (1989: 13–38); Nixon and Rodgers (1994: 393–436)

Ephrem: *Hymns against Julian* – Lieu (1989: 105–28)

Epitome de Caesaribus – Canisius College Translated Texts series, www.roman-emperors.org/epitome.htm

Eunapius: *History* (fragments) – Blockley (1983: 2–150)

Eunapius: *Lives of the Sophists* – Wright (1921: 343–565)

Eutropius: *Breviarium* – Bird (1993)

Festus: *Breviarium* – Canisius College Translated Texts series, www.roman-emperors.org/festus.htm

Gregory of Nazianzus: *Against Julian* 1 and 2 – King (1888)

Jerome: *Chronicon* – Donalson (1996); www.tertullian.org/fathers/

John Chrysostom: *Homily on St Babylas* – partial translation Lieu (1989: 59–79)

Julian: works – Wright (3 vols 1913–23); French translation Bidez, Rochefort and Lacombrade (4 vols 1924–65)

Libanius: selected works – Norman (1969) and (2 vols 1992)

Malalas: *Chronicle* – Jeffreys, Jeffreys and Scott (1986)

Orosius: *History against the Pagans* – French translation Arnaud-Lindet (3 vols 1990–1)

Philostorgius: *Church History* (summary of Photius) – Walford (1855: 429–528)

Rufinus: *Church History* – partial translation Amidon (1997)

Salutius: *Concerning the Gods and the Universe* – Nock (1926)

Sextus Aurelius Victor: *De Caesaribus* – Bird (1994)

Socrates: *Church History* – Zenos (1890: 1–178)

Sozomen: *Church History* – Hartranft (1890: 236–427)

Theodoret: *Church History* – Jackson (1892: 33–159)

Theodosian Code – Pharr (1952)

Zonaras: *Chronicle* – Translation of Books 12–13 DiMaio (1977: 1–60); ed. Pinder and Büttner-Wobst (3 vols 1841–97)

Zosimus: *New History* – Ridley (1982)

Essay Questions and Exercise Topics

Family

Questions

1. What was the status of the descendants of Constantius I and Theodora during the reign of Constantine the Great? Why were so many of them killed following the death of Constantine?
2. Does Constantius II deserve his negative reputation?
3. Why did the empress Eusebia assist Julian in the 350s?

Topics

4. Analyse how Julian describes the emperors Claudius Gothicus, Constantius I and Constantine the Great in his writings. What opinions does he hold about these emperors? Account for these views.
5. Identify the cases of intermarriage within the family of Constantius I. How prevalent was intermarriage in the family? Why was it valued?

Education and Conversion

Questions

6. To what extent can the course of Julian's early education be reconstructed?
7. Why did Julian convert to paganism?
8. How central was Mithraism in Julian's religious identity?

Topics

9. What chronological problems confront the historian of the early life of Julian? Why do these problems arise? What solutions do you favour?
10. Identify the key relationships that Julian established with individuals in the field of education, prior to his becoming Caesar in 355. What was the nature of these relationships? How did they develop, if at all, in his later life?

Gaul

Questions

11. Has the poor condition of Gaul prior to Julian's arrival as Caesar been exaggerated by both ancient and modern historians?
12. How much authority did Julian possess during his time as Caesar in Gaul?
13. Did Julian plot to usurp imperial power?

Topics

14. Read Menander Rhetor's advice on composing a *basilikos logos*. To what extent does Julian's first panegyric on Constantius II follow this advice? How should one understand the divergences that exist? Do you agree that the panegyric had a diplomatic purpose?
15. Make a list of the campaigns Julian conducted during his Caesarship in Gaul. Locate these campaigns on a map. Do the campaigns have clear strategic objectives?

Imperial Style and Reform

Questions

16. How did Julian's imperial style differ from those of his predecessors? Was this difference Julian's greatest failing rather than his greatest virtue?
17. Did Julian have a clear programme of reform?
18. To what extent was EITHER Alexander the Great OR Marcus Aurelius a model for Julian?

Topics

19. Analyse the career and activities of the eunuch Eusebius, grand chamberlain of Constantius II. Why did eunuchs come to prominence at the imperial court in the later Roman period? To what extent, and why, did Julian seek to diminish their power?
20. Consider the iconography of Julian's bull coinage. What meanings have been attributed to it, and why? Do you think a definite meaning can be established?

Religion

Questions

21. To what extent was Julian's paganism shaped by Christianity?
22. What was the purpose of Julian's teaching edict?
23. Was Julian's restoration of paganism bound to fail?

Topics

24. Read the sources relating to Julian's involvement in the rebuilding of the Temple of Jerusalem. What reasons are given for the emperor's interest in

the project and for its lack of completion? How valid do you think these reasons are?

25. Make a list of the incidents of Christians being attacked and/or killed by pagans during the reign of Julian. How authentic do you think the accounts of these incidents are? Do they become elaborated over time?

Persia

Questions

26. Was the Persian expedition a misguided undertaking?
27. What were the objectives of Julian's Persian expedition?
28. How good a soldier was Julian? (Answer with reference to his entire military career.)

Topics

29. Attempt to map the course of Julian's Persian expedition after the departure from Ctesiphon. What problems arise in attempting this exercise, and why? What do you think Julian's objective was on this leg of the expedition?
30. Analyse the different accounts of the death of Julian. What variants are there, and how can one account for them?

General Questions

31. 'Of the great figures of antiquity few are so abundantly documented … as the emperor Julian' (Bowersock). Why is Julian so abundantly documented? What particular problems does the nature of this evidence present?
32. Assess the historical significance of Julian and his reign.
33. To what extent is it possible to understand Julian psychologically from his writings?
34. Why does Julian continue to be a figure of such interest for historians?
35. Select a work (or works) of art inspired by Julian (e.g. Ibsen's play; the painting of Armitage; the poems of Cavafy; Gore Vidal's novel) and analyse the depiction of him. Account for the depiction given. Why do you think the artist was attracted to Julian as a subject?

Bibliography

Amidon, P. R. (1997), *The 'Church History' of Rufinus of Aquileia, Books 10 and 11*, New York: Oxford University Press.

Arnaud-Lindet, M.-P. (1990–1), *Orose Histoires (Contres les Païens)*, 3 vols, Paris: Les Belles Lettres.

Athanassiadi, P. (1992), *Julian: An Intellectual Biography*, London and New York: Routledge; originally published in 1981 as *Julian and Hellenism*, Oxford: Oxford University Press.

Aujoulat, N. (1983), 'Eusébie, Hélène et Julien', *Byz* 53, 78–103 and 421–52.

Austin, N. J. E. (1972), 'Julian at Ctesiphon: a fresh look at Ammianus' account', *Athenaeum* 50, 301–309.

Baldwin, B. (1975), 'The career of Oribasius', *AClass* 18, 85–97.

Baldwin, B. (1978), 'The *Caesares* of Julian', *Klio* 60, 449–66.

Banchich, T. M. (1993), 'Julian's school laws: *Cod. Theod.* 13.3.5 and *Ep.* 42', *AncW* 24, 5–14.

Barnes, T. D. (1976), 'Imperial campaigns, A.D. 285–311', *Phoenix* 30, 174–93.

Barnes, T. D. (1981), *Constantine and Eusebius*, Cambridge, MA: Harvard University Press.

Barnes, T. D. (1987), 'Himerius and the fourth century', *ClPhil* 82, 206–25.

Barnes, T. D. (1993), *Athanasius and Constantius: Theology and Politics in the Constantinian Empire*, Cambridge, MA, and London: Harvard University Press.

Barnes, T. D. (1998), *Ammianus Marcellinus and the Representation of Historical Reality*, Ithaca and London: Cornell University Press.

Baynes, N. H. (1912), 'Julian the Apostate and Alexander the Great', *EHR* 27, 759–60, reprinted in *Byzantine Studies and Other Essays* (1955), London: The Athlone Press, 326–7.

Bernardi, J. (1983), *Grégoire de Nazianze, Discours 4–5: Contre Julien*, Paris: Les Éditions du Cerf.

Bidez, J. (1930), *La Vie de l'empereur Julien*, Paris: Les Belles Lettres.

Bidez, J., Rochefort, G., and Lacombrade, C. (1924–65), *L'Empereur Julien: Oeuvres complètes*, 4 vols, Paris: Les Belles Lettres.

Bird, H. W. (1993), *Eutropius: Breviarium*, Liverpool: Liverpool University Press.

Bird, H. W. (1994), *Aurelius Victor: De Caesaribus*, Liverpool: Liverpool University Press.

Blanchetière, F. (1980), 'Julien philhellène, philosémite, antichrétien: l'affaire du Temple de Jerusalem (363)', *Journal of Jewish Studies* 31, 61–81.

Blockley, R. C. (1972a), 'Constantius Gallus and Julian as Caesars of Constantius II', *Latomus* 31, 433–68.

Blockley, R. C. (1972b), 'The panegyric of Claudius Mamertinus on the emperor Julian', *AJPh* 93, 437–50.

Blockley, R. C. (1977), 'Ammianus Marcellinus on the Battle of Strasburg: art and analysis in the *History*', *Phoenix* 31, 218–31.

Blockley, R. C. (1980), 'Constantius II and his generals', in C. Deroux (ed.), *Studies in Latin Literature and Roman History*, vol. 2, Brussels: Latomus, pp. 467–86.

Blockley, R. C. (1981), *The Fragmentary Classicising Historians of the Later Roman Empire: Eunapius, Olympiodorus, Priscus and Malchus*, Liverpool: Francis Cairns.

Blockley, R. C. (1983), *The Fragmentary Classicising Historians of the Later Roman Empire: Eunapius, Olympiodorus, Priscus and Malchus*, vol. 2, *Text, Translation and Historiographical Notes*, Liverpool: Francis Cairns.

Blockley, R. C. (1989), 'Constantius II and Persia', in C. Deroux (ed.), *Studies in Latin Literature and Roman History*, vol. 5, Brussels: Latomus, pp. 465–90.

Blockley, R. C. (1992), *East Roman Foreign Policy: Formation and Conduct from Diocletian to Anastasius*, Leeds: Francis Cairns.

Bouffartigue, J. (1992), *L'Empereur Julien et la culture de son temps*, Paris: Institut d'Études Augustiniennes.

Bowder, D. (1978), *The Age of Constantine and Julian*, London: Paul Elek.

Bowersock, G. W. (1978), *Julian the Apostate*, London: Duckworth.

Bowersock, G. W. (1981), 'The Julian poems of C. P. Cavafy', *BMGS* 7, 89–104.

Bowersock, G. W. (1982), 'Emperor Julian on his predecessors', *YCls* 27, 159–72.

Bowman, A. K., Garnsey, P., and Cameron, Averil (eds) (2005), *Cambridge Ancient History*, vol. 12, second edition, *The Crisis of Empire, A.D. 193–337*, Cambridge: Cambridge University Press.

Bradbury, S. (1995), 'Julian's pagan revival and the decline of blood sacrifice', *Phoenix* 49, 331–56.

Brauch, T. (1993a), 'The prefect of Constantinople for 362 AD : Themistius', *Byz* 63, 37–78.

Brauch, T. (1993b), 'Themistius and the emperor Julian', *Byz* 63, 79–115.

Braun, R., and Richer, J. (eds) (1978–81), *L'Empereur Julien: Études*, 2 vols, Paris: Les Belles Lettres.

Browning, R. (1975), *The Emperor Julian*, London: Weidenfeld and Nicolson.

Buck, D. F. (1990), 'Some distortions in Eunapius' account of Julian the Apostate', *The Ancient History Bulletin* 4.5, 113–15.

Buck, D. F. (1993), 'Eunapius on Julian's acclamation as Augustus', *The Ancient History Bulletin* 7.2, 73–80.

Burr, E. G. (2000), 'Julian "the Apostate" *Against the Galileans*', in R. Valantasis (ed.), *Religions of Late Antiquity in Practice*, Princeton and Oxford: Princeton University Press, pp. 143–55.

Cameron, Alan (1965), 'Eunuchs in the "Historia Augusta"', *Latomus* 24, 155–8.

Cameron, Averil (1993), *The Later Roman Empire AD 284–430*, London: Fontana Press.

Cameron, Averil, and Garnsey, P. (eds) (1998), *The Cambridge Ancient History*, vol. 13, *The Late Empire, A.D. 337–425*, Cambridge: Cambridge University Press.

Conti, S. (2004), *Die Inschriften Kaiser Julians*, Stuttgart: Franz Steiner Verlag.

Crump, G. A. (1975), *Ammianus Marcellinus as a Military Historian*, Wiesbaden: Franz Steiner Verlag GMBH.

Curta, F. (1995), 'Atticism, Homer, Neoplatonism, and *Fürstenspiegel*: Julian's second panegyric on Constantius', *GRBS* 36, 177–211.

Dalven, R. (1976), *The Complete Poems of Cavafy*, expanded edition, New York: Harcourt Brace and Company.

den Boeft, J., den Hengst, D., and Teitler, H. C. (eds) (1992), *Cognitio Gestorum: The Historiographic Art of Ammianus Marcellinus*, Amsterdam: Royal Netherlands Academy of Arts and Sciences.

DiMaio, M. (1977), 'Zonaras' Account of the Neo-Flavian Emperors: A Commentary', PhD thesis, University of Missouri-Columbia.

DiMaio, M. (1980), 'The Antiochene connection: Zonaras, Ammianus Marcellinus, and John of Antioch on the reigns of the emperors Constantius II and Julian', *Byz* 50, 158–85.

DiMaio M. (1988), 'Smoke in the wind: Zonaras' use of Philostorgius, Zosimus, John of Antioch, and John of Rhodes in his narrative of the neo-Flavian emperors', *Byz* 58, 230–55.

DiMaio, M., and Arnold, Fr. (1992), '*Per vim, per caedem, per bellum*: a study of murder and ecclesiastical politics in the year 337 A.D.', *Byz* 62, 158–211.

Dodds, E. R. (1947), 'Theurgy and its relationship to Neoplatonism', *JRS* 37, 55–69.

Dodgeon, M. H., and Lieu, S. N. C. (1991), *The Roman Eastern Frontier and the Persian Wars (AD 226–363)*, London and New York: Routledge.

Donalson, M. D. (1996), *A Translation of Jerome's* Chronicon *with Historical Commentary*, Lewiston/Queesnston/Lampeter: Mellen University Press.

Drijvers, J. W. (1992), 'Ammianus Marcellinus 23.1.2–3: The rebuilding of the temple in Jerusalem', in den Boeft, den Hengst and Teitler (eds), pp. 19–26.

Drijvers, J. W., and Hunt, D. (eds) (1999), *The Late Roman World and its Historian: Interpreting Ammianus Marcellinus*, London and New York: Routledge.

Drinkwater, J. F. (1983), 'The pagan "underground", Constantius II's "secret service", and the survival, and the usurpation of Julian the Apostate', in C. Deroux (ed.), *Studies in Latin Literature and Roman History*, vol. 3, Brussels: Latomus, pp. 348–87.

Drinkwater, J. F. (1996), '"The Germanic threat on the Rhine frontier": a Romano-Gallic artefact?', in R. W. Mathisen and H. S. Sivan (eds), *Shifting Frontiers in Late Antiquity*, Aldershot, UK, and Brookfield, VT: Variorum, pp. 20–30.

Eadie, J. W. (1967), *The Breviarium of Festus*, London: The Athlone Press.

Elm, S. (2003), 'Hellenism and historiography: Gregory of Nazianzus and Julian in dialogue', *Journal of Medieval and Early Modern Studies* 33, 493–515.

Ford, M. C. (2002), *Gods & Legions: A Novel of the Roman Empire*, London: Orion.

Fornara, C. W. (1991), 'Julian's Persian expedition in Ammianus and Zosimus', *JHS* 111, 1–15.

Fowden, G. (1998), 'Polytheist religion and philosophy', in Cameron and Garnsey (eds), pp. 538–60.

Gardner, A. (1895), *Julian*, New York and London: G. P. Putnam's Sons.

Geffcken, J. (1978), *The Last Days of Greco-Roman Paganism*, trans. S. MacCormack, Amsterdam/New York/Oxford: North-Holland Publishing Company.

Gibbon, E. (1781), *The History of the Decline and Fall of the Roman Empire*, vol. 2, London: printed for W. Strahan and T. Cadell.

Gilliard, F. (1964), 'Notes on the coinage of Julian the Apostate', *JRS* 54, 135–41.

Gleason, M. (1986), 'Festive satire: Julian's Misopogon and the New Year at Antioch', *JRS* 76, 106–19.

Gregory, T. E. (1983), 'Julian and the last oracle at Delphi', *GRBS* 24, 355–366.

Griffith, S. H. (1987), 'Ephraem the Syrian's hymns "Against Julian": meditations on history and imperial power', *VigChr* 41, 238–66.

Hamilton, W. (1986), *Ammianus Marcellinus*, Harmondsworth: Penguin.

Hartranft, C. D. (1890), *The Ecclesiastical History of Sozomen*, in P. Schaff and H. Wace (eds), *Nicene and Post-Nicene Fathers*, vol. 2, New York: Christian Literature Publishing Company.

Hopkins, K. (1963), 'Eunuchs in politics in the later Roman empire', *PCPhS* 189, 62–80.

Hopkins, K. (1978), *Conquerors and Slaves*, Cambridge: Cambridge University Press.

Hunt, D. (1995), 'Julian and Marcus Aurelius', in D. Innes, H. Hine and C. Pelling (eds), *Ethics and Rhetoric: Classical Essays for Donald Russell on his Seventy-Fifth Birthday*, Oxford: Clarendon Press, pp. 287–98.

Hunt, D. (1998a), 'Julian', in Cameron and Garnsey (eds), pp. 44–77.

Hunt, D. (1998b), 'The successors of Constantine', in Cameron and Garnsey (eds), pp. 1–43.

Hunt, D., and Drijvers, J. W. (eds) (1999), *The Late Roman World and its Historian: Interpreting Ammianus Marcellinus*, London and New York: Routledge.

Jackson, B. (1892), *The Ecclesiastical History of Theodoret*, in P. Schaff and

H. Wace (eds), *Nicene and Post-Nicene Fathers*, vol. 3, New York: Christian Literature Publishing Company.

James, L. (2001), *Empresses and Power in Early Byzantium*, London: Leicester University Press.

Jeffreys, E., Jeffreys, M., and Scott, R. (1986), *The Chronicle of Malalas: A Translation*, Melbourne: Australian Association for Byzantine Studies.

Jones, A. H. M. (1964), *The Later Roman Empire 284–602: A Social, Economic and Administrative Survey*, 3 vols, reprinted in 1973, Oxford: Blackwell.

Jones, A. H. M., Martindale, J. R., and Morris, J. (1971), *The Prosopography of the Later Roman Empire*, vol. 1, *A.D. 260–395*, Cambridge: Cambridge University Press.

Juneau, J. (1999), '*Pietas* and politics: Eusebia and Constantius at court', *CQ* 49, 641–4.

Kaegi, W. E., Jr. (1967), 'Domestic military problems of Julian the Apostate', *Byz Forsch* 2, 247–64.

Kaegi, W. E., Jr. (1981), 'Constantine's and Julian's strategies of strategic surprise against the Persians', *Athenaeum* 59, 209–13.

Kelly, C. (1998), 'Emperors, government and bureaucracy', in Cameron and Garnsey (eds), pp. 138–83.

Kent, J. P. C. (1954), 'Notes on some fourth-century coin types', *NChron* 14, 216–17.

Kent, J. P. C (1959), 'An introduction to the coinage of Julian the Apostate', *NChron* 19, 109–117.

Kent, J. P. C. (1981), *The Roman Imperial Coinage*, vol. 7, *The Family of Constantine I A.D. 337–364*, London: Spink and Son Ltd.

King, C. W. (1888), *Julian the Emperor*, London: George Bell and Sons.

Kolb, A. (1998), 'Kaiser Julians Innenpolitik: grundlegende Reformen oder traditionelle Verwaltung? Das Beispiel des *cursus publicus*', *Hist* 47, 342–59.

Krivouchine, I. (1997), 'L'empereur païen vu par l'historien ecclésiastique: Julien l'Apostat de Socrate', *JÖB* 47, 13–24.

Lane Fox, R. (1997), 'The itinerary of Alexander: Constantius to Julian', *CQ* 47, 239–252.

Lee, A. D. (1993), *Information and Frontiers: Roman Foreign Relations in Late Antiquity*, Cambridge: Cambridge University Press.

Lee, A. D. (2000), *Pagans and Christians in Late Antiquity: A Sourcebook*, London and New York: Routledge.

Leedom, J. W. (1978), 'Constantius II: three revisions', *Byz* 48, 132–145.

Lévêque, P. (1960), 'Observations sur l'iconographie de Julien l'Apostat d'après une tête inédite de Thasos', *Monuments et mémoires de la fondation Eugène Piot*, 105–28.

Lévêque, P. (1963), 'De nouveaux portraits de l'empereur Julien', *Latomus* 22, 74–84.

Liebeschuetz, J. H. W. G. (2001), *The Decline and Fall of the Roman City*, New York: Oxford University Press.

Lieu, S. N. C. (ed.) (1989), *The Emperor Julian: Panegyric and Polemic*, 2nd edition, Liverpool: Liverpool University Press.

MacCormack, S. G. (1981), *Art and Ceremony in Late Antiquity*, Berkeley/Los Angeles/London: University of California Press.

Matthews, J. (1989), *The Roman Empire of Ammianus*, London: Duckworth.

Meyer, M. (1986), *Ibsen Plays: Five. Brand; Emperor and Galilean*, London: Methuen Drama.

Müller-Seidel, I. (1955), 'Die Usurpation Julians des Abtrünnigen im Licht seiner Germanenpolitik', *Historische Zeitschrift* 180, 225–44.

Murdoch, A. (2003), *The Last Pagan: Julian the Apostate and the Death of the Ancient World*, Stroud: Sutton Publishing.

Nicholson, O. (1994), 'The "pagan churches" of Maximinus Daia and Julian the Apostate', *JEH* 45, 1–10.

Nimmo Smith, J. (2001), *A Christian's Guide to Greek Culture: The Pseudo-Nonnus Commentaries on Sermons 4, 5, 39 and 43 by Gregory of Nazianzus*, Liverpool: Liverpool University Press.

Nixon, C. E. V., and Rodgers, B. S. (1994), *In Praise of Later Roman Emperors: The Panegyrici Latini*, Berkeley/Los Angeles/Oxford: University of California Press.

Nock, A. D. (1926), *Sallustius, Concerning the Gods and the Universe*, Cambridge: Cambridge University Press.

Norman, A. F. (1969), *Libanius Selected Works*, vol. 1, *The Julianic Orations*, Cambridge, MA, and London: Harvard University Press and Heinemann.

Norman, A. F. (1992), *Libanius Autobiography and Selected Letters*, 2 vols, Cambridge, MA, and London: Harvard University Press.

Odahl, C. M. (2004), *Constantine and the Christian Empire*, London and New York: Routledge.

Paschoud, F. (1979–2000), *Zosime. Histoire Nouvelle*, 5 vols, Paris: Les Belles Lettres.

Penella, R. J. (1990), *Greek Philosophers and Sophists in the Fourth Century A.D.: Studies in Eunapius of Sardis*, Leeds: Francis Cairns.

Penella, R. J. (1993), 'Julian the persecutor in fifth century church historians', *AncW* 24, 31–43.

Pharr, C. (1952), *The Theodosian Code*, Princeton, NJ: Princeton University Press.

Piganiol, A. (1972), *L'Empire chrétien (325–395)*, 2nd edition, Paris: Presses Universitaires de France.

Pinder, M., and Büttner-Wobst, T. (1841–97), *John Zonaras Epitome Historiarum*, 3 vols, Bonn: Weber.

Rees, R. (2004), *Diocletian and the Tetrarchy*, Edinburgh: Edinburgh University Press.

Renucci, P. (2000), *Les idées politiques et le gouvernement de l'empereur Julien*, Brussels: Latomus.

Ridley, R. T. (1973), 'Notes on Julian's Persian expedition (363)', *Hist* 22,

317–30.

Ridley, R. T. (1982), *Zosimus. New History. A Translation with Commentary*, Canberra: Australian Association for Byzantine Studies.

Rohrbacher, D. (2002), *The Historians of Late Antiquity*, London and New York: Routledge.

Rolfe, J. C. (1950–2), *Ammianus Marcellinus*, 3 vols, rev. ed., London and Cambridge, MA: Heinemann and Harvard University Press.

Russell, D. A., and Wilson, N. G. (1981), *Menander Rhetor*, Oxford: Oxford University Press.

Seager, R. (1997), 'Perceptions of eastern frontier policy in Ammianus, Libanius, and Julian (337–363)', *CQ* 47, 253–68.

Shaw, G. (1985), 'Theurgy: rituals of unification in the Neoplatonism of Iamblichus', *Traditio* 41, 1–28.

Smith, A. (2004), *Philosophy in Late Antiquity*, London and New York: Routledge.

Smith, R. (1995), *Julian's Gods: Religion and Philosophy in the Thought and Action of Julian the Apostate*, London and New York: Routledge.

Smith, R. (1999), 'Telling tales: Ammianus' narrative of the Persian expedition', in Drijvers and Hunt (eds), pp. 89–104.

Stevenson, W. (1995), 'The rise of eunuchs in Greco-Roman antiquity', *JHSex* 5, 495–511.

Teitler, H. C. (1992), 'Ammianus and Constantius. Image and reality', in den Boeft, den Hengst and Teitler (eds), pp. 117–22.

Thompson, E. A. (1947), *The Historical Work of Ammianus Marcellinus*, Cambridge: Cambridge University Press.

Todd, M. (1992), *The Early Germans*, Oxford and Cambridge, MA: Blackwell.

Todd, M. (1998), 'The Germanic peoples', in Cameron and Garnsey (eds), pp. 461–86.

Tougher, S. (1998a), 'In praise of an empress: Julian's *Speech of thanks* to Eusebia', in Mary Whitby (ed.), *The Propaganda of Power: The Role of Panegyric in Late Antiquity*, Leiden: Brill, pp. 105–23.

Tougher, S. (1998b), 'The advocacy of an empress: Julian and Eusebia', *CQ* 48, 595–99.

Tougher, S. (1999), 'Ammianus and the eunuchs', in Drijvers and Hunt (eds), pp. 64–73.

Tougher, S. (2004), 'Julian's bull coinage: Kent revisited', *CQ* 54, 327–30.

Trompf, G. W. (2000), *Early Christian Historiography: Narratives of Retributive Justice*, London and New York: Continuum.

Urbainczyk, T. (1997), *Socrates of Constantinople: Historian of Church and State*, Ann Arbor: The University of Michigan Press.

Vanderspoel, J. (1995), *Themistius and the Imperial Court: Oratory, Civic Duty, and Paideia from Constantius to Theodosius*, Ann Arbor: The University of Michigan Press.

Vanderspoel, J. (1998), 'Julian and the mithraic bull', *The Ancient History*

Bulletin 12.4, 113–19.

Vidal, G. (1964), *Julian*, London: William Heinemann Ltd.

Walford, E. W. (1855), *The Ecclesiastical History of Sozomen and the Ecclesiastical History of Philostorgius as Epitomised by Photius, Patriarch of Constantinople*, London: Henry G. Bohn.

Wallis, R. T. (1995), *Neoplatonism*, 2nd edition, London: Duckworth.

Ward-Perkins, B. (1998), 'The cities', in Cameron and Garnsey (eds), pp. 371–410.

Warmington, B. H. (1977), 'Objectives and strategy in the Persian war of Constantius II', in J. Fitz (ed.), *Limes. Akten des XI. internationalen Limeskongresses*, Budapest: Akadémiai Kiadó, pp. 509–20.

Webb, P. H. (1910), 'The coinage of the reign of Julian the philosopher', *NChron* 10, 238–250.

Whitby, Michael (1999), 'Images of Constantius', in Drijvers and Hunt (eds), pp. 77–88.

Wilken, R. L. (1999), 'Cyril of Alexandria's *Contra Julianum*', in W. E. Klingshirn and M. Vessey (eds), *Limits of Ancient Christianity: Essays on Late Antique Thought and Culture in Honor of R. A. Markus*, Ann Arbor: University of Michigan Press, pp. 42–55.

Woods, D. (2000), 'Julian, Gallienus and the solar bull', *The American Numismatic Chronicle* 12, 157–69.

Wright, W. C. (1913–23), *The Works of the Emperor Julian*, 3 vols, London and New York: Heinemann and Macmillan.

Wright, W. C. (1921), *Philostratus, Lives of the Sophists; Eunapius, Lives of the Philosophers*, London and New York: Heinemann and G. P. Putnam's Sons.

Zenos, A. C. (1890), *The Ecclesiastical History of Socrates*, in P. Schaff and H. Wace (eds), *Nicene and Post-Nicene Fathers*, vol. 2, New York: Christian Literature Publishing Company.

Internet Resources
for Julian

There are an increasing number of Internet sites relating to Late Antiquity. Good starting points, which will provide further links, are:

Society for Late Antiquity, http://www.sc.edu/ltantsoc/
ORB Online Encyclopedia – Late Antiquity in the Mediterranean, A Guide to Online Resources, http://www.nipissingu.ca/department/history/ MUHLBERGER/ORB/LT-ATEST.HTM

For Julian, particularly useful are:

De Imperatoribus Romanis: An Online Encyclopedia of Roman Rulers and their Families, http://www.roman-emperors.org/startup.htm
This excellent site consists mainly of biographies of Roman imperial individuals. Of especial note is the biography of Julian (by W. E. Roberts and M. DiMaio), but also those of Constantius II (by M. DiMaio and R. Frakes) and Gallus (by T. M. Banchich). The site also contains maps, a guide to coins, and texts in translation. Of particular value are the translations of Festus (by T. M. Banchich and J. A. Meka) and the *Epitome de Caesaribus* (by T. M. Banchich), both part of the Canisius College Translated Texts series.

The Tertullian Project, http://www.tertullian.org
This site is run by Roger Pearse. It is of particular interest as it contains translations of other Christian texts, including Jerome's *Chronicon*, Gregory of Nazianzus' orations against Julian, and Photius' summary of Philostorgius' *Church History*: http://www.tertullian.org/fathers/

Also of interest is:

The Julian Society, http://www.juliansociety.org
This society is 'dedicated to the advancement of Pagan religion'.

Index